L. Studdiford McChesney

Under Shadow of the Mission

A Memory of Santa Barbara

L. Studdiford McChesney

Under Shadow of the Mission
A Memory of Santa Barbara

ISBN/EAN: 9783337039141

Printed in Europe, USA, Canada, Australia, Japan

Cover: Foto ©ninafisch / pixelio.de

More available books at **www.hansebooks.com**

UNDER SHADOW OF THE MISSION

A MEMORY OF SANTA BARBARA

BY

L. STUDDIFORD McCHESNEY

"SHE HAD HER WORLD OF ROSES
FOR HALF A WONDROUS DAY."

METHUEN & CO.
36 ESSEX STREET, W.C.
LONDON
1897

To

"*DOROTHY*"

Where do the old trails climb?
  Were spirits only bold
To mount as in the olden time,
  Should we reach the Hills of Gold?

If all the seas were crossed
  Through veering winds of Fate,
Would our hearts win—what hearts have lost,
  Beyond the Golden Gate?

Nay, could we backward sail
  Time's wide estranging stream,
Our Valley's gold would shine but pale—
  A dream within a dream.

CONTENTS

CHAPTER		PAGE
I.	EL DORADO	1
II.	FROM MY WINDOW	20
III.	WEARING WHITE	30
IV.	THE FIRST RAIN	41
V.	THE CHINESE NEW YEAR	54
VI.	THE MIRACLE OF SPRING	63
VII.	ORANGE BLOSSOM	71
VIII.	THE CHILDREN'S CAVALCADE	95
IX.	THE WEDDING RING	102
X.	EASTER AT THE MISSION	115
XI.	PORCH THEOLOGY	125
XII.	PORCH STUDIES	141
XIII.	ON FINCH'S HILL	157
XIV.	THE GREATEST OF THESE	182
XV.	KNIGHTS ERRANT	196
XVI.	A SPIRITUAL SYMPOSIUM	210
XVII.	EARTHQUAKE AT DAWN	231
XVIII.	ON THE SANDS	235
XIX.	LOST ON THE HILLS	245
XX.	OUR SKETCH	259
XXI.	MY CARCASONNE	270
XXII.	THE WINGED HOUR	275
XXIII.	LORELEI	294

CONTENTS

CHAPTER		PAGE
XXIV.	THE SIREN'S STORY	305
XXV.	FOLDED THOUGHTS	319
XXVI.	MIRAGE	338
XXVII.	RETROSPECT	353
XXVIII.	FOREBODING	366
XXIX.	MESMERISM	379
XXX.	THE SHADOW OF PARTING	396
XXXI.	THE LAST SYMPHONY	405
XXXII.	HEARTSEASE	415

PRELUDE

In bringing to the light of day this manuscript which holds our memory of Santa Barbara, from the yellowing leaves dropped phantom eschscholtzias, dim pansies, and loosened rose petals; and about them lingered still the faint scent of that far-off Summer-year. In that breath of fragrance, the past was present, faces afar were near, and eyes met — which will not meet in any sunlight nor by any sea. All are widely parted; and one — the Friend, unforgotten and beloved, who, under guise of the Spectator, sketched, chatted and smiled through these pages sleeps "until the day break" *under shadow of the Mission.*

CHAPTER I

EL DORADO

I BELIEVE in love, not only at first sight, but by prevision—else why, across years of waiting, has this Valley shone so fair, that through vistas of favourite galleries, above art talk of the London season, across the hurried, troubled current of New York life, a very mill stream, dashing to turn myriad wheels of action and speculation, it has still lured me with its vague spirit charm? I think we never really miss our own, so across continents and seas I responded to the call, met with answering eye, that long look of appeal.—You shall have the story of how Santa Barbara wooed and I was won.

We came, one August night, Dorothy and I, from the high winds and unkind fogs of the Northern Pacific Coast, and feeling still the dust and cinders of the trans-continental journey. There was the mysterious landing, with twinkling lights and confused voices, the pleasant stepping upon solid pier from swaying, dizzy plank, the quickened sense of expectation as we peered from the omnibus into the darkness of the village street with its long line of lamps, the blending of sweet garden scents with the salt breath of the sea, the sense of utter strangeness in a place where no face shone with welcome for us, and the thrill of seeing face to face the Valley of my love. The drive seemed long, with dull talk of fellow passengers upon rival hotels and various routes of travel—then, there flashed upon the night sudden lights, with shadowy outline of bay windows and festooned porch, and through the dimness of the palms, the drapery of rose vines, there rose "The Esperanza". Oc and Foo, known henceforth as our "Oriental Angels", took encumbering wraps and tourist's impedimenta, and our young host with smile of welcome and courteous greeting, transformed the strange hotel into the House Beautiful to tired (and—shall I confess it?—somewhat depressed) pilgrims.

Can you explain that feminine, or is it human experience, that just as some dream is wakening into reality, some ideal finding promised fulfilment, the heart doubts, withdraws and would elude, the very pleasure towards which all its longings have drawn? It is not the memory of past disillusioning, for young hearts confess it, to whom joy is still as assured as home garden or familiar lawn for daily treading. Is it the hereditary confession of disappointment, the human recognition of finite limitations, before one has learned from personal loss or imperfect gain, the preacher's epitaph upon life "vanity of vanities"?

In our unfamiliar rooms, the lost, shipwrecked feeling made us glad of quick good-night and coming rest.

In the morning Santa Barbara smiled. It has a habit of smiling, as if it held sweet secrets of its own, over which, if faith did not fail us, we too should smile with deep content. Since then we have loitered many mornings away on the porch, with pictures of foothills and mountains, framed in panels between the pillars, with arabesque of rose vines and clinging creepers, and a glimpse of the blue Pacific over the foliage of graceful peppers and stiff eucalypti, in which the town is sheltered.

This is the dry season, which I thought might be unlovely, not knowing the charm of California sunlight; and truly the roads are dusty and the hills brown and bare. No trees upon these slopes cast softening shadow, but a few dusky live oaks; except upon the eucalyptus grade, where one experimental grove makes a dark, solemn line upon the warm golden tints of the far hillside.

Now, our coming was weeks ago, as impatient letters remind me, but here the months have no sharp edges by which to mark their advent and their exit,—but all sleep with only two dreams to stir them; one of slumbrous sunlight, an earth all brown and gold, and one of sudden showers with quick, vivid green flashing across hills and valleys.

I find fairer reason than mines beneath the soil for calling this "The Golden State". For nine months in the year it is a symphony in yellow. Confessed, that the roads are dusty, and the fields are bare—through all the showerless months geraniums flaunt high their scarlet banners, lilies lift their undimmed chalices, heliotrope loses its maiden modesty in its high, hoydenish climbing, decoma blossoms unfold white petals with half-revealed heart of vivid red, great beds of garden marguerites turn to the unclouded sunlight their spiritual whiteness and golden glory, the pomegranate blossoms droop orange bells, and magnolia trees set fragant, pure blossoms in the cool, shadowy green of tropical leaves; and over all roses hold their queenship. But the characteristic charm of the season is in the tender blue of the cloudless sky, and the warm light, a glory on barren hills and undraped mountains. I did not know the sunshine was such an artist until I studied the delicate gradations, the ineffable tints of these bare peaks and brown foot-hills. For upon near view, and in absolute prose, they are bare and brown. But prose is always misleading. It is the finite fact, unrelated to mystery of space, or ideality of distance.

Seen from my window of enchantment, the undulations of the hills are in colour, yellow deepening into dreamy shadow, or shining under strong light with true golden softness; not metallic lustre of polished surface, but that deep luminous light upon the beaten gold of fine Etruscan workmanship.

California may be young among the States, but nature does not work here in crude, territorial fashion.

The Pacific is as dreamy in blue, the Islands as fair in sunset glow, the coast as soft and caressing in its clasp, as if Hellenic shore embraced Ægean Sea; and the sunset lights upon these hills have spirit kinship to the tender warmth, which I have watched, touch with ideal grace, then deepen into twilight shadow, the hills which circle Florence.

That plants and crops live, grow and ripen into fabulous richness through these rainless months may be by natural law, but appears to me to be by constant miracle.

In Santa Barbara County there is little irrigation, and in late loitering upon the porch I have felt no damp of dew. (Early morning studies I have not made). It is true, during the summer months, there is sometimes for an hour or two in the morning a poetic haze over the mountains, softening, not shrouding the sun. Cynics call it fog. It is more like our Indian Summer haze, touching all the landscape to more ideal grace, as friend's face shines through yearning dream. The mornings with this light, vaporous mist playing about the mountains, breaking their continuity and changing familiar peaks into weird, fantastic forms, I think the loveliest phase of Santa Barbara climate, its touch of mysticism. Then the Santa Ynez Range takes wild grandeur of outline, and through the mist I have caught the far whiteness of snow peaks. This effect was due to unusual drift of white clouds above the fog, like the gleam of glacier seen above lower mountains swathed in mist.

The sky here has few clouds, so the sunset lacks the strange transfigurations, which upon our eastern sea coast, and on the northern lake shores, give crimson light and purple shadows to celestial mountain ranges.

Here the sunset is a strange softening of the blue, sometimes into that tender, tremulous sea green, sometimes to pale pink or warm-hearted grey, that colour known as "ashes of roses". I always think that name is a true poem, a kind of dirge over roses which drop to ashes, though in those ashes is such glow of memory, such flush of tenderness, that one must know that dust once thrilled as rose petals in the air of June, and died only from excess of light.

I must give a lightly-outlined sketch of Santa Barbara, though one can only come to know it, as it unfolds its beauty in a soft, dreamy way to lovers like ourselves, willing to loiter along all its paths, to be lured into study of all its moods, and wait with smiling faith for its full revelation. For Santa Barbara is of a sensitive, poetic nature, and gives its full beauty to loving heart, not to critical eye. I should call it a village; though it has attained to the dignity of a city, and boasts a mayor as truly as London, though in a Republic we may not honour him as Lord Mayor. It has a State Street, broad and straight, rather more interesting than most village main streets, with variations in architecture from stately brick blocks to the low, tile-roofed adobe houses. From the foot-hills the town looks rather like Alice's chess-board in her Looking Glass World, as it is laid out at right angles. The houses are mainly cottage homes, unpretentious in style, but with climbing roses looking in at the chamber windows, and great bushes of scarlet geraniums, masses of heliotrope, beds of verbenas and the golden glory of the accacia, making the gardens gay, and the air faint with fragrance.

The valley is narrow and lies between the Santa Ynez Mountains and the sea. This range, though claiming no peaks beyond 3,000 feet in height, are true mountains in boldness of outline and grandeur of character. The lower spurs, called the foot-hills, give gentle slopes and crests easy for horseback climbing.

The mountains sweep around the town in a fine amphitheatre on the north and west. On the east they change into a high plateau, known as the Mesa. Under the shadow of this table-land is the richest farming land of the valley, lying along Mission Creek as it winds to the sea. Some of the slopes of the Mesa are terraced and planted with vineyards like the hills along the Rhine. Upon the south the valley has open gateway to the sea, looking across Santa Barbara Channel to the dreamy line of the islands Santa Cruz, Santa Rosa, San Miguel and Anacapa. The islands only give faint, far line, and do not seem to break the sense of the sunlit space of the open Pacific. The valley has as its ornamental trees, the pepper and the eucalyptus, and is beautiful with occasional orange groves and young olives among its wheat and barley fields. There are charming cañons penetrating the foot-hills, green and shadowy even in the glare and dust of the dry season.

The characteristic native tree is the live oak, an evergreen resembling in silvery-grey foliage and general growth the venerable ilex of Italian memory.

I could have dreamed months away on our porch and in my bay window, watching the tender browns across the hills, now lighted into gold, now, in the short twilight, deepening into purple shadows. But Dorothy was in the imperative mood, and, like all children, lives in the present tense. So out of my *dolce far niente* I was goaded and pricked into activity by fierce reminders of her own one hundred dollars and her desire for investment in horse flesh. After trying Palunino, a big, cream-coloured horse with fast, hard gait, a small buckskin pacer, various diminutive mustangs (one Nellie, with glorious mane, but most inglorious legs), the child, after a dash, mounted cavalier fashion and bare-headed, chose an iron-grey colt. Dorothy has with full faith endowed him with dauntless spirit, and christened him Ironsides. One day there came, with a gang of horse dealers, a small, yellow mare, quick-eyed, with graceful, dancing steps, which became nominally mine—but in truth Dorothy's; so with the big grey colt and the graceful pony, she controls matter and spirit in horse flesh! This little creature has been named Brownie after the beneficent Scotch fairy of tale and tradition—and Dorothy feels assured of triumphant future with "Ironsides" for martial daring, and "Brownie" for elfin adventure.

Now that I have given a glance at our outward environment, you must know the human elements which enter into our life—for I visit no more as stranger in this southern world. Do friendships too feel the quickening power of this sunlit air, and have quicker growth and rarer flower, that I so soon have found life opening into social gladness and true spiritual companionship?

Scenery is, after all, only a frame for humanity, so you shall take foot-hills and cañons, the smooth, fair beach and Montecito gardens as we have them, with comradeship and commentaries. To-day we walked to the pier, our party—whom you must know. The Crusader is our army man, whose fighting moods are like trumpet call to my feminine nature, and I long for ballot and musket, for place in the marshalled hosts, for right to the watchwords in humanity's fierce conflict.

He is sympathetic when not aggressive, chivalrous when not combative, poetic when not revolutionary; strong in personal magnetism, but giving his strength more to causes than to individuals. I have named him Crusader, though he is not enrolled beneath the banner of the Church—neither would any sepulchre, however holy, call him to conflict. Still, he is worthy to wear the red cross above his heart, which beats true for the living Christ in humanity, and for Him, his sword arm is strong. Walking with him is Themis, white-haired but flashing-eyed, the incarnation of justice; who brings all our desultory talk of theories and experiments to the straight lines of honour and right.

My companion, lately a stranger, I noticed in quiet walk up and down the piazza, while a warm warfare was waged on woman suffrage and kindred subjects. I felt his keen observation of the group, his fair measurement of the antagonists, his calm, unassertive mood, while with perfect good breeding he continued his walk, leaving our talk undisturbed. His fine poise, his English air of reserve, his dispassionate, critical attitude, led me to call him "The Spectator". I felt the setting up of a London standard in the Esperanza. While I was taking notes upon the characteristics of the stranger, and had named him to my satisfaction, I found that as listener to our talk he had dubbed me "Ultimata". Later he confessed, and justified his choice of name, by my fondness for the last word in an argument. The name clings—errors are so tenacious.

To-day we sat upon the pier with sea before us, with fine line of the hills sweeping to the beach, with side view of the town in the valley, with the ever watchful presence of "The Mission", as, white and phantom-like, it guards always its glorious past, and turns brave, sunlit face to the present of its decadence and shadowy power.

The Spectator took out book and paints to catch the mood of the hour in a sketch, while we sat round in idle chat.

After much general talk, Ultimata remarked, "The Catholic Church has never appealed more tenderly to me than here, The Mission a dim, ghostly presence, with shadows about it of Spanish supremacy and Indian allegiance; not standing as now with only ruined fountains and deserted garden to picture its loss, but set in smiling fields and fruitful orchards. The white walls, the graceful cloisters, the few haunting monks and the minor-keyed sadness of its services, all suggest so many questions as to what refuge man is seeking in place of the assured safety of the historic Church."

Crusader responded, " You mean what new retreat is humanity beating, in what new hiding place of cowardice will man shield himself against the sure, stern march of truth? What has any church or creed been but the last ditch in which fables and errors creep, rather than die in knightly fashion on the field? The Church has in turn allied itself with feudalism, with aristocracy, with slavery—now it entrenches itself behind capitalism and monopolies. The modern Church solves the problem of how to serve God and mammon. It serves God with its lips, its confession of creed, its uttered prayer; but with its power and wealth, its expensive, artistic formalism of worship, its flippancy of æsthetic ritualism, it serves mammon."

The Spectator dropped his brushes to ask in suggestive manner, " Has the Church fought no battle for truth? Does it show no roll-call of heroes and martyrs? Have the fiercest conflicts of the world not had religious watch-words as battle cry; often Religion blindly warring with itself, still dying for the truth with consistent testimony to the reality of 'Eternal Verities'? Are not the boldest theories of humanitarianism to-day the fruit of those germinal truths sown in Christ's teaching upon Syrian hillsides?"

Ultimata eagerly rejoined, "I find the eternal truthfulness of Christ's teachings in the fact that no modern breadth of sympathy, no recognition of brotherhood, no humanitarian effort outreaches the spirit of His words, that 'love' which 'is the fulfilling of the law', which now, in interpretation of legal code and social custom, we are slowly approximating."

The Crusader answered, "I was not attacking Christ's spirit, but the formalism of the Church in which they have buried Him. Once again He must rise and meet His own with touch and tone of spiritual nearness, break bread, pour the wine of true companionship with the common people—withheld from Him now by the formalism of ecclesiasticism."

Themis, who thinks with freedom, but holds with conservative steadfastness to the Church, now harmonised the discordant thoughts by saying, "How shall we ever reach underlying truth when we are all bewildered by the forms of truth and miss the reality? Two defend the spiritual sacredness of pure truth, as Christ taught it, while the Crusader attacks the dogmas and errors which have crystalised about the truth. Truth, for human acceptance, must have expression, and that expression must suffer from the limitations of thought and the imperfect development of those who gave it form. Would not the same efforts at reform made within the Church lead to broader, deeper creeds more worthy of the truth as apprehended by our later culture, while attacks from without threaten the stability of the Church, and of the truth which it incarnates?"

The Spectator replied with tender reverence, "I feel there would be great danger, even in change of form. Take the Liturgy of the Church of England, and to us, who respond to its solemn petitions, it represents not our narrow, personal prayers, but the prayers of the ages, our seeking in new bewilderment of broadening and diverging paths, the shining of the light."

"You make the very point I would urge," answered the Crusader, "I shall believe in worship where each man utters his own prayer, warm from his own heart. I believe in the living flame—not in the dead ashes."

"But the flame is living," pleaded Ultimata,—"the purified flame of thought which has warmed and lighted the world's wearied hearts—is the flame of the light-house not as worthy as the flickering of one's individual student-lamp?"

Themis, with practical wisdom, gathered up the wraps to move homeward, as she answered, "The world must have both lights, the individual light of independent thought, and the beacon light of accepted truth."

"That touches upon one of our old battle fields," said Ultimata, smiling up at the Crusader, "but we seem to have reversed our positions, for you, with military education practically defend centralisation, and I, with what you are pleased to call woman's waywardness of untrained thought, emphasise the value of individualism."

The Spectator sighed dolorously as he said, "The public spirit has pressed heavily upon my artist longings and I go home with an unfinished sketch."

The day's clear sunlight had softened into tender sunset tints; the blue, near the horizon, was etherealised into faint aqua-marine, with soft floatings of evanescent pink, flushing the sea into pale roseate light. The sound of the tide was a soft, rhythmic lapping against the sand, and sea gulls floated in slow, graceful circlings, showing white breasts in the dimming light.

"I think," said the Crusader, "that the sea gull, not the dove should be symbol of the Holy Spirit. It sweeps with mythical grace on its long, delicate wings, but the movement of the dove is short and broken, with sense of effort. The symbol of the Espirito Santo should suggest soft down sweeping, spiritual uplifting, a brooding, winged mystery; and that thought is not in harmony with the low, earthly flight of the familiar dove."

"You are an iconoclast," Ultimata cried, "if altar lights and haloed madonnas must fall before your desire for bare, undraped truth, spare that beloved symbol with its tender traditions! The dove! I close my eyes and watch its flight over unshored sea, until wet and wearied it flutters back to warmth of human hand; then, from waste of waters wins green hope for the waiting earth, the olive branch with its patient, shadowy grey of colouring, as if wan from sad, long watching; then its third flight, with hope of rest upon the new earth, fair and redeemed—call it a myth, seek record of the flood in older legends and other revelations, but its story is full of spiritual truth; the stain of wrong doing, the penance of purification, the patience of faith, and the promise of olive branch, dove, and bow spanning the reconciled heavens. What so tender and comforting, as that the familiar dove, which broods close to earth, flutters about home gables, and in its low, loving flight almost touches the fair, young heads of the watching children, should have rested on the sacred head while the voice from heaven called Him 'the beloved Son'!

" Dorothy—who is a kind of concentrated menagerie, and is horse, dog, and bird at will with such effect that I sometimes think the various metamorphoses are incomplete, and from other experiences she keeps the neigh, the bark, the cooing note—often talks of her faith in the immortality of animals. I express no doubt. How dare I, when in the ecstatic thrill of bird song, the loyalty of hound, the responsive intelligence of horse, I recognise that mystery of life, of which we only know that it is, and that outwardly it ceases to be? When we talk of the possibility of astral bodies, or spirit forms also for these who have suffered with us in the earthly life, her final argument is—'If there are no doves in Heaven, where did the dove come from to rest on Christ's head? No earthly dove could know, but every heavenly dove must know the Beloved Son.'

"I like the dogmatism of children, their persistent hold upon symbols of truth. I think in our proud desire to escape from the thraldom of legend and myth, we leave truth undraped and unwinged. My angels still wear floating robes, and lift brave, fearless wings."

"Yes," responded the Crusader in unrelenting tone, "but this symbolism makes too sacred for human use the dove, the lily, the haloed head, while we miss the message of other birds more daring in flight, and other flowers fuller in fragrance—and the Church has sacrificed the lives of toiling men and suffering women to the traditions of these haloed heads."

"No help from artist friend to save our symbols?" queried Ultimata.

"I am listening," the Spectator answered, "to add one to my American studies. This determined emancipation from all creed, from all legend, from the poetic fancy itself, is the outgrowth of Republicanism. After discrowning kings and disowning sceptres and calling on man to abdicate, or prove his right to sovereignty, it is natural that the same questioning should meet all symbols of power and authority. I am only waiting like an unregenerate Englishman, to hear our friend challenge the power of flight, and the traditional sunward glance of the American eagle."

Themis laughingly declared that the question under discussion was the Church and its symbolism, and that it was very unworthy of our English guest to make unwarrantable attack upon our national glory.

The darkness fell in soft, sudden folds, as on the San Miniato hills in the twilights of long ago. We passed the croquet ground, with the two Nellies, May and Grace just finishing their game, stood on the porch to watch a riding party dismount with gay, ringing talk, then passed in to dress for dinner, and I, later, to Dorothy's delayed lessons. Coming for her health, I have yielded to horseback exercise, to play with children and out-of-door life, all the sunlit hours; and strive to keep up a little French and German reading, some study of English literature, and feeble attacks upon fractions in the evening. But the scholar is sorely beset with the temptation of a single dance in the drawing-room, a peep at the illustrated papers in the reading-room, so radiant with student lamps and open fire on generous hearth. Then the teacher is not less assailed by temptation to an hour's quiet reading of art magazines, the "Atlantic", the "Century", and (true to my prophetic instinct) the "Spectator", always sent to my room by my English friend. Or, again, the lure is a quick, vigorous walk with Themis and the Crusader on the broad, shadowy porch, in the fragrant evening air. Then comes the pressure of neglected duty in the shape of to-morrow's Spanish lesson.

I am very sensitive to the southern, foreign atmosphere of the place. For, though ardently American in political convictions and social theories, there is an art-loving side of my nature, strangely unmet in our prosperous, right-angled cities; so for my own sake I love the lands visibly old; the pictured visions of art; the purity of classical, the manifold out-blossoming and the passionate upreaching of Gothic Architecture. So I love Santa Barbara better for the brooding presence of The Mission, the low-browed adobe houses, the southern faces and the musical vowels of the Castilian tongue. True, the Spanish blood is not of the purest, with its Mexican and Indian strains, and the language is lapsing into a dialect with its provincialisms and its Anglo-Saxon accretions. But the faces have still fine features, with sad, tropical eyes; and the language has a sonorous stateliness, in its contrast with the sharp curtness of our own tongue.

This is really a border town, where the Catholic and Protestant faiths, the Spanish and American races, the southern dreamy languor and the Yankee enterprise, touch and blend in curious complication.

The handsome, delicate-featured Spaniard, Cordesso by name, who acts as our groom, takes his orders from us with a chivalrous grace worthy of ancient Hidalgo. I fail to penetrate their life, and learn whether stoical acceptance of fate, repressed resentment, or recognition of the inevitable mastery of the Anglo-Saxon race, is veiled by the soft courtesy and gracious greeting of our southern neighbours. This I do feel, that only Latin, or Oriental people have right to leisure.

We crowd it, until pleasure becomes the most tyrannical of occupations; or leaving it unfilled, the higher natures toy with life in a weak dilettantism and the lower classes sink into masses of brutal ruffianism. But the southern natives have a genius for leisure, a picturesque grace of languor, which redeems laziness.

About the wine houses, sitting in grave groups are grey-haired Mexicans; their horses waiting them, with Spanish saddles heavily mounted with silver, and having in their massiveness and ornamentation some suggestion of the race's old mastery. Mingling with these meditative veterans, are younger, jauntier Spaniards with a touch of Americanism modifying them, but all have a perfect courtesy, a grace of bearing, which makes it a pleasure to ask one's way or to have a saddle cinched. Thus it chanced, with Spaniards about us, and a visit to Mexico looming in the near future, I thought of studying Spanish. So the first morning chat upon the porch, when the world seems all sunlight and roses, is broken for me by the coming of "Mi Sombrero" as my teacher is called, recognised in the distance by his broad-brimmed, becoming felt.

I thought once that sunlight and garden pleasures were the temptations of a child, but I know better now, that it is the tired shadowed life which feels such charm, and flutters on broken wing into the healing glory. So the Spanish lesson, though delightful in itself with the ardent, enthusiastic Professor, is sometimes unwelcome, when it calls me from the sunshine and social companionship of the porch. And the lesson to prepare at night after a long ride or the writing of home letters, shows me that my instincts are at present in favour of lotus eating. I should like, if indulgence were given now, to find release for blessed sunshiny months from sense of duty; not to be haunted by unwritten letter, by unread book, by unlearned lesson, to play with Dorothy, tell her stories, and listen to her more charming ones of fairy land, sit under the roses, dream in solitude, or talk at will, watch the shadows creep over the mountains, give all of myself a holiday and live only in cloudless sunshine and unbroken joy. The education into duty is so slow, so toilsome, so tearful, and then when one has yielded life to its government there is no escape from the stern, safe rule. What is the charm of southern sunshine, wealth of roses and luring hammocks, if the prosaic northern tyrant of duty shadows the sunshine, pierces one with the thorns of the roses and swings the hammock with measured movement as solemn as the pendulum of Time's horologe—"Never here, forever there"?

CHAPTER II

FROM MY WINDOW

TO-DAY, a day of convalescence after weeks of weary suffering, I sit at the open window and wonder how Santa Barbara looks to a tourist, not to a lover. My corner room on the quiet third floor, looks to the north and east. In the northern bay window, I sit facing the mountains, now my familiar friends. I love their moods, and even in this constant southern sunshine, there is subtle play of varying expression.

But I must resist their charm, and look down on garden, croquet ground and village street, that you may know the homelier life about me.

Here starts a riding party, for late afternoon climb up the foot-hills, or dash along the beach. I see the Spectator on "Daisy," the tried companion of last summer's camping trip. He, thoughtful of "spirits in prison" looks up to my window, and strives to lift that favourite helmeted cap, so vague in outline, so limp as to structure, that it reveals in itself the effect of Californian life upon the English temperament. For only in Southern California could such cap find favour in English eyes; but with short, rough coat, and the becoming riding leggings, it has an artistic grace. With him, in faultless habit, and uncompromising derby, with short, silver-mounted stick for whip, and gloved in tan-coloured gauntlets, with bunch of tawny marigolds, is Artista, whose costumes are all perfect studies in form and colour, and who, in the general laxity among invalids and wanderers, furnishes unvarying standard of city elegance. Chatting with her, in broad-brimmed unconventional soft hat, is Perdita. I hear the soft, musical laugh, the voice so southern in its cadences, and under the breadth of that brim, feel the dark, unfathomed softness of shadowy, brown eyes. Beside her is the slender form of her girlish mother, so sympathetic with youth, so charming in sweet unselfishness, and so fair in her personality, that her black dress garlanded with violets, the artists found lovelier at a late dance than all the maiden roses. Mounting with impatient grace is the Crusader, who rides with cavalry dash softened into knightly courtesy, as he tells campaign story, or quotes love-lyric to Artista, whom he joins. Now, on his white horse, the Fairy Prince takes place by Perdita, and the Spectator falls into line with Mater Violetta, who waves me salute, as in a cloud of dust they dash off; and I draw that long, deep, indefinable invalid sigh, and lean back to find a shadow creeping over the mountains, and fancy a touch of chill in the faint sea breeze.

Looking from my window, I am touched by the

sweet homeliness of some of the features of Santa Barbara life. The wild grandeur of nature often oppresses me. I long for mountain heights, for unbroken sweep of sea at times, for inspiration, for uplifting, but the human life looks so wan and frail a thing, beneath the awfulnesses of such shadows, beside the shoreless space of lonely sea.

After the first exaltation of mood passes in the snow Alps, my soul cries out against the inaccessible white heights. How lift and purify one's spirit for such companionship? Here, nature has a comforting familiarity, wild flowers take on garden ways, and roses and geraniums riot along the highways. Then the horses are so human and the children so coltish. In the large meadow opposite is a herd of horses, pastured there for two or three days on their journey from San Luis Obispo to Los Angeles. No nursery of children ever delighted watching mother more than their pranks have my sympathetic eyes.

They are evidently gossips (could they have learned it in only two days' stay in Santa Barbara?). One comes to the fence with outstretched head, eager eyes and lifted ears, another in questioning spirit joins him, and under the appearance of careless companionship peers intently up and down the street to learn the secret of the first one's observation, another strolls indifferently along. Then, young ones leap forward, not yet so well bred as to disguise curiosity under a mask of seeming nonchalance. So I have watched thirty gather to gaze, because one cast suggestive glance down the street. No group of gentlemen gathered in the corner window of a club house, benevolently intent upon their neighbour's affairs, ever gave finer studies. I see every aspect of human nature, from the truly sympathetic eye, to the uplifted eyebrow of the cynic.

But here come three Mexicans, dark-faced and keen-eyed, to catch certain horses to be offered for sale. Then that one instinct, stronger than love of one's neighbours' affairs, prevails, and self-preservation scatters the crowd in wild, confused careering. Here comes the manifold difference in intelligence. Some horses play a long-headed game, with wise studied moves, some dash aimlessly from corner to corner; others with aspect of mild submission are just caught, then quietly elude the swinging lasso.

I notice a peculiar expression in the eyes of men who deal with horses, not in the ignoble civilised fashion of stables, but upon open plain and in spacious *corral*. The eye grows keen, as accustomed to seek along a far horizon; yet determined, as habituated to fix itself with concentrated power of will, on one nature fierce and unsubdued.

The whole relation of man to animals will be better understood as magnetism is scientifically studied, and its positive laws evolved from the nebulous cloud in which the subject is now wrapped. Here come horses just released by their riders, trotting all caparisoned to their respective stables. They canter along in contented companionship to the corner, there part, several dashing into the Victoria stable on which my windows look, others to the Esperanza, while Dolly and Annita turn corners with wise discretion, until they reach Garden Street. Our own little Brownie was lately transferred from the stable of a private house, where she had been pet and playmate, to the stable belonging to the hotel. Three afternoons we had the groom take her, but the fourth day, Dorothy suggested that we should see if Brownie knew the new home. When freed by the touch of her little rider, she kicked up her heels in her usual frantic fashion, dashed along the walk to the road, half turned towards the old stable, pranced, lifted her head in questioning way, then in confident manner trotted off to the new home. As there was a watching group on the porch, Dorothy's triumph was great, when Brownie proved her power of thought and quick decision. The little creature is neither young nor sound, but all spirit and fire, responding to any mood and caprice of her young cavalier. For as Dorothy rides upon a boy's saddle, in Highland dress of the Campbell clan, she is Donald when mounted, and Scotch by birth; and woe to me, if I forget nationality and sex, and venture to give that laddie with kilted skirt and floating scarf, such order as would befit an American girl. So mounted, she rides with her friend Mae, who is a charming companion of uncertain ways, sometimes a big, buxom girl, brimmed with fun and frolic; sometimes, with change of dress or fancy, a prophetically outlined young lady, with airs of coquetry and desire for conquest.

The play between the child, with her sorrel Fannie, and little pet poodle Dot, and the young lady, with assurance of future generalship through difficult campaigns, is quite a comedy. But Dorothy, who is in love with childhood and swears by pinafores, is somewhat baffled by Mae's sudden dignities, with the advent of a belted dress, the borrowing and wearing with quaint style her mother's mull kerchiefs, and the final assumption of a real riding habit, and infinitesimal watch.

Dorothy insists that all her friends shall have their pictures taken, but this is a changing group. There is our neighbour Florrie with father of the humorous Charles Lamb type, who makes merry over rheumatism and French idioms, and mother of graceful artistic fancy whose cottage blossoms within with daisies, clover, and buttercups, eastern fields in Kensington; while the cottage without is framed in roses, and festooned with the Passion vine, with flame of scarlet blossoms. Florrie's passion is music; so fancy her a brunette, tall and fully developed, with violin as her symbol. There is Margaret, slender and graceful, with gazelle eyes and a flute-like clearness of voice.

One day, lately, at a lawn party they made her queen, unbraided the brown hair, crowned her with my heavy Norwegian necklace, draped her with oriental shawls, enthroned her on the horse-block tapestried with Roman scarfs; and in white pinafores, bright sashes and other gay attire, all knelt about her while she held a tall lily stem as sceptre. With a palm tree as background, and roses about them, the coronation scene was very charming. Dorothy clings loyally to crowns and royal robes, to knightly helmeted head and mailed hand, to plumes, to doublet and hose, to the trumpet call, the clang of arms, the test of lance in tournament and on field. Only in her enthusiasm for mediæval pageantry, for loyal vow and daring arm, for touch of accolade and song of troubadour, she always insists that she longs to be knight or crusader with dash of triumph or heroic death; but her imagination refuses with a shiver of apprehension, to re-create the woman life; the castle imprisonment; the tedious growth of weary tapestry; the watching by narrow casement; the waiting for armed tread of friends or dreading fierce foray of foes.

Oh! the perplexity of daughter-ownership in these enfranchised days. I think the woman mind is now in such bewilderment of hope, as both guides and misguides the sanguine prospector in newly discovered mining regions. With the removal of the old walls as to the limitations of sex, we are tempted with sense of sudden freedom, with space of broader horizon, to forget the limitations still of a finite condition, and of the average intelligence.

But, in the clashing of creeds, I respond heartily to the eternal, but imperfectly unfolded truth, that full development of individuality is the birthright of each spirit. Relation of sexes, domestic ties, social duties and political rights are all the growth from this primal root, the right to self-hood. Not in races, classes, sexes or political parties are we born into life; but singly, with faint fluttering of individual breath. Not in phalanx of the conquering, nor in pale affrighted group of the retreating do we pass from the field; but alone, with hero brow, or coward heart, meet the challenge of that last phantom foe. The deathly conflict others may press to watch, but its end of spiritual valour or of soul defeat is not of earthly record. Doubtless the daring strength, or faltering weakness of the earthly experience, gives the conditions of spiritual birth and of future life. Failure here, must, through long effort and later struggle, at last emerge into assured strength; and triumph of the spiritual hero must give power in more glorious conflict, and be foreshadowing of higher conquest. Hence the education of life must be primarily individual. Organization is needful to social development; but organisation under changing conditions, with such flexibility of structure, as allows the fullest expression to the individual, with regard to the social well-being of the many. Failing this ideal structure, the course of human development is through alternate formation and disintegration, as customs and laws find form from the fluctuating life of a people, then hardened into rigidity and lifelessness, yield to the pressure of aggressive individualism. This change is life; not the conservative preservation of dead forms, neither the revolutionary resentment against all form as barrier to growth.

Woman has long suffered from the thraldom of

outgrown laws and customs, and on certain sides still suffers from irrational restrictions; but as the walls fall and the fields widen there are other dangers in place of the old.

Undue narrowness of life, with accepted subordination to the natures and laws of the dominant sex, developed the virtues of patience under wrong doing, fortitude under suffering, and spiritual uplooking, as escape from the unjust conditions of life. But the acceptance of injustice develops faults likewise; the cowardice which seeks subterfuge, rather than dare hopeless conflict, and the moral irresponsibility which results from bearing penalties, so generally the result of the wrong doing of those in power.

A fine analysis of the much glorified feminine sweetness, would show not only true generosity and forbearance of nature, but an alloy of the vices of slaves; dissimulation of life, untruth of spirit. Now, woman nature must crystalise under new conditions, in bolder, stronger form. So the mother of daughters grows thoughtful with the possibilities of the future, holding for woman the broader hope and larger responsibility of a strong, self-reliant development.

The deep question of the purpose of education is unmet even by university curriculum, or professional training, because of the complexity of woman's nature and life.

Man moves with sure step to single aim, success in his chosen vocation. All things must tend to this supreme end. Marriage must wait its time home be located, social life accepted and political duties find place, in harmony with this ruling purpose. And the steadier this purpose, the surer is the hope of success. Concentration, even to the sacrifice of broader culture, is the secret of modern alchemy, transmuting baser metal to gold—that is, the gold of current coin, of outward success.

But while the intellectual power of woman sternly demands fuller development, equal development with man, and equal ownership with him of the whole earth as her rightful sphere of activity, that subtler stronger side of her nature, the emotional, holds beating close to her heart always, that other hope of wifehood and motherhood. This I conceive to be the problem: how to give woman a broader, stronger individuality, with opportunity of winning independent place and power, if she choose such career without sacrificing the elements of true womanhood essential to the highest ideal of wife and mother in possible waiting home. The "eternal womanly" we dare not sacrifice for temporal gain. Sex is a deeper fact, of mightier import, than possession of suffrage, or right to technical education. No plan for woman can be wise, which ignores or lessens the sacredness of potential motherhood.

Here comes the problem incarnate in restless form, as Dorothy dashes into the room, in company with Grace with face of flashing brightness, and Nellie with reproachful eyes, and wealth of floating hair. I yield to numbers, and put aside my paper to listen to the breathless, much interrupted narrative of their wrongs, upon the croquet ground; where the order of life is disturbed by the invasion of Goths and Vandals, in the shape of a domineering boy, who knocks the balls out of position, and cheats recklessly in the game. I am inwardly entertained, but express outwardly my lack of sympathy with three girls, who can be defeated by one boy. Dorothy rejoins resentfully, "But you forbid my knocking his balls, or hiding his mallet. We can't tease like boys or really fight, what can we do?" How can I teach them to hold their own against aggressive opponents, yet keep to the traditions of ladyhood in good little-girl form? What makes it more difficult is the frequent change of mood upon the part of the masterful boy; who one day outrages their sense of justice, on the next wins their hearts by some relenting of chivalrous attention.

CHAPTER III

WEARING WHITE

IS it December? By date of papers, by letters telling of the first snow and the gaiety of city shops all glittering with holiday temptations, and by Dorothy's talk which is a perpetual chiming of Christmas bells, I suppose it is. But by green lawns (for the Esperanza does irrigate), by breath of orange blossoms, by strawberries for lunch, and by the bouquet of roses on my table, and the bunch always worn above my rose-loving heart, I could disprove it. For three days we have had almost eastern summer; with languid, odour-weighted air, which quickens a longing for the cool breath of a sea breeze. Let me sketch our group on the porch. We gathered in numbers, this morning; I went down after a Spanish lesson, which consisted on my part of suppressed yawns, and furtive glances towards the window through which floated much merriment of talk and melody of laughter. Themis, against whose black garb I always protest, is in morning gown of vaporous grey, with faint flush of pink ribbons at her throat, and in the creamy softness of her little lace cap. These little matronly caps are the last refuge of coquetry. What is more fascinating than the ripened charm of an autumnal face, in which dark eyes still flash in defiant youth, with hair a fair white cloud, softening contour and complexion; surmounted by that delicate feminine crown of airy lace, with just a throb of colour through its whiteness. Caps indeed! They are idealising appeals to the fancy, pale premonitions of the far-off coming snow, with the tender flush of late, fair roses. Here there can be in the nature of things, no growing old. One only feels across the Continent the wintry breath, and over indefinably remote years, discerns phantom old age.

Since she could lisp, Dorothy has promised me, when I am a real old lady, charming caps with daisies for decoration. I have smiled for some years at this fancy, for caps are still alien to my thoughts; and the daisies, so incongruous with caps, I thought a sweet confession of a child's failure to picture the mother face as really old.

Artista, who is tall and slender, with stately grace of movement, is in a gown known years ago as a Dolly Varden, pale pink, brocaded with wild flowers. Close to her, and chatting with her, is the Spectator, framed by the vines which wreathe the pillars. He is in careless, artistic suit of grey; but thought worthy of being sketched, because of his cap or turban—(when we wear the same close-fitting, brimless headgear, we call it *toque*). It is light, soft grey, with fine embroidery in black.

Touch it, and by softness of texture and extreme lightness, you know that only in India was such wool woven and such delicacy of decoration enwrought. It is most becoming to the wearer, and I feel the pleasure of exquisite revenge in making this pen-and-ink sketch of him, as he ungallantly rejected my suggestion that he should be photographed, standing in the leafage, wearing the cap. Near him, sitting in the shade and writing, perhaps an acrostic of Nellie's name, perhaps an article on finance, is the Crusader; but just now comes a rush from the croquet ground, and the children carry him captive. He is strong and soldierly, heavily bearded, and with a step so stern and martial, that walking with him I always feel like a raw recruit, with wrong foot forward, and under the glance of the commanding officer's eye. In truth, the eyes of the Crusader alone, would demand for him a military career. At times they constitute a court martial from which there is no appeal; and once, when I had wilfully angered him, and he turned their fire upon me, I felt instantly like a whole, suppressed mutiny. Still they are genial blue eyes, with wonderful guilelessness of expression, when he is deluding the children with some impossible story. Dorothy never forgets his record in the army, and has asked me, under her breath, whether I suppose he has his sabre in his trunk; the real sword that clanked in its scabbard when he swung himself upon "Red Roy" to ride down the ranks, in the old war days.

Perdita is a southern brunette, with face of charming perplexity as a character study. On the surface it is sparkling and piquant, suggesting French readiness for epigram and repartee; but in the dark eyes, both luminous and shadowy, I see depths of possible self-sacrifice, with that light of ideality which will never see its heroes discrowned. I can fancy the flashing face always in sunlight, but sometimes I feel that it could be heroic under flame of martyrdom; and martyrdom has prominent place among the professions open to woman. This morning, she is in pale blue, with broad garden hat of white with bunch of vivid poppies. But I forget the purpose of this talk, which is to flash upon you the vision of myself in white, as proof that I keep still some girlish gladness, some undimmed hope. So I am in white even to my bunch of roses. But I do not love white roses as well as the pale pink, so maiden like in its faint flushing, the deep red, intense and passionate as woman's throbbing heart, or the glorious yellow, the symbol of high pride and fearless light. I think the regal rose must be the yellow. I have a passion for that colour. I always think that in the early Italian pictures there is such defiance of fate, such daring of soul, symbolised in robing heretics in yellow. Why was it chosen—was it suggestive of flame, and its purifying power upon unbelieving souls? Then I like the orange colours, the deep yellow and black—it is a bold triumphant chord—so I feel heroic possibilities in myself, when on black gown I wear yellow chrysanthemums or our own eschscholtzias. There must be spiritual significance in colour, when we have penetrated to its full meaning; a message clear and deep in nature's revelations, from the gaiety of buttercups shining in the fields, to the mystical blue upon distant mountain. Just here I will give the talk of our feminine group: for the Spectator has ridden off on Daisy, with such appointments of sketching books, paint boxes, folding stool and artist's umbrella, that he recalls the White Knight in "Alice in the Looking Glass;" and the Crusader is reading Mrs. Browning to Dorothy in the corner. She wakens me in the morning, when we room together, with the spiritual tenderness of "The Dead Pan," sounding so plaintive in the sweet child voice. She has reached in her thinking, the problem of evil; so submerged herself in the "Drama of Exile," and startled me by saying that Lucifer was her favourite character, and that when he was forgiven, she thought he would be more loving than Michael and Gabriel, who never sinned.

Ultimata gave the morning's text, by saying, "Themis, I do love to see you in pink ribbons; they are far more beautiful and becoming than your judicial black: they suggest 'justice tempered with mercy,' and give me a feeling of comfortable, personal hopefulness. With your high moral standard and uncompromising severity of judgment, I always dread even with your own liberality of thought, lest by looseness of social theory or religious heresy, I should suffer final condemnation; and I believe that you are that exceptional woman, whose heart is governed by her head. But your pink ribbons have a suggestion of sweet tenderness—a feminine relenting—do wear colours."

"Ultimata, if I did not know your strength of conviction on the great questions of the day, I should straightway condemn you for flippancy and flattery. You seem a mass of contradictions with your earnestness of nature and your outward nonsense. I think that Dorothy described you well the other day, when after flaming in sympathy with revolution, even when it included nihilism as an expression; you suddenly turned to her, watching you with dilated eyes of dangerous intensity, and expressed your faith in the reasonableness and possibility of a mother rebellion against small girl government—and she answered reproachfully, 'What makes you talk so, Mamma? You are a constant parody on yourself.'"

"Is this your sense of justice; in response to my compliment to your high-mindedness and pink ribbons to give such accusation?" questioned Ultimata. "I hate consistency—it is allegiance to mere form. However changeless truth itself, the human mind in its acceptance of truth must have moods and tenses.

"Now, Artista, as an apostle of the æsthetic, do give us your creed; though to be sure your dresses always express you. Each costume is a clause, and your general style suggests the underlying dogma. You believe in dress; but is it as benevolent duty, as conscientious art, or as unconscious expression, that you accept it?"

"I never did really enjoy creeds and catechisms, and thought that I had finished with them," answered Artista. "But I think dress is truly both a fine art and an expression of individuality. I think in some dresses I am most conscious of the harmony of colour, and enjoy them as studies—other dresses seem part of myself."

Themis, who often acts as chaperon to Artista, and will have facts before accepting theories, interposed—"Now, Artista, give some illustrations. We will forgive your talking about your own wardrobe, as it is only a means to an end, a help to us in our search after truth. How do you feel in this wild flower dress?"

"Oh, happy and careless, in gay summer mood, as something akin to butterflies."

Perdita, with utmost severity of expression, "You never think of work, else you would remember:—

>   'How doth the little busy bee
>   Improve each shining hour!'

From such a summer gown, you might have gotten whole hives of honey in suggestion; but you only think of the yellow butterflies, because they are more picturesque in their poise and flight. With your expenditure in dress, you might be a kind of Society for the Diffusion of Useful Knowledge—for instance, think of a robe with mulberry leaves and cocoons as pattern of the brocade: you might have a possible influence on the silk culture of the country."

"Now, Perdita, what does your own dress mean,

with its pale blue, and its scarlet poppies? You dress, just as I do, because you like it," said Artista.

"I had no severe motive in this morning's dress," retorted Perdita, "but I suppose the pale blue is an unconscious confession of my own calm sweetness of nature, like the unclouded summer sky. For you know that I travelled for months with you, without quarrelling; though you, like a characteristic Californian, gave me several ominous earthquake shocks: I think the poppies must suggest sleep and sweet dreams."

"Well, a dress with opium-eating suggestions, is not of the highest moral tone. Now I shall answer the question Themis put about my own relation to some of my own dresses," resumed Artista, "I never put on that tight-fitting navy blue, with the large silver shells as buttons, without a quickening of my restive longings. I may wear it only for a drive in my own village cart to the Ranch; but I feel anticipations of a European tour, and have vague visions of ocean steamers and foreign cities. It has the air of a dress entitled to adventures."

Perdita interrupted, "Should it only be part of the heroine's adventures, or should it meet with a hero? I fancy voyages of discovery to you, would always mean more sailing upon the deep waters of human nature (man nature) and studying newly discovered lands in the people you meet, than really caring for galleries and cathedrals. Now, don't be cross, for human nature is nearly as well worthy of study as Gothic Architecture or the Italian Renaissance."

"How ungenerous," protested Artista, "because you have had years of foreign travel, to decide that I am incapable of culture. But I shall talk about my dresses, since I am supposed to know nothing else. That costume in two shades of terra-cotta, which I wear always with chrysanthemums shading from pink to warm red, is like music to me. I feel in it the sound of deep, full chords, and love to look at its harmonious blending. That dress I enjoy selfishly, without thought of whether others like it."

Ultimata asked quickly, "Then you admit the possession of gowns which you wear with conscious study of their effect upon others? It is true that dress is a woman's armour and her weapons defensive and aggressive. When you are defeated in a controversy with some unchivalrous man mortal, who will attack anything womanly from feminine intuitions to fashion plates, I can fancy the easy triumph of conscious superiority in appearing at dinner in that deep cardinal plush robe, with its regality of train. So robed, woman's equality needs no proof. The burden of proving equality rests with the business suit; or if it is the night for a hop, the conflict may be a little less unequal with solemnity of dress coat, and redeeming grace of carefully chosen *boutonnière*. Seriously speaking, the subject of dress is a perplexing element in the woman question. Dress with its present demands, is fatal interruption to the earnestness of life and continuity of thought exacted by higher education. Yet dress is truly a power; and women cannot forego the old mission of draping and beautifying life.

"Themis, you find always more direct road than my meandering mind: what is to be the dress of 'the coming woman'? Then you are from Boston, and Boston must know."

"I think in this," answered Themis, "as in most other subjects under debate, the ultimate path must be one of compromise. The broadened, deepened woman will find a dress, expressive of herself, more individual, less conventional than that now tyrannically ordered by fashion; but it must be womanly, so I know 'the coming woman' whatever her power or achievement, will still wear the falling folds of the traditional feminine dress."

"You are right, Themis," replied Ultimata, "you always are right except when you condemn me. I see strongly, from what Dorothy calls my 'other-sidedness,' both the freedom and sense of suddenly broadened power, which we would gain by absolute release from the thraldom of dress; the greater leisure, the unwearied mind, the fairer field for intellectual effort. For inevitably now, we both judge and are judged by dress. We may subordinate the dress to individuality, may command recognition in spite of plain attire, or be found wanting under Worth costumes; but dress, with us all, is unfair help, or unjust hindrance in both social and intellectual life. We are unduly burdened for the competitive race with man in the outer activities, and among ourselves we are so disguised and masked by the fashions which swathe us, that there is waste of power, sacrifice of life, before we reach and know each other. Dress is unfortunately both expression and repression. With abundant income and refined taste, it is an unfolding in form and colour of one's self; but with narrow means, and other dominating interests, it is often only a confessed limitation to the broad, free life, which it burdens and does not beautify.

"But on the other side, I see the loss of poetry and sentiment in any radical change of dress. It would blur the fair traditions of art, and break the historic chain of costume, which links the woman of to-day with Greek goddess and Roman sibyl. It would touch with dimness our own tender memories, and take a thrill from love itself; which feels in the sweep of robes, the fluttering of scarf, something real and tangible of the beloved personality. I think poetry always conquers with me; so I advocate trains for evening dress, short costumes with grace of full drapery for usual wear, artistic tea-gowns to give glow of colour and consolations of grace to the invalid, and above all pink ribbons for Themis, and Santa Barbara roses for us all. Now, girls, don't take advantage of my leniency towards youthful love of dress, and natural vanity, by appearing in any startling toilettes to-night."

Artista, with unruffled dignity, but with evident relief from the anticipated homily upon the vanity of dress, exclaimed, "I came to join Themis and Ultimata for the good of my mind, to hear philosophy, or at least politics, talked; but the text has been pink ribbons, and the sermon such a justification of dress, that for the moral good of the Esperanza, I shall order to-morrow a new costume from San Francisco—I have a lovely idea in my mind."

Perdita quietly answered, "If new dresses and lovely ideas are synonyms, you are truly a creative idealist. I try to keep up some desultory study, so I thought as exercise to my memory and practice in arithmetic, I would keep count of your dresses. But your kaleidoscopic variety of costume has left me only with a confused impression of shivered rainbows. I shall feel it my duty to-night to wear solemn black or neutral grey, as a visible rebuke to the frivolity of pink and white matrons. I never allow my mother anything but violets or white chrysanthemums for decorative touches; otherwise, I could not control her girlish spirit. Oh! the responsibility of daughters in these days!"

CHAPTER IV

THE FIRST RAIN

FOR weeks past there has been a film of shadow over the pleasantness of life here, a dim foreboding, a vague unrest: for January was unbroken sunshine, from New Year's day, with its riding parties, its loitering in the porch, its German in the evening with bountifulness of floral decoration, and light gauzy costumes and the punch bowl in the hall, with its suggestions of Knickerbocker hospitality, through to its latest soft, dreamy sunset. Though such glory of sunlight was joyous to the glad-hearted children, who find life here all summer holidays, healing to invalids of sensitive lungs and faint breath, and restful in its blessed touch upon worn and wearied lives, who drop into hushed calm like some sweet, spiritual sleep, in which all consciousness takes the form of vague, smiling dreams: still, we all felt a ghost of sorrow, shadowing our gaiety, the dread of a dry year. Tourists and strangers felt that dread in a dim, apprehensive way; but Santa Barbara holds fearfully definite memories of the melancholy, deepening into tragedy, of dry years in the past.

So we saw a conscious shadowing of the faces of rancheros who recall other summers unquickened into green, ungladdened by waving crops; of the faces of merchants and business men, who know that California's wealth to-day, is less in the once fabulous mines, than in the fruitful downpour of the winter rain; of the faces of hay dealers, who mitigate their misery by buying up all the available hay, and, putting up its price to the despair of the livery stables, make the indulgence in saddle horses a serious item.

We realise the gravity of a dry year to the country, by the reticence of old Californians on this subject. They tell jolly stories of the old mining camps; and of the free life of the early days, when a man had all the mountains for his pasture, and turned out fearlessly the herds of wild horses to graze at will, with only a brand to prove ownership, and a dash over the hills to catch and claim his own.

But there is an ominous silence regarding the dry years. Only by much questioning, by chance expressions, by a look of sudden pain upon the bronzed faces of the pioneers do we conjure up some conception of that hopeless world, California in a dry season. From these weeks of waiting I could discern faintly the whole story: the eager longing for the usual rain, the confident prediction to sustain fainting hope, the unconscious studying of the wind vane, the quoting of the record of other years when the rains were late but bountiful, the ploughing and planting in sturdiness of faith that the rain was surely coming, the hopeless brownness of the baked earth, the clouding, blinding dust of the roads, the discouraged aspect of all the earth, and most sorrowful—utterly sorrowful—the suffering of the animals. To one who has ever felt the distress of a day's journey even, with a favourite horse, when wayside stable failed to give hope of hay, when pasturage lacked, still more where the arid dryness of alkaline plain gave no gleam of brook, or faintest line of running water, to relieve the thirst of the tired, panting creature, that one experience will give faint, sickening realisation of the agony of ownership, when there are great herds of horses and droves of cattle, with flocks of sheep, for which to find food and seek water through months of drought. Picture first the spirited dash of horses, with gambol of young colts upon these side hills, the contented loitering of motherly cows with mild-eyed calves, in the favourite meadow, close to the daily lessening stream of the little brook: then the loss of strength and spirit, as they seek nourishment from fields looking as brown as the dusty road itself; then the effort by careful economy of the high priced and long treasured hay to ward off death by starvation from the flocks, and the wearisome drawing of water from almost exhausted wells, to slake their deadly thirst. In such extremity, the grand generosity, the hospitable largeness of heart of real Californians have found expression; for neighbour has shared with neighbour, until the ruin was universal, till the thin, phantom-like horses and milkless cows dropped dead in numbers. One year, with heroic determination to save the poor dumb things that long suffering, and themselves the hopelessness of watching it, they drove whole flocks and herds off the cliffs into the sea. In all the romantic history of this State, from the first gold fever, with its frenzy of sudden gain, its despair of sudden loss, through all its agricultural experiments and triumphs, upon the surface scarred with mines and glowing now with tropical fruits and golden with wheatfields, there has been no leaf with record so sad, no picture so awful with shadow, as that of the famished, pathetic-eyed herds and flocks driven to that fatal leap. It forces me to believe in immortality for other of God's children than ourselves.

We dare not find bread for ourselves through horses' faithful, patient dragging of the plough and harrow, or the meek-eyed oxen bending their great necks to the yoke; milk from the udders of generous kine with much wronged motherly instincts, as weaned calves give appealing plaint; wool from the sheared and shivering sheep dumb before its shearers, and life itself from their lives sacrificed for ours, and then complacently accord ourselves immortality, but find no hope beyond their voiceless martyrdom. Life is in them also, a spark from that central flame, creative and eternal.

In conversation on this subject Dorothy calmly

announced to me the other day, that she preferred the Koran to the Bible. My nerves have ceased responding by sudden vibrations to any new expression of Dorothy's heterodoxy. I simply watch with philosophical calm the gradual evolving of her system of theology, as one of the expressions of the modern spirit, questioning all creeds, yet with reconciling touch bringing into related harmony all systems of religious thought. She is feeling in child fashion towards the larger freedom, the richer faith of a Comparative Theology. So I simply asked the why of her preference.

"Because," she answered, "when the Bible talks about animals and birds, it does it only as an illustration of something in our lives, as if they only lived for us; or if it says anything about kindness to them, it seems only as if unkindness and cruelty might hurt our own natures. But the Koran speaks of the life of animals and birds, of camels, hounds, and doves as if their lives were as real as our own, with true stories of joy and sorrow; and it promises them life beyond death. I suppose the Bible says nothing about their immortality, because if we learn the spirit of the Sermon on the Mount, we should know that the promises to the meek and the poor in spirit, must mean the great fine animals who serve us, and the birds with their sweet trustful ways, and their beautiful wings."

Well, the shadow lifted; if one dare call that shadow, which was only tender, brooding sunshine. I was conscious last night in my sleep of a peculiar home feeling, a sense of the East; I could not define it, until I wakened to hear the blessed rain upon roof and piazza, and pouring in gurgling streams over the eaves. I was simply flooded with gladness, the gladness universal of moist fields and quickening seed, of the summer's roses and the autumn's grapes; of comforted sheep and tranquil-eyed cows, of colts, lambs, and all the glad young of the fields: of exultant ranchero and reassured merchant, and of all the lovers of the rare Golden State. We shall watch now for the transformation scene. Can these hills of golden lights and brown shadows, these barren fields really quicken into sudden greenness? We shall see.

I wakened at intervals all night, only to hear the music of rain, be sure that it was no dream; then lulled by its monotonous melody, dropped asleep with heart rejoicing, which was true Thanksgiving service.

This morning the meeting was joyous from friend to friend; as if we were heirs, come into possession of sudden fortunes.

We all crowded out upon the piazza, to feel the damp air and see the freshened beauty of the roses; the shrubs and trees bending beneath the constant, heavy rain. There was the inevitable touch of sadness in seeing the ground white and pink with petals of roses dashed to sudden death in the universal gladness. Other roses, of deeper colour, of purer whiteness, of more fragrant breath and fuller life will bloom in their places. Still life was sweet to these roses to which the rain was of deathly fate, not of living hope.

The irrepressible children made dashes across the wet grass, raids into the shrubbery, shaking down on themselves the drops in sudden showers; and held out their hands, and lifted up their faces to feel the delight of the cool, good rain. Even the Spectator, who wears an air of deluding prudence, crossed the lawn in the heaviest shower, under pretence of examining his family of thermometers, barometers and allied mysterious recording instruments of nature's uncertain forces; but in reality, I know, with an Englishman's satisfaction in wet weather. Added to the natural enjoyment of moisture and misty effects, is his practical, personal sympathy in California's need, as a prospective ranchero.

I expressed to Dorothy my great sorrow that we had not bought the forty acres on the hill of which I wrote in rapturous rhetoric to the Family Financier, but was advised to wait his coming, since my judgment upon soil and my intelligence upon the water supply, he was pleased to doubt. But if we had bought it, I should have felt myself gaining some sure part of the financial result of the rain, of which, *Hans* said, when he brought my breakfast tray, "there's millions in it;" quite unconscious that he was using a phrase, now part of our American classics.

To be sure the side hill has only a magnificent group of boulders, and a few solemn, dusty-leaved live oaks; but to have been a property owner

THE FIRST RAIN

before the rain, would have enriched life some way, and quickened some harvests into growth.

Perhaps, as ranchera, I might have mastered some of the difficulties, comprehended some of the problems of Californian nature. I know there is a mystery in its water supply, that springs fail in places where water could be predicated, and gush defiantly when all water sources seem to fail. Then nature has been in a mood for chemical combinations or elfish experiments—for there are mineral springs of all possible blending: sulphates, carbonates, and chlorides; springs saline, alkaline, chalybeate and magnetic. There only lack mesmeric springs, with sure gift of sleep. No doubt, somewhere in her hidden laboratory, California holds such springs. When discovered, sceptics and scientists will spoil another fairy story, and explain the nap of the Sleeping Beauty and her Court, by the existence of mesmeric springs on the Palace grounds.

The water supply of the town of Santa Barbara comes from the mountains by an aqueduct through Mission Cañon. I smile, when I write the word aqueduct, with memory of those massive arches, giving such beauty of line against the soft Italian sky, such frames for Campagna pictures. This aqueduct of ours is primitive; uplifted on frail wooden trellises, or showing running stream in small, open red-wood troughs upon the ground. But the sound of running water is infrequent music during the dry season; so the aqueduct as it follows the bank, or crosses the stony bed of the dried streams, has its rhythmic charm. In this valley there have been, I think, no experiments in Artesian wells. Many of the houses have their own water supply from wells, lifted to desired height by windmills, and these windmills are notable features upon their ranches. I have not been able to understand the method of windmill activity. There seems, as a rule, no wind, and days and weeks the mills show unstirred fans, as a touch of picturesqueness, across lawns and over barns and stables. When they move, and how, is one of my California conundrums.

The air is so warm and soft that it is a delight to sit in the open window, and watch the familiar sunlit world so draped and disguised in this mantle of rain. The streets are almost deserted; for in a world of constant sunshine, people do not take kindly to umbrellas, waterproofs and overshoes. But I look with a sense of comfortable satisfaction, upon the ugly Scotch ulster and club-handled umbrellas, with which I burdened myself in Chicago midsummer, as special preparation for the rainy season.

There is a feeling in the reading rooms and halls of the Esperanza of being over-populated, as the guests are all restive prisoners (though there is a billiard room for the superfluous masculine element, and a reception room for the children's riots). Many are, like myself, with sudden sprouting of the long buried conscience, devoting the

THE FIRST RAIN

rainy day to home friends. For this is a community of exiles. Many are here for health, some for pleasure, some by chance loitering, Dorothy and I by fate. I cannot fancy myself without this experience. My life, for years shaping itself towards Santa Barbara ends, grew over-wearied for this rest, wounded for this healing, embittered for this sweetness; feeling itself an alien everywhere, to find the sweet sense of home in this far-off Valley of my dreams. I ought to have been born here, and should, but for some little entanglement in the threads of destiny.

But it is something to recognise one's rightful birth-place in spite of the accidents and dislocations of fate. That Dorothy is a Santa Barbarian by natural right is proven by her Mexican dash in riding, her harmonious relations with the mustangs in general and Brownie in particular, her physical need of sunshine and her calm disowning of all future interest in school-books, kid gloves and all representative features of New York civilisation. To be sure, she misses the theatres, known to her by thrilling matinees; and as she had chosen irrevocably the profession of actress for her future, I questioned how the change of environment would affect her plan of life. But with a pony given to circlings and curvettings, to dancing steps and daring manœuvres, the transition was easy to the role of dashing equestrienne in the circus of the future. She is a fearless rider, perhaps one might say, reckless. The Crusader often assures me, as she rounds the corner madly, and dashes towards the porch with a little sense of triumph at the glances of consternation which meet her, that some day she will be brought home in two packages, the body in one, the spirit in another.

But I have a proud confidence in the destiny of the daring spirit. Better dash to one's ends, with risk of fall, than creep through life, a safe, conservative coward.

It was happy fate that to such rider little Brownie should be given. The peculiar form that happy fate took in bringing about that end, was a kick received by Ironsides, given by Brownie. Such was the beneficent Brownie's first night's justification of her fairy name. We were warned that she was unfriendly to strange horses. Such unfriendliness, we thought, only proved the innate refinement, the delicate ladyhood of her nature. But Ironsides had the misfortune to be the strange horse, though he was in his familiar stable, and Brownie was the intruder. She settled their relative positions that first night, and in the morning we found poor awkward Ironsides standing upon three legs, with the other drawn up almost at right angles, the face a study with its abused, long-suffering expression. There was the look of a hurt child in the colt's eyes; the appeal and protest of one unused to pain, but meeting life henceforth with wise distrust, an element new in his hitherto innocent nature. I suppose it was part of the full California experience, to go with a young lady friend, humane by nature and wise by several

THE FIRST RAIN 55

years' Santa Barbara residence, with many adventures and some accidents in her own fearless, graceful riding, and doctor the colt. It was her brave, tender hand that rubbed on the arnica, then turned the hose upon the lame leg; while I suffered the pangs of helpless sympathy, and Dorothy, seated upon a bale of barley hay, talked tender love to Ironsides, her dear colt, and vowed vengeance upon Brownie, then my horse.

But all our care, and the visits of the veterinary surgeon, left him lame, though he grew happy and coltish in his ways again. Then he was sent to pasture. Dorothy, as the only practical compensation for his loss, confiscated Brownie. Then came swift relenting towards the criminal, many apologetic explanations of the way the accident happened, and at last the comfortable assurance that it was just part and parcel of Ironsides' masculine perversity and general awkwardness to get kicked. The same night Brownie kicked the barn door down; but no doubt it was due to the obdurate obstinacy of the barn door, or the timorous weakness of barn door hinges, that it should have had this experience.

At last Dorothy with pride pointed to the prints of the horse shoe high up on the door, and exclaimed, "If Brownie does kick, she leaves the loveliest prints of the daintiest hoofs."

For two months, Ironsides ran in real colt-fashion over the hills. Then, as the pasturage became very poor, and he had a healthy boy appetite, we thought we would bring him into the stable. So Dorothy, with the melancholy faced, handsome Spanish trainer of horses for the Esperanza stable, went in search of him. They had a long afternoon's dash down the ravines and up the slopes; but brought the captive back, very rough as to his grey coat, and so spirited in the use of his legs, that he showed himself not only convalescent, but prepared, I thought, for Brownie's mode of warfare. The dark-eyed, grey-bearded *Jose* assured me—with a twinkle in his eye, that the *Señorita* rode like the *Diablo* and some day "she would spoil her neck so," giving a significant gesture to indicate a broken neck.

But that reckless side is not all of Dorothy—to-night she is sitting with me in still companionship. Perhaps we are weary with the over-pressure of this crowded day in the Esperanza—perhaps some roots of eastern memories are stirring with the fall of the first rain. But in place of dinner with glare of gas and crossing voices, we had tea in the shadowed lamp light of our restful room.

Now I am content, sitting silent with slippered feet on the fender, while Dorothy is absorbed in copying her poems. Do not smile, the little maiden has written some charming child lyrics. Out of the full content of her simple, young life she upreaches on wing of ideality, or sweeps sometimes toward dark, shadowy mountain gloom. It shows her "other sidedness," that the gay, sunny nature should sing yearningly of the "Distance" or utter, like solemn refrain of life's incompleteness, her "Discontent." In these, the thought outreaches her power of form

THE FIRST RAIN

and they are suggestive, but imperfect. But some of her little Summer songs are perfect as trill of robin, or daisy's disc of light. I am very proud of my kinship to these child verses, and feel that some time I shall be grandmother to real "grown up" poems.

CHAPTER V

THE CHINESE NEW YEAR

IT is still pouring rain, to the great satisfaction of the grateful earth and the expectant rancheros, but to the disappointment of our Celestials; for it is the Chinese New Year, "a movable feast," as it falls upon the first new moon, after the sun has entered the sign of Aquarius. Early this morning, Oc and Foo, Chin Foo and Byng began their salutations and the offering of their gifts. Every room is decorated with large bowls, where in water, among piles of pebbles, are roots of the Chinese lily, with stalks of pure, white blossoms. This lily is a kind of narcissus, and the flowers, with deep yellow centres, on long, straight stems with lancet-shaped leaves, are truly a beautiful greeting, offered in bowls gay with eastern colouring.

The faces of our oriental angels shone with the smile peculiar to this grave people, a smile like sunlight upon deep, shadowy waters; giving surface brightness but no revelation of the depths. With the lilies were plates of a Chinese nut, which has for kernel a small, sweetish fruit like a prune but with an astringent flavour; and confectionery, looking like candied orange peel, and a thin, hard paste with flavour of cocoanut. I tried to gain some information for inquiring minds about this fruit in a nut shell, or this nut with a fruit kernel, but I failed to elicit any facts; for though they all speak English, it is routine English in answer to demands for wood, for hot water, for matches, and taken beyond these familiar phrases, they understand but imperfectly and give uncertain, broken answers.

I have made but limited study of the Chinese, my acquaintance being chiefly with Oc and Foo, who answer the office bells. I once thought, when I had seen only three or four stray Chinamen in New York as imported curiosities in the tea stores, that I could not distinguish one Celestial from another. I was so strongly impressed with the strangeness of the national type, that I could discern no individual differences. But I see now the variations of the national type. Foo is a kind of factotum in the Esperanza, and in addition to ordinary services, brings refractory locks to reason, changes the features of the wrong key with deft touch until it slips with perfect right-mindedness into the waiting key-hole, screws up to safe tightness the drop light of loose tendencies, and I have known him cure a smoky chimney by turning his almond-eyed gaze up its dusky depths. He has not the usual Chinese physiognomy; the solemn face so like a mask. He is round-faced and merry, stouter than the usual type, and altogether more human in aspect. He is full of fun, and delights in playing pranks on Dorothy. She has a weakness for a glass of milk at night, with a slice of bread; haply a stray piece of cake. So when she rings her bell at night, Foo generally appears with the irregular and surreptitious feast. But sometimes he comes empty-handed and solemnly announces, "No bread, no milk, no cakee, dining-room lockee, all darkee." Then when the shadow of disappointment steals over the hungry face, somewhere from the depths of his innocent white jacket sleeves, drop down full goblet and loaded plate. I think he has a gentle sense of humour over Dorothy's disorderliness, for in making a transit through her room, I have known him to stop and pick up a pair of buttoned boots from under his feet, and set them gravely as ornaments upon the brackets on either side of the looking-glass, gather up various wandering hats and hang them upon the branches of the chandelier, and lay dress, pinafore and Tam O'Shanter in startling resemblance to a small girl, restfully, tenderly upon the bed.

Oc has a more delicate face, and a smile of curious remoteness. I try sometimes to analyse it, but it baffles me. I think that he is a born diplomat and enjoys a sense of secret power, when one appeals to his finesse of management.

The gas at the hotel has ways of its own, a certain capriciousness of nature, manifested in alternate high flaring and dim, depressed burning; in triumphant hiss as it flames beyond control, or plaintive

THE CHINESE NEW YEAR

sigh, as it escapes unlighted from the burner and refuses all recognition of the wasting match. I wanted a lamp, but lamps are dangerous in wooden caravanseries, so my request was met by Foo's appearance with a drop light and his illuminating smile. In vain I clamoured for a lamp. He answered as he calmly adjusted the drop light, "Very good lampee, no fall, no breakee." So I lighted my drop light and bided my time. It came one evening, when the rebellious gas positively refused to burn. Candles were hastily distributed through the house, but Oc appeared in my room with a large lamp which he lighted, watching me with his suggestive smile. The next evening the gas burned, but I said to Oc, "Very good lamp, Oc, but no shade." He darted a look of intelligence upon me, entered into the intrigue and said, "I get big shade, very fine, I hidee him," so he disappeared and returned with a beautiful ground glass shade, with delicately engraved pattern. It is a lamp of that mysterious kind which winds up from beneath like a clock, and gives in burning a solemn, significant click as of marking off the passing minutes. Oc always fills and attends to this lamp himself; and winds up its mechanism with his diplomatic smile as if we were allied powers in some secret treaty overreaching duller and more open-faced nations.

I have no opinion upon the Chinese question in the abstract; but I am enjoying my studies of this, to me, new and enigmatical national type. From my own experience in the hotel, I should call them perfect servants, going through their duties with the regularity of finely constructed automata. Still, without the touch of a woman's hand on any part of the machinery, I could not unravel the mystery of this house, but for the presence of the Fairy Prince—for so we call our charming young host, whose true personality was discovered by Dorothy through her familiarity with fairy lore. All the house servants are Chinese and the waiters are of every known nationality, Irish, Spanish, German; and our own at present is a Russian, of whom I must later give a sketch. Chin Foo, who attends to our rooms, is as impenetrable as the Sphinx, and brought his New Year's offering with a gravity fitting some solemn religious ceremonial. The day will be observed in their own quarter with Chinese crackers, fireworks, the clashing of instruments in a discord which they call music, and by the presence of Chinamen in the brocaded jackets of their gala days.

A journalist would put on mackintosh and rubbers and make notes on the spot—damp, depressing notes—but I, from my familiarity with the Chinese quarter and the memory of past Fourths of July, shall in dry garments, by the wood fire on my hearth, proceed to construct the Chinese New Year.

The Chinese quarter is one of the streets of the old town, with low adobe houses. It has by day a deserted look, as most of the Chinamen are employed as house servants, but there are two or three Chinese stores, and in these there are always groups of the Celestials: I have never seen cards or opium pipes, which should be there to complete the picture. Before Christmas I ventured into the stores, hoping to find hidden in their mysterious depths some temptation in the shape of oriental goods. There were the usual soft crape neckerchiefs, fragile cups and quaint China tea kettles, sandal wood fans and those of the common decorative style, silk panel pictures with graceful butterflies and birds on wing, or those with women figures in the cumbersome enveloping of the national costume, and some river scenes with mountain background, which obtruded itself with sense of equal right upon the observer's eye, as Chinese art is not held in thraldom to rule of perspective. I discovered a charming sandal-wood casket for a little sister about to pose as bride (it surely must be in childish tableau, only), and panels with their oriental pictures for the other young sisters, acting their little comedies as matrons and mothers; for they seem children still at play, to my eldest sister heart. I sent to Pater Familias a charming tea pot, in quaint kettle shape with well padded straw cosy. The kettle, filled with real Chinese tea, I thought a truly significant gift, for his weakness for tea is quite feminine, and his fondness for telling long stories between his uncounted cups, makes it a problem how to continue to furnish the beverage hot, and of its original strength. But with this padded cosy, the tea will simmer with undisturbed warmth of temperature for five hours; so it will give time for real geological development of good stories. I was glad to escape from the atmosphere of these stores; with mingled odours of tea, sandalwood, dye stuffs and the invisible opium. One sees occasionally on the street, Chinese women, dressed, as is the custom among the lower classes, exactly like men; but with the long braids fastened about the head with sharp, glittering pins. With them are sometimes the queerest, quaintest children, dressed in the same loose, wide-sleeved jackets and ample trousers; little embryonic Celestials, so droll with their serious faces and grown-up style of costume, that I have always wished to buy a pair for mantel ornaments.

From the newspaper letters, and the enthusiasm of eastern tourists, returned from the Pacific slope, I thought the labour question was settled here, as far as domestic service is concerned, by the advent of perfect house servants in the Chinese. But I find in Santa Barbara, and I believe the same conditions exist in all smaller towns, that owing to the inadequate number of the Chinese to meet the demands of the place, and the legal restrictions now limiting their immigration, the balance of power between employers and employees is much disturbed. The Chinese are restless and ambitious, making frequent changes, with outside investments claiming their attention; and maintaining an attitude of indifference and independence toward the house holders whom they serve. They are admirable servants in the almost mechanical regularity with which they attend to their duties, are quiet in movement; and with a sense of order which gives the kitchen of a Chinese servant an artistic pleasantness.

The immobility of countenance, the monotonous tones of voice, the even, unhurrying movements, all seem part of their admirable mechanism. But faces that never flush; steps that neither hasten with anticipation, nor lag from unwillingness; natures alike unstirred by enthusiasm and incapable of discouragement, do not appeal to our human sympathies.

When I think of the warm-hearted race by whom we are served in the East, whose thunder-cloud of temper and lightning-flash of words startle the serenity of home life, I recall also the quick beating of their human hearts with ours in every time of sorrow, the gracious service of warm, strong hands for us when sick room shadows creep about us, or deathly coldness touches the faces used only to our passionate kisses; and I forgive the Irish tongue and temper, for the sake of the love and loyalty of the Irish heart.

I do not deny the Chinaman the possession of a heart. It is there, with its devotion to his country and his family, with his reverential worship of his ancestors; but it is a heart as yet unreached by us. There is a Christian Chinese Mission in Santa Barbara, much frequented, since it teaches reading and writing, those roads to the practical end of money getting; but I question how far their methodical, controlled natures, educated in the inflexible rigidity of the ethics of Confucius, respond to the awakening, spiritual touch of that faith which is life-giving to the individual spirit. The Chinese seem like conscious, resigned, law-ordered atoms of the safe, strong, unchanging national whole. One pleasant feature of their lives here is their success upon their infinitesimal ranches. In all our rides through the Valley, we come upon little bits and strips, much irrigated, and densely green with the growth of vegetables; the property of Chinamen, who bring to the generous breadth of the new land, the habits of close economy of space, and careful culture, which make the overcrowded soil of China so productive and beautiful, as to justify its poetic name of "The Flowery Kingdom." The vegetable gardening here is chiefly in their hands; and the green-laden waggon and most melancholy mustang of the Chinese vendor is a familiar feature in Santa Barbara streets.

But here comes Oc to wind up and light our international lamp. I ask him if he went to China Town to keep his New Year. He answers with undisturbed serenity, and without the appearance of having been excited by the explosion of a single cracker, or depressed by the fall of even a passing shower, " Yes, many China boys, muchee rain, goodee time." So to the enigmatical Chinese mind, the combination of fire-works with rain, constitutes a good time.

CHAPTER VI

THE MIRACLE OF SPRING

OF all nature's processes as watched in many lands, I have seen nothing so like miracle as this sudden transformation of the brown, dusty earth into vivid living green. After the first rain, which lasted two days, came a week of warm sunshine.

First across the hills there passed a sudden change, too faint to be more than a prophecy of Spring. The surface was still brown, but along exposed ridges and upon the sunniest points, appeared a tender faint green, only visible in a strong light, as upon the outside line of fold in drapery. There was a moist, sweet smell in the air as of fresh, upturned earth, and an expression of expectancy across the still barren fields. Then came another week of variable weather; heavy rain alternating with quickening, glorious sunlight. I never tired of watching the moist effect of these wet days, the mountains blotted out, the hills a blur of cool wet grey, and the late afternoon light, when the rain ceased, giving the nebulous distance of an English landscape. For several days, the heavy rains, or frequent showers, with clouds low upon the mountains gave a veiled charm to nature. Then came a morning of triumphant sunshine; not light between the showers, but full-hearted, glad, assured sunshine. For the first time in days the mountains were visible; with every wrinkle upon their faces, every point of their crests in clear outline. But where beneath their guardianship was my golden world? The hills were radiant in clear tender green, luminous it seemed in its shining, so full of light and thrilling with life; and across the green, touches of faint yellow and purple, a little later to unfold in such masses as made the foothills a carnival of colour. Then followed six weeks of Edenic beauty. I write from memory, as in those weeks I could only live, bud, and put forth leaf of joy in nature's unconscious way. I could not make an herbarium for scientific study from that living, palpitating bloom.

The fields were fresh and glad, with eager horses enjoying the green peas and salad of their table; for evidently the succulent, young grass was such dainty to them. The roads, clean washed from adobe dust, after the rain hardened into firm surface which rang under the horses' hoofs like asphaltum pavement; and along their sides were borders of grass, like miles of unrolled shimmering ribbon. Then nature in her joy grew vocal with running water, as streams ran merrily over stony beds through the many cañons; and Mission Creek flowed visibly into the sea.

Then came rides through yellow clouds of wild

mustard above our heads; while the horses made æsthetic lunches of the sunlit beauty of the feathery blossoms.

One ride I recall as a vision of glory, to a bee-ranch, six miles from town. Before coming to California I had romantic expectations of the charms of bee-ranches; from a "Century" article with suggestive illustrations of wild flower fields, and fertile valley vistas. The way thither was through sunshine, spring bloom, and air thrilling with conscious creative life. Of course we were all young; with that immortal youth, the birthright of us all in hours of true spirit revelation. The disguise of mature years fell from us, and I know under the ecru veil twisted about my wide-brimmed hat, was the visionary brain of twenty years ago; and beneath the bunch of eschscholtzias, the glad girlish heart, with dower of love's young dreams.

We were all part of the glad, growing, quickening spring; with its budding promise, its hope of ripening summer with gain of bountiful harvest— for here harvests are not autumnal, but part of the midsummer glory— as spring lavishes its perfect joy in February. Can you see with me this vision of California Spring? Green, green everywhere on the foothills; in the fields of young barley and wheat, in the shining, freshened leaves of orange trees, of figs, of silver-leaved eucalyptus and solemn, dusky live oak, upon the vineyard slopes and across the meadows of the valley. There are masses of palpitating radiance where the eschscholtzias—the State's symbol flower—lift their light-brimmed chalices; and dim shadows of pale blue blossoms, called by me the wild hyacinth, but ruthlessly re-named by botanical friend the wild onion. (Scientific people are as uncomfortable to deal with as statistics and other uncompromising facts.)

Near the beach is a bewildering growth of lupins, purple, blue and white, an ice plant with pale pink blossoms and thick leaves shining as with hoar frost; and everywhere that emblem of æstheticism, the wild sunflower. Then in less number, with a touch of patrician beauty, is the Mariposa lily, three petalled, white, shading into pale purple. But nothing could give such impression of the daring glory of California's wild flowers as the Spectator's water-colour sketches in the Ojai Valley, where he spent three weeks of nature's budding and sudden bloom; going after the first rain, and not returning to us until a faint, yellow shadow was dimming the freshness of the spring world. These drawings have gone to England, and I fancy them on the walls of the Old Water-colour Society flashing their prodigal beauty, their unshadowed sunlight, among the cool green and gray of English lake scenery, the deep blue mountain shadows of North Wales, or the purple glow of heather-clad Highlands. Of two or three I will give faint outlines. One was the valley, an amphitheatre girt with strong steadfast mountains; their lower slopes, green with the moist, vivid tints of early spring, and the broad valley foreground a bewilderment of blossoms, a colour orchestra, evolving variations upon the same theme of southern, sunlit life. The sense of light in the atmosphere, of strength in the mountains, of gladness in the fields, the undimmed blue of sky, the unshadowed green of earth, give that keen, ecstatic joy, always so akin to pain. Why that touch of grief in the utmost thrill of joy? Another Ojai Valley view was a study of hills in strong midday light, with brown, upturned fields for foreground, with the labourer, horse, and plough giving that comforting human touch to the beauty of nature. It was the prayer and promise of its answer, "Give us this day our daily bread."

After years of familiar study of foreign cities, with their centuried confession of man's effort in art and architecture, and of unrestful life in our own cities, still in the molten state with seething of hot streams and flame of volcanic activity in fierce speculative life, I find much rest in the primitive gaining of bread through upturned sod and buried seed.

Yet I know modern life has not left nature to work out her own ends of generous fruitfulness. For there are cruel "corners" in grain (gambling with the daily bread of His giving), and hot strife between railroad monopolists and rural "Grangers." Still it leaves undisturbed the comforting relationship between the farmer and the soil; the soothing, calming touch of mother earth upon those who clasp her closely, and trust to the bounty of her motherly heart.

There may be a bucolic slowness in purely agricultural regions; but after study of the characteristic physiognomy of various communities, a rural neighbourhood has to me a solid comfortable restfulness of expression, compared with the keen-eyed, metallic sharpness of faces, in regions where mineral resources tempt with that lure of sudden wealth.

I do not quite accept Ruskin's condemnation of the unfolded coal mines of England, because of the ruin wrought in scarred lawns and stained mountain brooks; for one understands the value of iron and coal to the manufacturing interests of that island kingdom. But on a new broad continent, with forests still unfelled, and fertile plains untilled, I question the gain of delving for uncertain mineral wealth, below the soil; with surer, steadier gift of waving grain and ripening fruit above. There seems a natural, healthful expression to the communities which rest upon the sure unfailing foundation of agricultural life. It gives a peaceful, smiling nature, homes framed in gardens or set in golden fields, wild flowers for the children's gathering, berries for parties of simple pleasure, brooks for the boys' fishing, and paths across the fields for neighbourly treading. Then in a farming community there is the peaceful hearth side, with place for the grandmother with knitting and stories of the far-away, fabled age " when I was a little girl"; for the wife with her housewifely interests and her sympathetic presence which makes the house a home; for the group of children with their winsome ways and shining curls, to keep the hearts from growing old. There are herb gardens

THE MIRACLE OF SPRING

with their gift of gentle healing, kitchen gardens with their grace of climbing peas and odour of bean blossoms, and front yards gay with flowers. There are well worn paths to the village church and the home of the sleeping dead; and sheltered, fragrant lanes for lovers' twilight walk.

But a mining camp is fearfully, aggressively masculine; earth torn and scarred with his impatient seeking, and heavily laden with tons of problematical ore; streams degraded to turn speculative stamp mills, the hills disembowelled through sinking shafts, digging ore and other methods of prospecting; and shanties and huts giving meagre shelter to men, who for such seeking have sold their birthright of home and love.

What place here for watching wife, or clinging child? No strength and leisure for such encumbrance; but wronged man nature asserts itself in the physical acceptance of the marred, stained type of womanhood, which comes by natural law to meet the lowest needs of lowered man. I know there is often a hopeful outcome in prosperous mining towns, in properties which pay good dividends, in gradual transformation into civilised centre with homes and schools. But the curse strikes deeper than through the desolation of deserted mining camp, and despairing, luckless prospector. It has fevered the blood, and maddened the brain of American men in speculation; and brought alienation and antagonism between the overheated lives of eager, hungering men, and the shivering, apprehensive lives of watching and waiting women, chill with the possible loss of uncertain future. No calm, steadfast home rests upon the quaking foundation of mining stocks.

I cannot now—in the early Eighties—in this smiling State, with its wide wheat fields and its groves of oranges, almonds and olives, re-create the California of the "Forty-niners", and of Bret Harte's stories. Its old unrest is calmed, its old scars healed with nature's tender touch.

California may have less play of light and shadow, less dramatic unfolding of story, than in the days which made Sutter's Mill the Mecca and Medina of mammon worshippers. But its prosperity is deep rooted, with healthful branching and weight of golden fruit.

Who would ever think that the swift, sweet awakening of our southern spring could have called forth such moralising? I wandered from the Spectator's pictures. I shall return to their poetic rendering of California life. I recall one (though of the dry season), taken, I believe, on Mount Pinos, at least somewhere in the Santa Ynez Range. It was the course of a river or stream, seen through a group of sombre pines in the foreground, winding on and on through sunlit fields with sinuous course, until, a faint, far thread, it was lost in dim, dreamy distance. I called it "Beyond", for it lured with its shining devious line the thought on and on, till it seemed like human story lost in infinite sea or eternal space. Upon close study, it proved to be not the flowing of the stream but strong sunlight

THE MIRACLE OF SPRING

upon the white, stony bed of a dried stream: not the movement and unrest of life itself, but the worn channel and wavering course of a power now at rest; part of the earth's written record. One, more daring than the Spectator's usual mode of treatment (for he carries into his art something of the repression and reticence which characterise him in social life), was a strong sunset study of lurid, intense red. I remember only that glow of impassioned colour; as if day of mild, mid-summer light, had at sunset given way to tragic mood, and revealed in death, soul of heroic daring. I know that to many repressed natures, especially woman lives, death must be a triumphant experience; the first full, unfettered expression of themselves.

CHAPTER VII

ORANGE BLOSSOMS

THIS heading should mean the budding of that romance, for which I have waited. But with youth and beauty, meeting manly strength and knightly courtesy, all the elements of romance touching in the sunlit air of this rose garden of a valley, I see about me frank friendship and glad companionship, but no love story for my happy telling, and your sympathetic listening. These orange blossoms are burdening the air with their suggestive sweetness, deep hidden among the glossy leaves; while on the same tree shine last year's late yellow oranges.

The orange trees in the Esperanza, as in many home gardens here, are purely ornamental, and planted only for the beauty of their blossoms and glow of their fruit. For the orange here lacks the luscious sweetness of that of San Diego, grown in the rich red ferruginous soil of that more southern valley. Here, upon certain ranches, with careful culture, they are sweet but never large. We have had from the Esperanza's paternal ranch, "Glen Annie," some delicious in flavour; and those from the Dinsmore ranch, deep sheltered in the cañon of the same name, are far-famed for their excellence. But, either because of distance from a good market, as we are (happily for the peaceful beauty of our valley) remote from a railroad, or because other crops bring better returns, the orange culture is not characteristic of Santa Barbara County.

Lying under the shelter of the Mesa is one ranch, most southern in all its aspects, with beautiful orange grove and fine vineyards, and low, large rambling building as vinery. We passed this on our first morning's ride in Santa Barbara; and how Italian the whole scene was, like vineyard on the hills of Tuscany; the more so as we saw oxen ploughing, and laden donkeys, with dark-faced contadino-like driver, passing along the road.

In Montecito, the beautiful valley near Santa Barbara, there are several orange groves; most decorative features of the country, but I do not know the quality of the fruit. An orange grove in itself, from the stiff stateliness of the trees, I think less picturesque, than an orchard of wayward, gnarled old apple trees; and in blossoming time, the pink-tipped buds, and drift of white blossoms of the home orchards, I think lovelier than the symbolical blossoms of the orange. Still the presence of the orange tree is dear to me always, as true sign of southern environment. It makes the most visible distinction between the landscape of Northern and Southern California. The one is our land, with cherry, peach and apple orchards, with pink and white blossoms shining with the early summer promise of our young years; the other, the fragrant mystical south, with suggestions Italian and Hellenic. Sometimes, I think Southern California, with its dry, warm slopes, its browsing sheep and goats, its vineyards and olives, its blue sea and dreamy islands, though with a kinship to Italy as I know it, must be, in its colouring and local features, still more like pastoral Greece or the Sicily of Theocritus.

I remember years ago, when Dorothy was lingering on the outermost verge of baby days, a friend raised from an orange seed a little slip, which when it put forth two tiny timid leaves, was brought to the delighted child as a real Brooklyn orange tree. I do not remember its fate, but I presume it died from hourly watering and much caressing. At least, I do not remember any weight of golden fruit upon that tree of tender care and large hope. The child never doubted her future ownership of fresh oranges every day; and moved about with tender broodings of prospective gracious hospitality, when she could stand under that tree, pick its golden fruit and gladden all our hearts with her generous gifts.

I think, in a land of orange groves, she has found less joy in the fruit of earthly growth, than in the faint foreshadowing of oranges upon her two-leaved slip.

Artista brought, in her usual generous offering of flowers from the home ranch, many sprays of orange blossom: so we all went down to dinner decorated like bridal party on its way to church for the fateful service—and still no romance quickens. Can it be that my presence as an authorised reporter of such romance, has a nipping effect upon the bud?

Madame de Staël thought one might do without happiness in Paris: so perhaps in the valley of eternal summer and immortal roses, one might be content without love.

The best justification that I can offer for deluding you with orange blossoms, without veil and wedding favours, is to picture for you the fair young bride now of our household. Naturally, the groom is with her, and shall come into the picture as restful shadow. What but shadow can even bridegrooms be, while nothing more picturesque offers in masculine attire, than blue yachting coats, and grey shooting jackets? I have tried to inspire the Spectator with the fancy for a brown velvet studio coat; but he treated the suggestion as a new proof of feminine flippancy, though he is quite at home in giving hints for charming costumes to the ladies, and I am carrying in my mind two or three ideal toilettes, until a trip to San Francisco, and the presence of the Bi-metallist of the family, shall give me the creative power to materialise their beauty in Indian silk and China crape. Some weeks ago, as he stood with Artista under the vines, which have a trick of framing graceful groups, I heard him give her the *motif* for a charming costume, quite Californian—"a symphony in yellow." It was to be of lemon colour and Indian yellow, in soft material with possibilities of artistic draping (nun's veiling and India silk, I thought to myself), and I saw in fancy the stately brunette, robed in the golden glory, moving through the mazes of the dance with the artist of its creation. Artista confided to me her plan to startle the Spectator by appearing in the costume of his fancy. In a moment of confidence, I whispered to him the compliment awaiting him of seeing his thought incarnate. So we have watched and waited while Artista has coquetted with blue, pink and cardinal, with crushed strawberry and terra cotta, with olive green and chocolate brown, has grown guileless in white and penitential in black, and still we wait the shining of the yellow robe. Is she waiting some hour of triumph in harmony with its vivid beauty, or some mood of daring in which to flash upon us its gorgeous glory; or is it some lenten penance not to gratify her own latest caprice? If no light dawns I shall work out its mystery in a novel, to be called "The Heroine of the Yellow Gown." It sounds like own cousin to "The Woman in White."

But to return to the orange blossoms. The bride is fair, with true Marguerite fairness; hair brushed smoothly back from the girlish forehead, and blonde braids wound about the small head, so gracefully poised upon the slender neck. She only needs the loosened braid, the girdle and Marguerite satchel to be perfect in the garden scene; and there is a dark-browed, mysterious eyed South American in the house, who would be an irresistible Mephistopheles. But this is Marguerite of kindlier fate, having, it seems, a life all garden bloom, with right to jewel casket, holding youth, fairness and love, worldly gifts of outward fortune, and grace of inner loveliness. The companion sketch to hers should be according to accepted novel rules, of one strong and stalwart, with dark hair and eyes as shadow to her fairness. But her knight is tall and slender with hair and beard of light brown; and with the same look of fragility and grace which characterises the bride. They are so alike in fairness of colouring and delicacy of feature, with the same unconscious grace of those who hold by habit and natural heritage the good gifts of life, and with such freedom from the sentimental tenderness of manner which makes confession of the joy of new ownership, that I should have called them brother and sister. I do not know them; they belong to the gay young world, but they belong also to mine, since I have chosen them as the points of high light in my picture. Over most lives here I see some shadow brooding: with some only the lengthening shadow of the late day itself, of those who walk in the sunset light, over some shadows of old sorrow resting like idealising haze, upon some heavier darkness of storms now gathering in sudden gloom, over other lives now in sunlight, I see faint premonitions of the shadows which shall be. For there are those of poetic temperament, of sensitive organisation predestined to pain.

Given life as it is, and to an idealist needing always heroes to crown and saints to worship, the disillusioning process of living is keen agony; not the less agony that one may still find humanity an intensely interesting study, with its blending of good and evil, its strange hidden roots of motive, its uncertain, imperfect growth. But between the liturgy of worship towards ideals, with which all young hearts begin life, and the deepening, widening charity which holds sacred, lives discrowned and disinherited, lives of outward loss and spiritual failure, there is an interval of personal pain, of passionate doubt. So I see faces shadowed with tenderness of sympathy, and others shadowed more sorrowfully by the cynicism in which there is no sympathy.

But it is a relief to let the eyes and heart rest sometimes upon undimmed gladness, to bury one's face in the roses and feel no thorns, to look into a child's eyes and see only childhood, and to watch young love, as if youth and love were alike immortal. I find so much of the selfishness and bitterness of natures, resulting from the inevitable need of struggle, the heat of conflict, the pressure of other lives, that I sometimes wonder what the strange, sudden development would be, if some morning we should waken to the possession of an earth uncursed by thorns; a generous earth which should give bread without that sweat of brow; a sunny unshadowed earth, true garden of Eden, with no angel with drawn sword between its perfect beauty and our exiled hearts. Could any life be selfish, where all lives found generous place; could any hand be grasping, where all hands were filled; could any spirit be ungracious, where none had dread of failure? Could any unfaith be, where sod and sky kept perfect faith with man? One year's bad harvest in the wheat fields, of failure in the golden corn, brings such dread pressure of poverty on the poor, such apprehension of loss to the rich; that the poor grow defiant in their bitterness, the rich selfish in their anxieties, and the truth of human brotherhood seems but a mocking fable. The effect of wealth may well be hardness of heart, dimness of spiritual vision; where we have the poor always with us as phantoms at every feast, shadows upon every joy. To the many the result is selfish indifference, to the few unavailing pain. For charity itself works with outstretched hand, but with questioning, protesting heart. What joy in abundance when others lack, what gain in golden harvests when others fail of gleanings? With the tendency of the modern mind to study facts, accumulate statistics, from which to deduce laws, we are told there must be a certain proportion of failures, of criminals, of suicides in each generation; such proportion being exactly determined by laws of heredity, and the facts of environment. Think of the pathos of it! With life as it is, we dare not all be glad, we cannot all be good.

But I sometimes see, among lives which have ripened in constant sunshine, such sweetness of nature, such purity of mind, such graciousness of courtesy and restfulness of manner, that I draw a deep breath of longing for a life so sunny and spacious that all humanity could wear such glad, confident smile. I know much of this is only seeming, the well-polished surface of life, not life itself; and that those charms of voice and manner, significant of sheltered drawing-rooms and curtained windows, conceal often the unrest and incompleteness of inner life, while they reveal its outward perfections. Then if grace, sweetness and pleasantness are developed by a life of inherited or assured wealth, we find in the shrouded courts and dark alleys of our great cities, among the criminals seeking shadow, and prostitutes, whose faces lift only in the gas light, strange revelations of loyalty and tenderness; and towards the hard working poor, I feel absolute reverence, I have seen such power of persistent sacrifice, such strength of loyalty, such patience of long suffering.

But to return to our group:—Last night was glorious moonlight, with soft, fragrant air. The piazzas are generally deserted in the evening, as ours is a community of sensitive lungs and invalid throats. But Themis has perfect health, as well as finely balanced mind. She is a most harmonious unity, with physique which gives free movement to her eager, but controlled intellect; and a mind, which by its just, equable activity neither burdens, nor unmercifully exhausts the physical. She is strong in her emotional nature, but with her emotions dominated by her steadfast will. I find her a tower of strength. Most women as friends, give responsive sympathy; but such friendship is often only the play of reflex feeling upon natures highly elated or deeply depressed, an intensifying of ourselves. But Themis has a steadying, controlling touch upon the lives of others, because her own life, ordered according to law, is so perfect a unity.

I am nocturnal by habit, and feel my best in cool evening air. I think the day wearies with its excess of light, bewilders with its multiplicity of details, gives too strong an outline to the lives touching ours, to give us full self-development. I like the shadowed, withdrawn possibilities of life, in evening walk or twilight companionship. Under the deepening darkness, one dare assert a stronger, more accentuated individuality than when in daylight we study the faces that watch our own.

The Crusader, though in love with Santa Barbara (or he would not have found place in my talk), finds the little village not a broad field of action; so night after night is heard upon the piazza, his tramp, tramp, tramp, as in walk, solitary or companioned, he expends his restless, resistless energy. Last night our trio walked together, and I think the breath of the orange blossoms must have suggested the theme, for some way the talk drifted to the subject of marriage.

We are none of us young, judged by the candles in our birthday cakes, if an ungenerous world gave cakes and candles, and we have all known the experience of marriage with its "better and worse." Then we are fearless friends, and talked in the cool, calming moonlight with that pleasant rhythm of measured step.

Talking of collegiate and professional education for women, and the deepening and broadening of woman nature under such development, Themis remarked, "Its finest result you may find in the unfolded nature of the woman—its larger, fuller blossom: but I think the practical, tangible gain is deeper than that. It is in her having now a root of her own, the possibility of independent growth. I believe that these thoroughly educated daughters of ours, will not be dependent upon marriage for happiness, neither as opening the only possible career, that of domestic duties and social power."

Crusader, with most advanced theories regarding women (but unconsciously to himself treating them personally, and as subjects under discussion, with sense of masculine supremacy), retorted, " Women seem incapable of considering the great questions of higher education and political enfranchisement, without assuming a position of antagonism towards men. Why glorify intellectual development as an escape from marriage, which is the highest and only natural life for woman? Why in her broadened, deepened life, should she treat man as an enemy? Are all her acquirements and attainments only so many weapons, stored in the armoury of the future, to be used in a conflict against man?"

Ultimata, who has a reprehensible habit of interrupting, broke in, "Why for six thousand years have men been incapable of seeing women in any light, save that of their accessories? Why to-day must the question of woman's development assume the query as to whether this stronger, grander type is equally fitted for wifehood? If it is not, it must find another career; for this stronger, broader type is the woman of the future. The symbol of the vine is henceforth obsolete, since women know that the moral strength of the world has been their own; that by popular assent men have vested in women moral integrity and spiritual strength, reserving to themselves the intellectual attainments and practical possessions of the world. This moral force of theirs has been the world's conscience. Men have never fought for any cause, save nerved by woman's power of faith, sustained by her strength of sacrifice. But this same spiritual power, which has been the world's heart, beating true under all the outward vicissitudes of nations' growth and nations' death, beats now with a stronger, mightier throb, since beating with conscious, recognised individuality. Men thought the division of labour eternally wise, when they elected to do the fighting and bade women do the praying. But praying has its danger, since it may lead to fuller understanding of His teaching, who came not to bring peace into the world, but a sword. The same holy sense of duty which kept women in political subordination, illumined by stronger spiritual light, may make them rebels."

Themis, who is socially conservative, though so

liberal in thought, answered, "But I see no reason for glorifying war measures, since the way is opening to women now, into all departments of labour, and into all professions. I only trust that the developed, enfranchised woman may be truly woman. You know, while I favour woman suffrage, that I think with apprehension of the short haired, loud voiced type of woman, developed by public conventions. But even the Crusader concedes now the right of woman to full citizenship."

"I long denied that right, as you know," replied the Crusader, "on the ground that the national safety demanded that the voting force of a country should be equalled by its fighting force; that every ballot should have behind it a possible musket. Service on the field unfits a man for taking merely sentimental views of citizenship. I have seen too many men pay with their heart's blood for this right, to think it is one which should be lightly conferred. But in our Federation of States, the experiment of woman suffrage can be more safely tried than elsewhere; since, should any State fail of the armed force to sustain the decision of its votes, the National Government could be called upon to give the aid of the Federal Army, as in the famous Dorr Rebellion in Rhode Island."

Themis said rather dolorously to Ultimata, "You called the Crusader your convert to woman suffrage; but he is certainly not an enthusiast in the cause. How did you meet his favourite argument that the rights of citizenship rest upon the ability to bear arms? Did you promise him a brigade of Amazons?"

"No," answered Ultimata, "I insisted that he should define his position as pure materialist, or as a believer in spiritual powers. You know that he accepts Spiritualism and is more of a mystic than a sceptic. So he readily admitted the reality of spiritual forces. Then I asked him in a long letter, of which I can only give the main points, how he dared assert that the victories in our civil war were due only to the visible and marshalled armies of the north, since the hearts of American women were uplifted in faith and prayer; and none knew through their appeal, what hosts invisible, what higher powers took part in the conflict, when not national life alone, but liberty and the brotherhood of man, were in deathly peril."

"Yes," the Crusader answered, "I think the argument valid, that if we recognise spiritual powers, we should admit the possibility of an alliance with unseen forces, through the faith and loyalty of those who bear no arms. But war has been to me so awful a reality, that I would by all thoughtful statesmanship, defend the nation against another appeal to arms. We have been so reckless in our political experiments, and learnt wisdom at so high a price, the best young blood of our nation."

"In your warmest moments of spiritual insight," Ultimata said, "you recognise the power of woman as an ally in the conflicts of life, political as well as social; but in your realistic reactions you fall back upon the Gospel of Avoirdupois, and really think us less, because we weigh less. But whatever the relative power of man and woman, the whole question of woman's development was subtly stated in an old 'Atlantic' essay. 'Ought Woman to learn the Alphabet?' It was, I believe, by that gentle Knight, Thomas Wentworth Higginson. This query enfolds the whole problem. Once given the seed of the fruit of the tree of Knowledge, and women can be denied no part of its awful growth and fateful fruit."

Themis, who always brings us back from our devious paths, asked, "But how does that bear on the future relation of the sexes? Will men seek women less because of their larger culture, or will they seek more earnestly, with professions and independent careers as their rivals?"

Crusader said, "I honour the broader, stronger woman; but she must wear her wisdom in womanly guise, as drapery, not as armour."

"But," Ultimata objected, "if worn as drapery, it might only embarrass her, entangle her in the march of the future; but worn as armour, it might win her recognition from the champions of 'the fighting force.' But let us be practical. A broad sympathetic but vague education may make women more charming in home life. I almost think it does. It gives flexibility and grace, with quick adjustment to the thought of others. But the real test of the value of education is, will it make women capable of self-support?"

Themis, in amazement, "I never suspected you

of bringing anything down to a money basis. Do you really narrow the woman question to that mercenary point?"

The Crusader joined in the protest, "Yes, for an idealist, an advocate of spiritual powers, I think that is a strange recantation of the faith."

Ultimata answered with resolute firmness, "I do narrow the subject to just that point. You two can afford to ignore it, since you both inherited fortunes and have never felt the common pressure of life. But I know that woman's larger life depends upon her power of individual action. The power to make money, is the power to own one's own life; to hold it free from false entanglement and outward thraldom."

The Crusader asked, "Do you desire this power of financial independence in women, as a defence against marriage?"

Ultimata fiercely, "No, I desire it as the only justification for marriage, since only a woman financially independent, or with power to win such independence has any right to marry. Then no man can make her slave, or hold her wearily as his life burden. I have yet to see the man so chivalrous, that his wife has never felt her dependence either as slow, dull heart ache, or as keen, quivering pain. I have yet to find the man so generous as to ratify in fact, that ecclesiastical fiction 'with all my worldly goods I thee endow.' If at the altar, he said 'with half my worldly goods I thee endow', and made it legal contract, it would lessen the activity of the divorce court, and hasten the millennium."

"I fully concur with you," answered the Crusader, "in your attack upon the falsity of a service, which endows a woman with visionary property rights, to which she has no legal claim. But let me press the question, to which you have given indirect or evasive answer: do you desire marriage for this coming woman, or do you think it a sacrifice of this higher strength to give its fulness to home life?"

"Ultimata has a way of circling all round a subject until she dizzies herself," said Themis. "Until she regains her steadiness, I will answer you, that for the noble girls, in whose future I have an interest, I should choose for them single life, not of enforced struggle for financial independence, for I would have fathers protect daughters from that need; but single life of broad study, of scholarly culture, of calm friendship. There will always be girls for seeking in marriage, emotional and unintellectual, whose only aim is wifehood."

The Crusader asked, "Then shall the future generations claim only the weaker, narrower type of womanhood for mothers; and shall the deepened woman nature miss the tenderness, which comes through experiences of wifehood and motherhood?"

Ultimata replied seriously, "The whole question is a perplexity, but I see two or three gleams of light, which I will flash on your darkness. I believe in love and marriage, but that is only one article in my creed; I believe also in woman's independence, her fitness for single life, but to true woman it will be always the highest joy to choose wifehood, in place of independent career; but it must be in genuine marriage, the mating of peer with peer in equal companionship, in equal experience of life's weal and woe, in equal ownership of all life's goods; with full independence of thought, full right to all expression of such thought in word and deed, in creed and vote. When it comes to the possibility of professional career for a wife and mother, I question the wisdom of such dual life (except where unusual gifts or positive genius would make repression a pain to itself, a wrong to the world). I know that a wife needs her fullest strength, her finest touch, for that creative work, the making a home; and that a mother needs leisure of heart for child care and child caressing. I fully feel that such marriage broadens a woman, beyond the most successful single career. But for such marriage, there is a practical lack; the lack of men, so broad, so strong, so sympathetic as to be peers to the women of to-day."

The Crusader said reproachfully, "I thought you were growing so wise, so womanly, but you have a trick when you give a rose of always piercing me with the thorn."

"Then," added Themis, "practically, in the absence of these heroic men not yet evolved from lower forms, you would agree with me, that single life is for cultured, intellectual women the calmer, surer path."

"Yes I would," confessed Ultimata, "yet I instinctively pity any woman who misses motherhood; and there is much spiritual gain, much true development, often much sweet companionship even in imperfect marriages; but I am haunted always by the dream of a high ideal marriage between natures strong and generous; upbuilding of a home on sure, deep foundations with possibility of broad, blessed love."

Crusader, somewhat sardonically, "Then you would justify woman at present in accepting marriage as a certain cross, more or less mitigated in the bearing, but surmounted by the possible crown of motherhood?"

"There is the advantage of legal training!" said Ultimata, "How strongly and concisely you always express my ideas for me! I accept your abstract of my creed."

Themis laughingly rejoined, "I think Ultimata by her concessions has only weakened the cause of woman, and evoked the ungrateful sarcasm of the only representative of men, whom we thought worthy of a voice in our symposium; while I feel a calm, rational satisfaction in my consistent defence of the scholarly possibilities and the intellectual independence of single life."

When we said good night in the lighted hall, I thought the orange blossoms wore a tired, discouraged unappreciated air.

CHAPTER VIII

THE CHILDREN'S CAVALCADE

TO-DAY has been high festival, for the children have had a picnic, with our neighbour of the Charles Lamb humour as commander of the ranks, custodian of the supplies and guardian of the camp fire. The entertainment was not a purely Arcadian pleasure (though in seeming so openhearted and guileless), but a deep laid scheme of revenge upon " the grown ups" as Dorothy respectfully designates us. Two weeks ago, an excursion was planned to the great representative ranches of Elwood and Glen Annie. This involved so long a drive that the children were excluded. Though the refusal to take them was part of that general system of benevolence, organised by parents and teachers " for their own good", this aspect of our unselfishness did not reveal itself to the subjects of our benevolence, as with four-in-hand, waving flags, and a trumpet (borrowed from one of the deserted children) blown vigorously by an amateur postilion, we dashed off in the morning sunlight.

My head had yielded to the combined parental wisdom in declaring this trip too wearisome for the little ones; but my heart rebelliously allied itself with the group of wistful-eyed children on the side walk, who waved us farewells in lingering, pathetic fashion. I had all day a suppressed heart-ache, and felt no pleasure until, on the homeward drive, two or three miles from Santa Barbara, we were startled by a dashing cavalry raid, and the glad-faced children gave us mounted escort home.

They seemed so gay in their greeting that I thought them truly magnanimous, until at bed-time Dorothy unfolded their plan of retaliation. They had arranged a picnic for all day on the hills or in a cañon; and as mothers do not bear fatigue well, and are subject to various head-aches, fainting fits and hysterics from over-weariness, and fathers alone could never bear the strain of a day's care of children, " the grown ups" were to be excluded " for their own good."

Still, a certain nobility of nature asserted itself, as the fathers and mothers under discipline were to be allowed to pay for the picnic; and I was graciously requested to make an immediate and generous contribution. I was glad by this peace-offering to bring my judicious brain and self-reproachful heart into reconciliation. I was the children's advocate with the other less sensitive and penitent parents; and consent was given with the saving clause, that someone must go, to see that the horses were properly tethered, and the camp fire kept under control. After consultation and a popular vote, Florrie's father was chosen, for which many reasons were assigned; one was that he was funny and would make them laugh; one that he was used to camping out and could make real good coffee; and still another that he was sure to take a French novel, which would keep him part of the time amused and out of the way.

So with this concession, the picnic was arranged; and the cavalcade has just dashed past the porch and out of the Esperanza grounds.

I wish discipline always took so picturesque a form. It was a charming picture. Mae, a simple-hearted hoyden to-day, in short dress, mounted on Fannie, with her curly poodle Dot in her arms; Margaret on restive little Gipsy; Florrie on Irony (for by this gentle satire of name, because of his most unmartial ways and unheroic moods, Ironsides is now familiarly known); Bertha, a tall, slender girl with pathetic eyes, in which childish joy is dimming and womanly earnestness deepening, was on Bruz, a favourite stable horse. Harry, a fine handsome boy, sure of a political future, as he hails from Ohio, was on his gentle-eyed Jennie; little Blanche, a most fearless, dashing rider, was on her spirited Dick, and that feature of the place and delight of the children, the Lucas donkey cart, brought up the rear, well filled with Elinor and May, Nellie, Grace and Mabel, with two large rag dolls. Prue and Priscilla by name, very flat as to profile, and very voluminous as to Mother Hubbard drapery.

Dorothy—or Donald, her other self—was tempting Brownie, already excited by the crowd, to her wildest careering. The Adult Concession drove an open buggy, alone, except for the dinner baskets, the wraps and the inevitable yellow-covered, French novel. The girls were all in short dresses for freedom in play; so skirts of blue, of red and of bright plaid, with flash of cardinal stockings, and floating of sash and scarf gave brightness of colouring; while broad-brimmed garden hats with gay ribbons, and white pinafores gave summer fairness to the donkey cart.

What an exodus it was, what rallying and dispersing, what consultation and discussion, what sudden starts and precipitate returns for forgotten whip or added word of good-bye; and finally what a flash of conscious triumph on their faces, as they dashed off, leaving the deserted "grown ups" to wave their dejected farewells from the porch.

A sudden silence fell on the Esperanza; and I thought a shadow crept over the garden, as the gay cavalcade vanished and the merry voices died on the summer air. I came up to my room, resolved upon letter-writing, as an escape from the solitude and silence. For with gay groups and glad voices all round me, with the passing of the children out of sight, I felt myself in sad, strange exile.

Would the most fearless imagination dare picture the world one day without its child life? What unnerving of the man's hand for action; what fainting of the woman's heart. So much is written of the mother's influence upon the child, so little of the reflex, the child's touch upon the mother's life. Children are often thought interruptions to life. In an outward sense they are. Their need of hourly care, their plea for love's expression, their childish frailties, and their sweet persistency of presence, leave no unbroken space for action or achievement to those to whom, in the eternal plan, children are given. But it is only in the clear shining of child eyes, that I see unity and meaning in the woman fate. Broaden her life as you may, strengthen it to the utmost, and she lacks the steadfast power of man, his continuity of action.

I believe this tidal law of her nature, its ebb and flow, its subtle variations give her a recognisable power of her own; the power of delicate analysis, of fine sympathy, and the tender touch both in literature and art, in unfolding the complex, involved human nature of this age, both mystical and sceptical. Better than man, with his unity of outward life, his simple directness of aim, does she in her apparently broken and disintegrated life, comprehend the hidden depths, the folded meanings of human nature, with its immortal power of flight, and its limitations of earthly horizon.

Man, with his control of outward destiny finds it possible to make of life a narrow but completed sphere. Woman in home life, failing of any perfect outward expression, must be only a broken arc; but an arc, I believe, of a grander, broader circle. The bird always free for flight and song, wings its way from tree to tree, or to the crest of low, familiar hill; but the bird brooding over its nest, denied all power of flight, sweeps in her quiet watching with her mother heart, the utmost space of summer sky.

Do not call me inconsistent, that I believe in the rightfulness of public career for women. Each woman is individual, with right of choice between the life of outward activity and direct results and the life of motherhood, hidden and lost, as regards personal achievement, but with its compensations of spiritual power and infinite upreaching.

There is a tangible gain in the accumulation of money, the exercise of political power, the expression of self in book or picture, which prove the validity of life; and woman in generous expenditure of herself in inspirational power upon others, leaves her own life often with a vagueness of outline, which gives her only a phantom self-consciousness. This sense of loss, this feeling of the useless evaporation of woman's life in small social duties and home cares, is comforted by the child's touch upon the mother.

With the baby's little upcurled hands both folded in one of her own, its warm, soft head pillowed upon her arm, she is consciously mother, but unconsciously part of budding, fruitful nature, akin to the Creative Power. There must be leisure of heart and life, for true motherhood, the possibility as with bird mothers of much quiet brooding. It is this need which makes me doubt the possibility of holding wise, generous motherhood in harmony with the pressure and activity of professional career.

I know that women doctors from education and practice, are much wiser on all sanitary and hygienic points, that, with knowledge of physiology and the physical laws which govern life, they are better mothers to the children's bodies than others can be. But I remember once when we were at home in the house of a lady doctor, a grand, brave representative of that noble profession, that the children came in one evening as I was reading fairy stories to Dorothy, supplemented in answer to her plea, by some of my own weaving.

They begged me to go on reading, and I felt the flame of their eager excited eyes as I read; then came the stories of our own fairy world, for Dorothy and I often wander there. When it was over, and they came to give me sweet, ardent good-night kisses, they asked, "May we come again and listen," adding in tones both proud and tender, for they gloried in their doctor mother, "of course, our mamma has no time for fairy stories."

I had suffered often from self-conscious worthlessness, when my invalid life with only motherhood to give it any meaning, had been brought into sharp contrast with the active, ambitious life of my friend; winning public honour, and doing positive good work for suffering humanity. But that night I rocked Dorothy to sleep with comforted heart, contented with the secluded, shadowy life, which gave generous place for fairy stories.

Does it win a smile from you that instead of

practical power and recognised service, I should accept as adequate expression to life, the weaving of twilight fairy stories by the open fire, for the child cradled in my lap? It may not be adequate expression to the mother to tell such stories, but it is genuine need of the child's heart to hear them. And the broader, stronger life of woman to-day, through the unfolding of true culture, has, as not the least beneficent of its ends, the power to tell sweeter and more significant fairy tales to the children at her knee. If men understood how truly the mother's nature is the child's world, they would give all possible atmosphere of tenderness, all genial warmth to the wife's life, that its breadth of thought, its power of light might make the child-world sunny and spacious.

I was glad at lunch to find a gay party, "booted and spurred" for afternoon ride: Artista, Perdita, the Spectator and Fairy Prince. They were in animated discussion, regarding the respective advantages of home life and foreign travel. I believe the talk had commenced by some humorous narration by Perdita of her experience while studying music in Stuttgart.

She said as I entered, "I can fancy you, Artista, mounted in fine style for the equestrian display in Hyde Park, an ornament in Worth costume to the Champs Elysées, driving in languid elegance in the soft afternoon light to the Cascine in Florence, or posing in classic grace, to watch the sunset from the Pincian Hill: but I cannot imagine you a student in a bare room, with the cold cleanliness and the frigid order of the *Hausfrau* about you, sitting on the hard sofa with benumbed feet on the solitary strip of carpet, taking your seven o'clock coffee with crescent bread, at a table with exercise books, German Grammar, Schiller's Dramas and *Nathan der Weise* suggesting the day's occupations. I cannot locate you in one of the barren rooms, with only the glacial looking, white porcelain stove to give it warmth. You need colour and sunlight. You may think that you want the advantages of student life abroad, but I think you would gain foreign culture with coral of Naples, the mosaics of Rome, the filigree of Genoa, or, if you will be antiquarian, the long, pendant earrings of the peasants of Albano, or the slowly strung pearl necklaces of Florentine maidens, like the threaded years of passing generations."

Artista with her most scornful smile retorted, "You like to talk as if it needed the courage of a stoic, to spend a few years of school life in Germany. But I remember gay enough stories of the year at Heidelberg, the walks over the hills, with afternoon coffee in some garden overlooking the river and valley; and then your trip with artist friends to sketch the Renaissance Court of the Castle, with its English memories. And yet you wish to strike a chill to my heart, with your pictures of the cold barrenness of student life in Heidelberg. I call it jolly."

Then turning to the Spectator, Artista added—

"But you look critical — are you listening to make cynical studies of American girls?"

Spectator in conciliating tones answered, "I have been only a year in America, and met really very few American girls, so my mind is still studying them, not quite fairly, as unknown human specimens, but with delicate, critical faculty, as variations of the Daisy Miller type."

"Oh, we quite forgive you," retorted Perdita, "for of course we watch constantly for the out cropping of English prejudices under your polite exterior, and for some manifestation of belligerent John Bullism towards our colonial crudeness. But you are rather disappointing in your pleasant way of taking things. I shall re-read "American Notes" to quicken my mind in re-creating the English tourist. You will not answer in that character at all; slender and dark, quite contented with a Mexican mustang, and reconciled to a sun which persists in shining in this undisguised fashion. You have wandered too long, you are quite de-nationalised."

"If he requires to be identified as an Englishman," said the Fairy Prince, "I am prepared to do him that friendly service in return for his lessons to us in the English language. If you doubt his nationality, watch the way in which he detects Americanisms. I spend most of my time in reading Richard Grant White, to be prepared with refuting quotations from that "well of English undefiled" Chaucer, to show that our so-called slang is early English from pure unmuddied sources."

Ultimata, who had been turning over the leaves of "Democracy" to leave the young talk undisturbed, now joined forces with Fairy Prince by saying, " I have a deep reverence for the purity of a language; still in a young nation with new developments and outgrowths a living language must bend to its needs, broaden with its growth and bear in its changes and accretions, the record of new forces and elements. The inventive nation of the world can rightly patent a few new words. The ranches of California, the lumbering camps of Oregon, the cotton fields of Mississippi, the copper mines of Lake Superior, the breadth of Western prairies, the shadows of Red-Wood forests, will scarcely take possession of an old language without breathing into it the free life of this broad and varied people. It is no use being sensitive about our youth and imperfections. We are English with something lost, but something gained. We owe reverence to the traditions of our English past; but we owe faith to the possibilities of our American future."

The Spectator quietly rejoined, " To listen to your defence of faith and youth, one might think America quite shame-faced in her guileless maidenhood. I have not noticed that expression, but perhaps it takes more than a year's residence, to reveal to an obtuse Englishman, this characteristic American modesty."

Artista exclaimed. " All Perdita's compliments are quite lost upon you. You are sneering at us, in the average English fashion, and yet you often say you like our open-hearted, open-handed ways."

"If I said anything else," answered the Spectator, "I should be very ungrateful to the genial friends who have made their little valley rank next in my heart to my Warwickshire home."

Fairy Prince, looking at his watch—as if he needed to note time in the human way—rose, saying, "As recognition of that graceful compliment, let us confine our talk upon our ride to pure, unquestioned English."

Ultimata added, "Then you must not venture to have 'a good time.' How can a nation be happy without that expansive and inclusive phrase?"

In the afternoon the lights were so tender upon the hills, that I thought it would be a charming time for a quiet ride, and then I would go and have a look at the picnic. So I ordered Pacer, and started on a slow, sauntering walk; as I like to loiter when alone, though I enjoy a good dash when riding with others. I knew the meadow they had chosen, after many prospecting parties to find a place with good shade, with generous pasturage for the horses, with running water, with safe, open spot for camp fire and freedom from poison oak.

So I turned off the main road into a narrow one, scarcely more than a shadowy lane, though broad enough for careful driving. Far off I heard the jubilant voices, and saw through the dusty foliage of the live oaks, the flashes of colour as they darted about in eager play. I rode quietly to the fence before I was discovered. Then there was a rush forward, as I supposed to offer the hospitality of the camp, but no, it was a confused narration of adventures and narrow escapes; with faint apologies that the lunch was all eaten and the coffee cold.

Then from the shadow of a comfortably remote tree, the Minority of One appeared, French book in hand. He gave satisfactory report of the community. Nothing more serious had occurred than a few of them wetting their feet in crossing the brook on stones; except that the solitary boy had fallen in and been spread out in the sun to dry. Dorothy had alarmed him with her reckless climbing, but when rebuked had answered, "It does not do nowadays to interfere with children's climbing, since any school-girl knows that we are descended from monkeys, and surely ought not to lose the accomplishments of our ancestors."

The camp, if it offered no hospitality and showed not even a glimmer in the embers of its fire, gave a picture to reward me for coming. Some of the horses, quite free, were moving about the open field, choosing choice spots for nibbling; others less trusted were tethered in green places with the tasselled *riatas* of Mexican manufacture. The cart, gay with wraps tossed in at random, made a spot of bright colour in the sun; and the happy donkey was browsing quietly, looking so diminutive and droll among the horses. The children returned to their play, but suggested that I should finish my ride and then come back to make part of the cavalcade home, but "real late," for the day was warm and the fun hardly commenced. So I turned back to the San Francisco road, and quickened Pacer into a brisk lope. I love this stretch of road; especially one bit where the mountains seem to sweep across it, until nearing the seemingly impassable range, it gives open road with billowy lines of softly rounded hills upon both sides.

To think these beautiful hills should have human ownership; but I believe they are part of the Hope Ranch. I rode till the lengthening shadows forced me to face the reproaches and arguments of the dissatisfied children; for I knew that no definite hour, while a ray of light lingered, would be accepted by them as " real late " and time for return. But I rode back with unrelenting resolution, as it was half past five. Then came the bridling and saddling of the freed horses, the harnessing of the donkey, the gathering scattered wraps and lightened baskets; and in the tender evening light we dashed into the hotel grounds, after a slow ride home, as we sauntered, not to hurt the donkey's feelings. Then came hurried farewells and the cavalcade broke ranks; as some dismounted and set their horses free to find their own stables, and others cantered homeward.

CHAPTER IX

THE WEDDING RING

I WAS sitting on the porch this morning with the Crusader, when a letter was brought me. The handwriting was unfamiliar, the postmark unknown. I opened it and turned to the name, then again to the ardently warm affection expressed in the opening lines. Puzzled, I again glanced at the envelope, lest I might be appropriating love meant for another, but the address was undoubtedly mine. Then I read the letter with sense of bewilderment which yielded to mingled joy and pain. When finished, I remarked, "That letter is a life history"—Just then my Spanish teacher carried me captive, but under the vowelled sweetness of Castilian inflections, my spirit was studying the moods and tenses of woman nature and woman fate—For my friend, long silent, and I thought lost to me in the wanderings of this many-pathed world, had written strange suggestive words—she had, she confided to me, failed to regain her health but had won her freedom, and gave her maiden name and new address.

—She told no story of suffering, showed no strain of agony in breaking the close relation—but wrote simply and gladly of the joy in her emancipated life, and her happier environment. I recalled with a pang at heart our old merriment in the days of our foreign comradeship, when I drew under my matronly wing her fair, glad beauty, too girlish for unprotected wandering—I learned then, that her loveliness, and the absence of the traditional wedding ring had quickened English criticism into censorious condemnation.—I entered the lists in her defence, by divulging the fact that in our country, Puritan protest against the symbolism of the Established Church, had long banished the ring from all marriage services save the Catholic and that of the Church of England; and that marriage is still legal without that outer seal.

Now the unringed hand claims its unwed freedom— Some tragedy underlies this simple record, some awfulness of alienation before this exultation in loneliness, some agony of spiritual disruption before this joy in self-ownership. Depth of feeling she may lack. Her nature when I knew her had never been sounded by plummet of pain or loss. I saw only the surface brightness, the unstirred sweetness. With my memory of her girlish gaiety, her quick sympathy and her rippling bewitchment of merry laugh, I cannot picture her with loss of faith, lack of love, and all the sweetness turned to bitterness. What wrong has left her life in the fulness of its fair womanhood without wifely right of name, without shelter of home, or sanctity of love? More failed in such marriage than wedding ring. What alloy has dimmed its own gold, and weakened to frail breaking that circlet of wedded love? My heart aches, but involuntarily I smile. I had heard so much of the strange social conditions of California, owing, I was told, to the circumstances of its settlement, the influence of Spiritualism and the laws in favour of easy divorce. I said always before coming, that I had only one friend in California, that she was a good Presbyterian, and not divorced. Alas for my permanency of social foundation, my pharisaical self-gratulation! It is strange while my interest in Spiritualism is forcing upon me deep thoughtful consideration of the present unrest in home life, the failure of spirit unity in modern marriage, that this letter, with its light but significant confession, should press the same subject upon my heart, with the painful questioning which comes from personal love and tender sympathy. Later in the day, I saw the Crusader wandering about uncompanioned.

As soon as he saw me in the remotest corner of the porch, he joined me, noticed the shadow on my face and said, "I fear the morning letter has saddened your day, Ultimata." The story, but without name, was frankly told him, for his nature is as broad in sympathy as his life in experience; and his treatment of social questions is fearless in strength, fine in spirit. I never fear to discuss with him any subject which touches human weal, socially or personally. It is a hopeful sign of the free thought, the higher purity of the age, and one result of the larger co-operation of the sexes in all questions of reform, that man and woman together frankly face the problems which earlier would have been imperfectly met by the single thought of each, but refused joint recognition. One step beyond, when to woman's sensitive nature and spiritual intuition is given the right of expression in all that pertains to the national welfare; and the higher morality, the loftier life of our people will prove the wisdom of the age, which avails itself of her finer, subtler power.

One thing I notice on the Pacific coast, that it offers an open field for the working out of social questions; a field comparatively free from traditionary growth of opinion and prejudice. It makes social life here, especially in San Francisco, varied in elements, uncertain in form; but to one interested in the development of a transitional age, vastly interesting.

Ultimata said, after narration of her friend's story, "When we are young, such confession of an individual life touches us keenly, stirring quick responsive sympathy; but it is sad only with its own sadness. But in later life, each individual expression is weighted with the human loss and pain, of which it is only a single throb. It is not only the suffering of one single soul, but symptom of a social malady. Is there any hope of a happier, more healthful social condition in which lives may develop naturally; not be nipped in the bud, or blighted in the flower?

THE WEDDING RING

Is marriage itself a failure or is the lack in the conditions of the age? We have the traditions of happy homes, but to-day the startling record of the divorce courts. I realise that the difference between marriage in our time, and that known to us by tradition, is more seeming than real. In earlier ages, especially the first generations in a new land, there is full, hard employment in outward ways, the man on his farm, the woman in domestic activities: so the life is one of mutual dependence and helpfulness. But we have reached a time of speculative activity among men, and larger leisure among women. Man's work is not primarily for the home, nor woman's interests centred there. Man is fevered and restless with the largeness of his possible achievements, and woman ennuied with a life broader in its culture, than in its demands of duty. Man is dizzied by the fierce excitement of money-making, and woman dazed by the unreality of her life. He misses the peace of the inner life, and she the healthful pressure of the outer. Then this is an analytical age, which takes cognisance not only of results; but discovers by fine process the elements which enter into its organisation.

"Society includes vivisection in its scientific culture; and numbers the heart-beats and studies the quivering nerves of those frenzied or stupefied by its own experiments. Heart ache is the universal human ailment, not characteristic of one age; but now it is not suppressed and concealed, but recognised and revealed. This disclosure of the social malady is painful, but still a step towards health and healing."

"As a woman," asked the Crusader, "do you see any remedy for the unrest of women; this discontent in the marriage relation, which must be rightful, if the natural condition of man and woman?"

"The relation must be more difficult," answered Ultimata, "with the greater complexity of life, the larger unfolding of woman. Her nature must be met at more points, reached upon a higher level. With woman's power for independent career, she is not satisfied with simple domestic wifehood. She demands fuller, larger companionship: while man's outward life of excitement and unrest leaves him no strong, calm power for true communion and spiritual unity. He makes home life only an interruption to his career, and its relations justification for still fiercer strife for money, that he may give wealth and luxury as compensation for the withdrawal of love and tenderness. Let no man think that woman accepts the most generous bestowal of externals as compensation for the loss of the strength and rest of his own presence in the home. Many women failing to win the real joy of life, amuse themselves with its drapery and decoration. Then, with discontent at heart, leisure of life, and a fully unfolded nature emotional and intellectual, comes the temptation to social experiment, the loosening of the marriage-tie and the frequent appeal to the divorce court. Which is wise: enforced acceptance of heart exile in nominal homes, or the avowal of the truth, with disruption of the tie and freedom to choose other conditions and form other relations? It seems all bewilderment, with no sure guidance in the individual life, in social customs or in the absoluteness of legislation, since each State forms its own code of morals."

"That question must be slowly answered by the age," replied the Crusader, "not impulsively by an individual, but my own conviction is, that all movements, social and legislative, tend towards individualism; and that customs and laws must have a larger elasticity to admit of more freedom of thought and action in the personal life. Have you never felt that the root difficulty in marriage is permanent, legal ownership; and that many of the disasters of the relation and the agony that now attends the disruption of the marriage tie, would be wisely met by legal, limited contract in place of the life-long bond? Would not the uncertainty of tenure lead in marriage to the same self-control and courtesy which characterise betrothal?"

"I see no hope for woman, but only deepening despair," said Ultimata, "in the acceptance of any relation between the sexes, but that of marriage. This relation as it exists presses heavily upon woman for many reasons, among them her financial dependence and legal irrecognition; but it gives some basis of life, some root of growth. Man has in his profession or vocation, an expression of life, a continuity of power denied woman. A relation limited to a few years' companionship, would withdraw from woman's life, the elements of stability and outward restfulness."

"Do you feel sure then," asked the Crusader, "that if the bond were not doubly riveted by Church and State, there would be always repudiation of the tie and rupture of the relation, between those drawn together by love, and living in conscious freedom?"

"I believe," answered Ultimata, "that such relation would result disastrously, except with the loftiest and most finely adjusted natures. Woman's love is more spiritual than man's. She loves always an ideal man, sees the possibilities of his grander, truer self in the eternal unfolding; and to this ideal is often true, through all life's disillusioning experiences. Then as motherhood is the supreme experience in a woman's life, the father of her children holds her with a power beyond the strength of his nature, or the charm of his presence. But man's love is more physical. He loves a real woman, and would have her outwardly fair and eternally young. Fatherhood is with few men the strongest expression; but that controlling feeling (call it love or own it passion) towards woman. I therefore fear that man would not be so strongly held by the mother of his children, were he free, without social odium or legal penalties to choose those of fresher, fairer faces. I think the relation by limited contract would give stronger temptation and less restriction to man's passion, and surer more fatal pain to woman's more constant, because more spiritual, nature. Then it would practically leave children's lives unhoused. How would you insure their welfare under this system?"

"I am assured," replied the Crusader, "that living

in freedom, with conscious self-ownership and the right of change if the relation proved inharmonious, would quicken the man's chivalry and tenderness by his uncertainty of hold upon the woman of his love; and that the woman would have incentive always to keep her graces and charms undimmed, which won his love. So the relation might and would be often permanent, through the gracious compliment of renewed giving, not the absoluteness of an accepted thraldom. Then the children would have always a home of love and concord; not a prison to hold hopeless, embittered captives. In case of the dissolution of the tie, the children must according to the decision of the law, become the charge of either parent, or the wards of the State."

"A lovely mother the State would make," cried Ultimata, "where is the mother lap to climb, the mother arms to hold, the mother voice to sing lullabies. It makes me shiver and turn cold: I seem to see the clinging, wistful-eyed children, nestling for warmth and comfort in the statuesque marble folds of a gigantic goddess of Liberty. No, I believe in the permanency of even the shadowed, sorrowful, earthly home of to-day for the children's sake."

"You cannot believe that father and mother living in antagonism or infidelity, can give true and healthful homes to young lives. Better the coldest, bleakest asylum, than a home which is a battlefield of warring natures," replied the Crusader.

"I admit that, when marriage is absolute antagonism between the natures it binds," answered Ultimata. "There are two classes to whom the limited contract would give rightful relief: those of highest ideality, to whom an uncongenial marriage is the fire of martyrdom without its purification, and those held in outward union with inherent and inveterate hatred, making the relation a mocking lie, an impure thraldom. But the greater number of marriages are not unholy, but simply imperfect. There is divergence of thought, many disappointed hopes, much difficulty of adjustment; yet often the possibility of true living in reciprocal self-sacrifice, in charity of judgment, in wise control of emotion and action. There is, I am assured, often the development of grander strength, of finer spirituality in the quiet acceptance of unsmiling duty, than in the impatient demand for happiness. But the limited contract, to pleasure-seeking natures, would be a temptation to make life a series of conquests, an epicurean festival of new and delicately varying emotions. That temptation would assail man more than woman, since in man, by nature or long social custom, is more developed the love of the chase: and the temptation would not assail alone men of the lower type. I have heard a man of chivalry and honour confess, that the utmost joy in life, was not possession, but the excitement of assaulting the impregnable fortress. The unwon woman was the fortress. Women with the most personal charm and social brilliancy would be subjected likewise to the temptation to make life a series of triumphs, not loyal-hearted devotion to home. Then I feel so strongly that the welfare of children should dominate both lives: for the loss or lessening of happiness to two in mature life must be less sacrifice than the future of children, to whom the loss of home influence and home atmosphere is cruel disinheriting. Since father and mother are fate to children by their creative act; they should be kindly fate also, as protecting providence. And I have known those held in imperfect and disappointing marriage, rise through love to the children into high and helpful companionship."

"But the instinctive demand for individual happiness is so imperious," objected the Crusader, "that humanity will not generally be ruled by its sense of responsibility to the coming generation. The feeling which draws man and woman together is the irrepressible longing for the nature which meets and completes its own; which finding is bliss, which missing is unendurable pain. In limited contract, the loss would not be final; since across the present failure, would shine the hope still of freedom and self-ownership, or the higher joy of spiritual unity in some later relation."

"Another objection which you will call sentimental," replied Ultimata, "is that the idea underlying limited contract would give to the first rapture of love, a question of its own reality, a chill consciousness of possible change.

"The utmost thrill of love is its instinctive faith in its own immortality, the sense of eternal fealty which makes spoken vow too feeble, finite life too short for its utterance. Would you win the woman of your love with the implied scepticism, and to the uncertainty of a limited contract?"

"Not now assuredly," answered the Crusader, "since a man may believe in the need of martyrs to social reform, but will not light the flame about the form he loves. No man could, with present social conditions, subject the woman of his love to the misapprehension and irrecognition which would follow the acceptance of such a relation. But personally I would willingly woo her to years of companionship, at their end to claim her still by the unshadowed love and the undimmed joy of the relation; so through life be still winning her love, still won by her charm."

"Contract would fail, as surely as marriage does, of perfect happiness," said Ultimata, "since the failure is less in the relation or the rite, than in the incomplete and inharmonious lives, which would still lure, and still disappoint.

"If the experiment were generally made of a series of contracts, lives would be hopelessly broken and their relationships sadly entangled; and the end would still be loss of ideality or pain of disillusioning. But I see in marriage, even though a partial failure; steadfastness of purpose, loyalty of life, and recognition of duty. Many marriages, I confess, should be broken. The determining question is 'faith or unfaith?' If there be faith between the natures, however temperament or condition may mar their outward harmony, I recognise the truth and honour of the relation. But unfaith (not of necessity outward disloyalty), but the absence of confidence, the lack of abiding trust, should always justify separation, most of all for the children's sake, to whom the atmosphere of truth alone is spiritual life."

"We are not so far apart in thought as we seem," remarked the Crusader. "I am suggesting a remedy for the evil as it exists: marriage without the reality of spiritual unity. You are defending marriage as it should be, with dower of faith and loyalty. You worship somewhat the symbol for spirit and make a fetish of the wedding ring."

"Yes," confessed Ultimata, "to me it seems so much. I sometimes feel when I see it on a worn woman's dead hand, how it has bounded her world, been her earthly horizon. Within that little golden circle has been held her utmost joy, perhaps also her inmost pain; but its wearing means loyalty of life to the maiden promise, steadfastness of faith to the woman fate, and the rightful glory of motherhood.

"I think it must have been this little glittering ring of wifehood on Vittoria Colonna's dead hand, which withheld Michael Angelo from touching her lips with the passion and the pain of his unavailing kiss. Yes, I hope through all the ages, woman may still be won with the old, sacred words, 'With this ring, I thee wed,' but that by fuller love, by finer harmony, marriage may be at last worthy of its symbol, that perfect golden circlet."

CHAPTER X

EASTER AT THE MISSION

SANTA BARBARA holds Easter service all the year. One forgets here the fact of wintry death, and misses the deep joy of spring's awakening. But to-day is Easter, when the fairest blossom grows fairer with spiritual significance, and earth wears a smile of previsioned joy. We went to the Mission for morning service, hoping to see the ghostly whiteness of the church radiant with the glad sunshine, and fragrant with the breath of living flowers. But the church was cold and shadowy; and the few lilies on the altar looked pallid and phantom-like, shining among the lighted candles. There was no glory of decoration, no warmth of human gladness. Sad old Mission, once the root of living, hopeful growth, now only lifeless pressed flower; recalling in its fair pathos the glamour of sunlight faded from fields once green with the promise of future harvests. There seemed among the straggling worshippers no quick, responsive warmth of acceptance, as among the contadini at church feste in Rome.

EASTER AT THE MISSION

The Catholic Church, speaking a language of symbolism, needs always glorious music, altar pictures, grand processional and rich vestments. It requires fulness of life, majesty of movement. It must strike full, daring chords. In decadence, it is unlovely and pitiful; like discrowned royalty in faded purple and tinsel crown. Studied from without, the Catholic Church appeals to me strongly: but within, when I would kneel at its altars and lose myself in faint amen to the inflexible rigidity of its creed, the unchanging ritual of its service, I find my desire for worship defeated by my own individuality, which asserts by intellectual questioning, by defiant doubt, the facts of American birth and Protestant ancestry. In Catholic countries I own its grandeur: I feel its charm as long as I am conscious spectator: but the effort to yield to its claim, to feel through spiritual sympathy or quickened imagination, the restful faith of believer in the power of its sacraments, the validity of its authority, is vain, and the fact of individualism rises up against ecclesiastical tyranny, the freedom of spiritual truth against the imperfection and incompleteness of all church organisations. I think the Catholic Church and the Quakers hold the two complementary truths, regarding the relation of the human mind towards the Infinite: the one the imperative need of the individual to find rest and strength in the visible Church, in formulated creed and accepted ritual; the other the right of the individual to hold undisturbed its close personal relations with the Eternal. The one builds upon its partial truth, the absoluteness of the outward Church; the other from its acceptance of spiritual freedom, abolishes all priesthood. The one gives the comfort of "the Communion of Saints," the other the unclouded shining of "the Inner Light."

But since churches exist as pathways for humanity towards spiritual truth, no one path can be absolutely best for all minds; since human nature is not an absolute entity, with assured power and unvarying relations to "the Eternal Verities", but is the aggregate of natures both akin and alien to each other, with hearts of individual throb, though of one human blood. To many natures, self-distrustful and sensitive, there is unspeakable comfort in the rituals and sacraments of an established church.

There are features of the Catholic Church, which appeal to me, with promise of consolation missed in Protestantism: one, the presence of the Virgin Mary among spiritual powers; the apotheosis of the womanly. Is it not wrong enough that woman has been disinherited on earth, but that the wrong is projected into Eternity: that the Supreme Being should be always in thought of worship, in confession of creed as in vision of artist, masculine in form? Theodore Parker's bold, tender prayer, "Our Father and Mother, who art in Heaven," is the needed broadening of the conception of the Infinite to meet the true human need. If one cannot create ideal of earthly home, without the brooding sympathy of the woman nature, as well as the outward activity of the man's; that Infinite Heart, the ultimate home of all humanity, must hold in its perfection the Motherhood as well as the Fatherhood of the race. Not only do women seek women in their utmost need for sympathetic presence, for helpful touch; but men also, in failure and loss, appeal from the rigid law and cruel judgment of men to the larger comprehension, the deeper sympathy of woman.

The commandments on Sinai, delivered, through prophet of Jewish race, to a people honouring only the masculine elements in humanity, are positive, absolute, with the sharp outlines of human law; but the Beatitudes in the Sermon on the Mount given by the lips of the Divine Teacher are feminine in tender, vague spirituality. One cannot honour Christ, and refuse honour to the woman type in humanity, since His blessing rests upon humanity's power of forgiveness and self-sacrifice; the virtues, in which men have generously given women the possibility of full development. I have longed often for the sweet, familiar habit of the Catholic heart in its appeal to the Mother of Christ.

Again, I feel the blessing, while I know the perils of the Confessional. I would choose for women, always a woman confessor; and I would make confession, not a frequent, formal act, but an occasional blessed possibility; the opening of the flood-gates, when high tide and rising current threaten hopeless devastation, unless path is made for the pent-up waters. If one under pressure of suffering confide in home or social life to friend, it is like throwing down the safe walls of defence, which guard the individual life. It makes future companionship difficult between the two sharing such confidence; since on one side there is sensitive pride, on the other conscious power requiring the utmost delicacy of expression. But under the seal of confession, it is not individual disrobing the soul of accustomed outward drapery before the critical gaze of another; but the unveiling of the spirit to a spiritual healer. Without holding to the rite of absolution, one may believe in the confessional, as offering release from unbearable suffering, relief from burdens beneath which the life is fainting, and the true spiritual gain of sympathy and assurance of forgiveness.

I think an open confessional might often keep defeated, reckless lives from the temptation of suicide, if human help were as accessible as the cold, sullen river.

Then I honour the practical wisdom of the Catholic Church, in utilising by organisation, the lives of single women. One may, as Protestant, regret the cloistered lives of women fitted for human homes and motherhood; but I am sorrowfully conscious of the loss of power in the lives of single women, who seem too often to lack basis of action.

True, in the broader possibilities of to-day, careers and professions open to the self-reliant and ambitious; but a great mass of single women remain who fail of active possibilities from the very structure of society. After youth is passed, a single woman must create interests for herself to justify her existence.

She may, with wealth, take philanthropy as her field, with more or less wisdom in her single and unsustained efforts; or if scholarly, choose literature; or if artistic without original power, may toy with art in amateur fashion.

But these efforts of ordinary women are too often like children's gardens, gay with stems of flowers thrust into the soil without root, and so without hope of growth. Then, on the other hand, there is such call for help from the unnursed sick, the unhoused poor, the unmothered children.

The Catholic Church, has by its system of gathering its single women into sisterhoods, made them a power for good among the poor in hospital, in asylum and school. I cannot sympathise with convent life, with its rigid seclusion, its narrow rules, its enforced devotions. The routine, and withdrawal from warm home life must be dehumanising. But I know no life more bountiful in good, more blessed in the living, than that of the Sisters of Mercy.

But I must give the Mission as it looks to us in the sunshine of this Easter morning. It is a large white building, Spanish in style, with arched cloisters and *campanile*. It is stuccoed and whitewashed; but from description you can hardly fancy how beautiful it is, set in fair fields, with broad view sweeping to the sea. Was it by grace of God, that the Catholic Church has chosen always the fairest sites for convent and monastery? H.H. has drawn charming pictures of the old Mission life under the

Spanish Government, reaching a fair chain of civilisation across the wild, new coast.

One sees through her sketches the heroic self-sacrifice of the early Fathers; their judicious sowing of the wide, fair fields to golden grain and planting fruit orchards; the wise administration of power in their own societies and their just government over the communities of Indians, who tilled the fields, lived in smiling villages and became part of the prosperous, happy Mission life. Then, these Missions formed the garden spots in the wilderness, and offered hospitality of shelter and food, and often gift of horse to the passing traveller.

I feel comforted to know that the decadence in the power and prosperity of the Missions antedated the American possession of California; and was caused by the Mexican Revolution, and the withdrawal of the Spanish subsidies, which had been the foundation of their wealth.

Doubtless I am glad to have this fair, sunny coast part of our country: but I do wish that our part of conquest and progress was less shadowed by injustice and wrong doing. One can scarcely feel, however plausible the explanation of purchase by settlers, of transfer of land through loan and mortgage, that it can be right to have fertile valleys and whole mountain ranges owned fifty years ago by the Spanish and Mexican natives and swept by their immense herds of wild horses, now in undisputed possession of Americans, with their fruitful orchards and great grain ranches. There are not more than two or three of the original Spanish families in Santa Barbara, who now hold much land. Most of the Mexicans are poor; and I feel their dark pathetic faces, their graceful picturesqueness and their sweet southern courtesy, a shadow upon the brightness of the Valley. For I hate the money sharpness, the commercial shrewdness of the Anglo-Saxon race. Their success is well for the material development of the country. But I mourn the poetry which is dying out with the Spanish race; its grace of life, its national games, the dark-eyed beauty of the South and the Catholic traditions of the old Mission days. I think with nations, as with individuals, the charm is often with those predestined to failure.

I am sure there are no two types of humanity so uninteresting to me as the successful, self-made man of large wealth; and the popular society woman. Ordinarily the successful man in business is strong by his lack of sympathy with others, self-poised by his insulation from the currents of feeling and thought which sway sensitive minds; and steady in purpose from narrowness of aim. And the brilliant society woman achieves triumph by treating life as a kind of decorative art, to give becoming background to her style of beauty. She is incapable of understanding the emotional nature of others, except as an instrument for her skilful touch. The successful business man grows hard from ignoring the lives of others; the society woman cruel from making the lives of others elements only of gain and triumph to herself. I am certain that sensitive, highly-organised natures become unnerved for action by their intuitive altruism. They are deterred from any effort which would seem to wrong others, and diverted from steadiness of purpose by their instinctive understanding of the lives which touch their own. They are deflected from their true course by the influence of others upon their responsive natures.

In truth, it is a delicate question how far any life can carry its ambition, without spiritual discourtesy to other lives. Fortunately for the world's work, there are many of massive make, and unwavering will, who never pause to question their own right of way. As with individuals, so with nations: and this commercial, colonising Anglo-Saxon race is awakening countries into self-conscious activity, after centuries' dreaming of southern life. But I like better the pathetic southern eyes, with lingering of dispelled dream, than the eager hardness of our own. So I love in Santa Barbara, the shadow of the Mission, the old adobe houses, the sad-eyed, grey-bearded Mexicans, and all the lingering of Spanish colouring and Catholic traditions. It helps, with orange orchards and olive groves, to make the place foreign and southern.

There are two or three pictures one would cross the Continent to see. In one of our rides soon after the rain, we went along the Mesa to the Light House. I see it all, the valley just quickening into tender green, the far sweep of the blue sea, and against it a cloud of tender pink, an almond grove in blossom. I think the almond should be symbol of joy. Its outblossoming is so sudden; so complete that unfolding of fair, radiant colour, without premonition of leaf or shadow of green; like the breaking forth of some great joy, the budding of quick, ecstatic feeling. This tender flush of pink was the herald of the fruit blossoms, giving to the landscape the most exquisite bits of colour across the green. I am sure you will mourn with me, that the almond is not a good paying crop, and in many places they are uprooting them to plant the English walnut.

Never mind, upon one ranch there will be that lovely flush contrasting with the silvery grey of the olive leafage (fortunately for our finances the olive offers something more tangible than its suggestions of Italy, and is a profitable crop).

Then I have another fancy, known in the family as my speculation.

Long ago, when we wintered in Cannes, and I saw the thousands of acres given to verbenas, geraniums, mignonette, and heliotrope, and orange trees, planted for their blossoms, not their fruit: I planned with my usual vagueness as to date and detail, that some time I would go to Southern California and raise flowers as in Cannes, for the various perfumes and essences, and establish a "Lubin" of my own on the Pacific Coast. I am so far on the road towards the success of my speculation, that I am in Southern California. The climate is the most important element in the speculation, my creative self the second. No doubt the flower culture and the *Fabrique* will follow. I should call it an ideal industry. Then think of the Attar of Roses distilled from Santa Barbara roses. I am sure no Attar from Araby the blest, would ever by its breath quicken such vision of bloom and beauty as a single drop of Santa Barbara essence. It would quite rival the Elixir of Youth, with its power of sunlight, its concentrated fragrance of the spirits of a whole summer's budding, falling roses!

CHAPTER XI

PORCH THEOLOGY

ULTIMATA went down this morning hatted and gloved for church, after compromising with Dorothy, who was to write the absent Papa a letter, and learn a favourite psalm. She loves the Liturgy of the Church of England, especially the solemn beauty of the litany, but she has an inherited dislike for sermons; not on the spindle side, for a girlhood spent in "the City of Churches," gave her mother a fondness for sermons which she thought an indication of the loftiness of her spiritual nature, but which she learned later was the satisfaction of individual needs and artistic tastes in an outwardly narrow life. For wandering into country churches, with only the mediocrity of average sermons and the singing of a village choir, she has learned by self-condemnation to distinguish between worship and intellectual sympathy. But her fondness for sermons abides, and no books travel more constantly with her than Newman's, Robertson's, Martineau's and Philips Brooks' Sermons. The Spectator has met a confessed need in life by sending her Temple's Sermons to Students; many bearing the date of his own listening to them at Rugby. These, with their concise brevity ("ten minutes with a leaning to mercy"), their clear simplicity and tender spirituality, have won Dorothy's approval. To these she listens eagerly and to Philips Brooks. One Sermon of his, "The Pillar in the Temple," has so captivated her imagination, that she repeats the pages of solemn, exquisite beauty, in which he describes the sunlight and shadows, playing over Cathedral pavement and upon the pillar of strength (part of its grand unity); and the passing and fading of human life, while steadfastness of pillar is unstirred, and glory of temple undimmed. These said in a solemn recitative, sound like Milton's blank verse, or the far-off roll of organ music. But to require Dorothy to sit through a sermon, delivered after the full morning service, is to develop in her a strong family likeness in suppressed restlessness and variations of significant protest against modern martyrdom, to a Field Geologist, sometimes caught and ruthlessly tethered, for a morning in church. Ultimata's own attendance at service has been irregular for years from invalidism; but she never hears church bells, without a longing for the hope and helpfulness of the morning lesson, and the right of response to those petitions in the litany, which sweep so broadly, touch so tenderly, the universal human needs.

But while waiting for her two-mule chariot, the

street car, the Crusader joined her. He was far from well, and in restless mood. In impatient step, in resentful tone though without word of confession, he uttered the masculine protest against weakness and its restrictions. He said sarcastically, "I cannot understand your wish to go to church, as I suppose you have not indulged in buying a new bonnet in Santa Barbara, and can hardly plan to study the latest fashion in this remote valley."

Ultimata answered, "I always adhere to a habit formed in England of very plain church dress, generally simple black; and I would myself favour a church costume of the severest simplicity, that none should attend service for display, and none be deterred from act of worship by plainness of wardrobe."

"Will you tell me once frankly," mildly thundered the Crusader, "what you expect to gain by purely mechanical responses to a worn-out creed, and listening to a sermon which by its orthodoxy will compel you to the hypocrisy of outward assent to what your mind denies?"

"A full answer to that would lead to a long discussion between us," replied Ultimata, "and I see the car in sight."

"No mortal man, whatever his need of enlightenment," retorted the Crusader, "could expect a woman with spotless ecru gloves and Prayer Book in finest crushed levant, to take off her gloves, lay down the Prayer Book, and help another nature in its honest questionings, rather than join the ranks of outward conformists to the undoubtedly respectable habit of Church-going."

Ultimata said, "My life is one of broken power; and if of service at all, it is in irregular ministrations to others, not in acceptance of established forms. If you will talk with me seriously about the mission of the Church, its imperfect good, its partial failure; or reverently of spiritual truth, whatever its finite manifestations, I will sacrifice gloves and Prayer Book to a missionary service on the porch."

The Crusader for answer, gathered a spray of yellow roses and said as he offered them, "There is a text. Now let me bring out your favourite rocker, and we will choose a shady place," for Crusader and Ultimata both glorify southern sunshine, but both like to sit in shadow, while they look out upon the sunlit garden, the glimpses of the hills, and the far-off, luminous blue of the sea.

"Now," said Ultimata, as she touched with brightness the sombre church dress, by fastening the roses against the black lace scarf at her throat, "I will take your own text, the yellow roses. You are the apostle of culture even in your choice of the fairest, fullest flowers. You know the value of continued effort, of centuries' experiment in horticulture, the worth of scholarship in the education of to-day, the need of organisation in political parties, and the gain of accepted conventionalities and courtly traditions in social life: then why deny the advantage of similar organisation of recognised continuity of effort, in the history of the Church? Must not spiritual growth be allowed the same conditions of conscious striving, and of outward expression, as intellectual development or social unfolding?"

"I cannot give a full affirmative even to that question," answered the Crusader, "since schools, political parties and social conventionalities give expression to truth known to be partial and imperfect, since of merely human growth, and therefore yielding to slow modification of thought, to impulse of intellectual renaissance, or to outbreak of political revolution. No college, no society, no government holds to absolutism in its power; but the Church claims its right to authorised expression of divine truth and is autocratic in its sway."

"But though the truth be divine," responded Ultimata, "since the medium of its revelation (through prophet, apostle, and seer) is human; must not the same charity of judgment be extended to the shortcomings and errors of the Church, which you grant to all other forms of growth?"

"Define your position," said the Crusader, "you women are so delightfully vague in an argument. Do you appear as defender of the faith as held by the Church, or of your individual belief, which would not find expression in the accepted creed of any Christian denomination?"

"I am an advocate for the right to spiritual growth under the same conditions, and with the same limitations which mark other forms of human development," responded Ultimata. "I am an American, though I am conscious of certain characteristic faults in our young, broad land. I am a Republican, though I discern perils in the Republican experiment, and I am a Christian though I admit the imperfect, inconsistent expression of Christ's spirit in the teaching of the Church; but I did not think any Protestant needed to avow disbelief in the infallibility of the Church. I thought Protestantism had established the right of individual judgment."

"Yet, in this morning's service, would you not respond by solemn 'Amen' to mysteries of faith as held by the mediæval Church? Before Confirmation, must not the mind bewilder itself with the labyrinthine windings of the Thirty-nine Articles? Does not the Church still darken by its theological dogmas the clear shining of Christ's pure, spiritual teaching?" asked the Crusader, with tone of suppressed scorn in his voice.

"Doubtless," replied his antagonist, "the Church holds to old forms of expression, but allows great liberality of interpretation."

"And this liberality," interrupted the Crusader, "leads to insincerity of spirit; since the creed has in the minds of many worshippers an interpretation, which is its own refutation. I believe an utter negation of faith is higher spirituality, is certainly purer morality than the covert doubt, the simulated belief of many Christians. I believe that accuracy of expression is in itself moral training, and looseness of expression a spiritual peril."

"Let us settle two points before we can understand each other," said Ultimata. " You believe that truth must have outward expression, and that full, spiritual truth can only have imperfect, earthly utterance. You would therefore justify creed and dogma, though it gave finite limitation to infinite truth?"

"Yes," answered the Crusader, "I would justify such creed and dogma, if held always open to question and flexible in form, to meet the broadened, deepened thought of each new generation. I am always defending living truth against dead error, or perhaps I should say the palpitating life of to-day, against the fossilized life of the past. For all creeds once throbbed with blood, once thrilled with life."

"Yes," broke in Ultimata, "I feel the intense vitality of other systems of faith, by Dorothy's creative imagination in the study of mythology. Apollo and Minerva, Thor and Freya are to her full of individual life and significant, spiritual meaning: to me they are only interesting myths. To return to our foundations: you believe in the necessity of organisation, and therefore in the worth of the visible Church with its growth of outward ritual, its language of rite and sacrament?"

"Under the same conditions," said the Crusader in a tone of dissent, "the consciousness of imperfection and the possibility of change, I believe in the value of the Church, as I do in the expression of creed and dogma. But I believe that the world needs always a vigorous protest against the accepted errors and the autocratic authority of the Church."

"I wish," said Ultimata, "that your crusades were more clearly defined as against the errors of the Church, and not the Church itself. For you must feel that the Church meets a great human need."

"I find even that statement difficult of acceptance," protested the Crusader, "since I know that the moments of spiritual uplifting in my own life, have been oftener on some lonely mountain with wide sweep of horizon, or before the pentecostal flame of sunset, than in the minster's shadow, or under the pictured glory of cathedral windows; and I am sure the lives of highest spiritual power I have ever touched, have been those unfettered by church traditions, who trusted to their own spiritual wings. Inspiration does not come by appointment."

"I grant the possibility of both experiences," replied Ultimata, "that you find the highest spiritual truth in individual flight, and that many natures have personal illumination through power of faith, through clearness of vision. But you are a born aristocrat, in spite of your anti-monopoly sympathies, and I am a true democrat. You condemn the Church because the highest natures do not require its help: I defend it because average human nature, weighted with materialism, burdened with care, finds strength and faith through its teachings. I know, that in the pressure of practicalities, the absorption in business interests in the life of man, the wearying routine of duty in the life of woman, that the Church speaks a language of comfort and hope. In the materialism of the age, its very iteration of spiritual truth is a watchword, wakening and rallying the higher powers to activity and conflict against the visible forces of mammon and self. At least you must honour the Church if it marshals its forces on the side of spirituality against materialism: for whatever our difference of creed, practically we both accept the dualism of Persian theology, and recognise the endless struggle between light and darkness, between life and death."

"Yes," answered the Crusader earnestly, "the history of human thought is only the record of that fierce conflict between good and evil in forever new incarnations; but I cannot forget that in our land, the Church was ranged on the side of slavery against freedom, of monstrous, moneyed injustice against simple human right."

"I admit," said Ultimata, "that the Church is not always on the side of right on each individual battle-field of humanity; but after all, it has from the prophets' days to our own, yes, from the acceptance of the earliest sun myth to the most spiritual conception of Christ, been for light not darkness. It has held sacred spiritual truth, though often through broken imagery of symbol and legend. You know that the highest, finest development of each nation has been in its time of full faith in its own system of religious thought, whether classical mythology or Christian creed. Faith is creative, scepticism destructive."

"Yes," admitted the Crusader, "we find common

ground in personal acceptance of the awful dualism of life, in sympathy with the powers of light against those of darkness. I fully believe that each strong true life adds to the reservoir of spiritual force from which the future may draw; and that each weak, yielding life lessens the power of good, and lengthens and intensifies the struggle. It gives a fearful solemnity to the individual life; but I fully believe a struggle is impending between the impurity and imperfection of accepted religious thought, and the power of truth of the independent soul, so I think one may oppose the Church and be on the side of justice and right."

"I know," sighed Ultimata, "that this is an age of turbulence of thought, of transition of form; and doubtless the Church must accept some changes in sympathy with the age. But I still feel it to be a stronghold for spiritual truth; and believe that it may need to extend its outworks and uplift bolder towers for outlook and defence, but that it will still guard as sacred the revelation of divine truth upon earth. That it can change its forms and modify its creeds is proven in the past, and it still exists, a vital and life-giving power on earth. You must feel that it is allied with spiritual forces against materialism and unfaith."

"Theoretically yes, practically no," asserted and dissented the Crusader.

"But life is at unity with itself," asserted Ultimata, "so if the Church is theoretically right, the right theory must conquer the outward wrong."

PORCH THEOLOGY

"You know," said the Crusader, "that life is not at unity with itself; that, on the contrary, life is unrest and struggle, and that sometimes the theoretical right succumbs to the practical wrong. The Church must return to truth and simplicity of outward life, or the theoretical teaching of such truth is only darkening the vision and deadening the spirit. It must accept the universal law of life, and dare the conflict against mammon and materialism."

"This reminds me," Ultimata said, "of John Swinton's account of his visit to Karl Marx, just before his death. After talk of the uprising of popular thought in communism, socialism, and nihilism, as well as the deep, underlying discontent (the central flame beneath these volcanic breakings), the visitor asked what is the law of life? They were upon the beach, a restless crowd about them; before them the unresting sea, forever purified by its own discontent of movement. Marx bared the bold, brave forehead and white locks as he answered solemnly, 'There is but one law of life: Struggle.' —Is that also the law of eternal life?"

"I believe not," replied the Crusader. "I know that we think together so far as to believe that the Supreme Power works with effort and against resistance—or perfect, harmonious right would rule His universe. He also struggles against antagonistic force of evil, or weight of matter; but I believe that He will evolve perfect, full life in each individual soul as in His universe."

"How grand, after all, is the old story of Genesis,"

said Ultimata, " how we fall back upon its language, whether of simple narration or of spiritual myth. How better describe the working of all power in the universe to ever finer forms and higher types, than the calling of order out of chaos, setting sea and land in bounds, and making light triumph over darkness? But sometimes I feel that the conflict must be eternal, for the imagination fails to picture life which is not struggle, the physical life of casting off exhausted matter, assimilating new; the spiritual life of accepting good, rejecting evil. The power of choice in the effort to evolve individual life from helpful elements and against antagonistic forces, seems to rule from the growth of a crystal to our highest conception of the Supreme Power. I long for rest, yet the effort to picture it suggests a vision of closed eyes and quiet hands, which we call death. I think the joy of eternity must be the outlook upon conflicts won, the uplook to broader fields of grander victory. I cannot picture peace, and I am sure you, with your fighting instincts, cannot, save as transient rest under flag of truce to gain strength for the morrow's march and the coming battle. Our rebellion here is against the uncertain and unjust ends of the finite struggle, the defeat of true hero, and crowning of unworthy victor. But with assured gain to the right, triumph of the highest, can you think of any grander law of life than struggle?"

"Yes," answered the Crusader, "I think the harmonious adjustment of the powers of life would be restful peace; the peace of life, not death. I think the perfect relation of sun and planets in their ordered movements, the law which governs even meteors in their flight, suggests final, infinite harmony."

"But," said Ultimata, "our friend Dr. Winslow has written a strong, bold book, 'Force and Nature,' to prove, from planetary movements in their order, and volcanic eruptions in their aspect of rebellion, two universal laws, repulsion as well as attraction. So the peace and order would be still the result of the struggle of two opposing forces."

"Well," laughingly responded the Crusader, "I believe the law of your nature is struggle, you have a genius for contradiction. You will not agree with me even when I propose a compromise in remotest space. But certainly upon earth and with ourselves, there is no cessation of hostilities. In the human spirit as upon earthly soil, it is conflict still between the thorns accursed and the promised bread."

"You know," said Ultimata, "that Dorothy has a metaphysical way of stating things. She had this even in her infantile days. I can give you two illustrations of her spiritual vision: one recognising the conflict, one foreseeing the peace. When she was about six years old, we were walking in Central Park, and she stopped me to look at a tree, which in its growth had rent the heart of a huge granite boulder. I was in a brown study at the time, and paid little attention to her exclamations until I heard her say in low solemn tones (and when she speaks with that hushed voice, I always listen, for then she is often my sibyl), 'But the stone had to give way to the tree, for the stone is dead and the tree is living; life is stronger than death.' I watched that afternoon, the growth of green in the meadows and leaf upon the trees, with a kind of spiritual joy.

"When she was two years old, I took her to England to have the beloved friend, whose name she bears, hold the child as god-mother at the christening. The day of this solemn rite, I saw an exquisite little font for holy water, a shell held by an angel in robes of pale, shining pink. I bought it as visible memory of the day, which would appeal to the child's heart. It always hung in her room, and she had long talks with her pink angel. Once, in unpacking after a journey, when she was still less than three, I laid, for safety, the angel far over on the bed. She leaned on her dimpled elbows, looking wistfully at her treasure out of reach, then said, with a real human sigh, 'Don't put my pink angel on the bed. Angels with wings don't get tired, only little girls with feet.' So she could fancy movement which is not effort, and flight without weariness. But I cannot conceive even of angel pilgrimage, without the instinctive thought of pausing for breath and rest, when one has faced the free wind on long sustained flight. I evidently lack celestial imagination."

"I think," answered the Crusader, "that you talk with Dorothy too much upon spiritual subjects.

The child is suffering from 'other worldliness.'"

"Well," Ultimata responded, "that reproach should not come from you, for the other day she came upstairs with a brooding look of perplexity on her face, and with embryonic lines showing between her knitted brows. Soon she said, 'Mamma, the Crusader puzzled me so: was he in earnest, or trying to make me think for myself? He had been talking of the struggle between good and evil, and I told him you had read me something of Zoroaster's philosophy in "The Ten Great Religions of the World", and I thought the idea was wonderful. I like to think of life as a battle-field. Then he said that the powers of good and evil are so at war in us, that he believed when we die, part would go up and part would go down: but that after æons of purification, the part that went down would also grow fine and pure, and then we would be united, be all of ourselves. Now that makes me feel very queer and uncomfortable.'

"Soon after, one day fractions were peculiarly 'vulgar' and 'improper' in their insubordination to her comprehension, and she had grown impatient and unreasonable. When the lesson was over, she said with a quiver about her lips and a laugh in her eyes, 'I think if I had died this morning, Mamma, there would have been nothing to go up.' So you see what seed you have planted, to grow up in grotesque fancy and in serious memory. But here come the Church people, and I wonder whether our theology on the porch has been rightful Sunday service. It has been rather defining doubt, than a confession of faith."

"It has been, you mean," said the Crusader, "thinking your own thoughts, not speaking the words of others: it has been breathing pure air, not the musty atmosphere of a closed church: it has been feeling the warmth of June sunlight, not the chill of theological shadows. The text was a spray of yellow roses. Now I will prove my liberality of creed, by bringing you as part of the service, roses, red, pink and white." So he strolled off and soon returned with a manifold argument in favour of out-of-door theology, in a generous bunch of roses.

Ultimata bravely held her ground, and with disused Prayer Book and discarded gloves in one hand, and roses in the other, defended herself against the accusations of desertion to the enemy, as the groups of church-goers passed her on the porch. But in her own heart as she walked upstairs was the stirring of an unanswered question; how far the exercise of individual freedom in thought and habit might be right, and when its exercise would be grievous wrong and spiritual wound to those, who missing the outward services of the Church, might miss also the inner truth and the shining of the eternal light.

CHAPTER XII

PORCH STUDIES

I NEVER tire of sitting on the porch and watching in dreamy fashion the play of life about me, especially in the summer, when there are fewer strangers, and I attain by continual observation to clear outlines of the personal characters which form the ever-changing groups. I generally have a book, as apology for my withdrawal from the active social life, for hours of talk exhaust me, and I like better the possibilities of quiet study; though I listen critically to the voices, so much is revealed in the natural tones. More learn to mask the face than to control the voice. One sees human nature in its pleasantest aspect in these sunny out-of-doors studies. After giving greeting to the various groups, I generally pass for a few minutes' low-voiced talk, to the far, shadowy corner, where the invalid rests whom we are watching sorrowfully through the slow gathering shadows of the dark valley.

He is a German, but in delicacy of feature, with black hair, and eyes with a flash of lightning through their depths, he is more Italian in type. He has been a man of large, active business interests, accustomed to command, and has an autocratic power, sheathed by his present weakness. He is facing death calmly, with constant thought of the future of those near to him; with longing for his own release, but with no irradiation of spiritual hope. His attitude of smiling expectance towards death, not as a transition, but as an end, is to me an interesting study, though fraught with unspeakable pathos. He talks with lingering tenderness of his home life; with fond pride of sons and daughter, and has a loyalty, still flushed with a lover's admiration towards his large, fair-haired wife. She is the picture of a *Hausfrau* so restful and helpful, so stored with practical wisdom, so suggestive of good house-keeping; and through all weariness and sadness of watching, the quick-moving, gifted hands weave such intricacies of fancy work, create such marvels of delicate embroidery. The daughter I have called Saint Cecilia, from her musical culture, her fine, clear voice which by its power should have the breadth and fulness of church service for its utterance, and from her right to saintly aureole. Her strength of self-sacrifice has not been called forth by any enthusiasm of religious appeal, but is inherent, part of her nature and development. She is a fine linguist, an ardent student; having taken a severe course of art training, and given years of devotion to music. Many girls in these days, sent to college or given professional career, accept student life from their atmosphere or environment. But this girl, in her father's home, with German devotion to the duties and details of home life, has quietly carried on a plan of solitary study. With her scholarly culture, she has no interest in the great questions of the day, and is as untouched by the fever and strife of woman suffrage and kindred conflicts, as if she were a mediæval châtelaine of a castle on the Rhine. Her sense of duty is supreme, and her life has a repose, a quiet strength and womanly dignity in strange contrast with her unshadowed girlish face. She has a type of face I much admire: regular features, olive complexion, eyes of dark blue; but so shadowed with heavy lashes, and strongly outlined brows, as to seem black in intensity of shadow. She wears her hair cut straight across her forehead, which accords well with the somewhat severe lines of her face. Her mouth is beautiful, with tender, childlike curves in repose, quick gladness of smile, but with a power of scorn under indignation. Her dress is very expressive; rich and elegant, but with a certain maidenly reserve about it. In her manner to gentlemen she has perfect unconsciousness of self, and neither poses for effect, nor plans social triumph. With her quiet power, her restful charm, I yet feel a lack. She has not strength of emotional nature. In love she will be quietly won, won to life-long loyalty, but will never be swept by any high tide of feeling.

Once when I was speaking with reverential admiration of her strength of character, her scholarly culture, the Crusader said, "Yes, but she has not even embryonic wings." Imagination fails in the rare blending of her nature; and I almost feel if imagination fails there cannot be any breadth of sympathy. There is in her nature true tender sympathy with those of her own world; but I doubt her power to enter deeply into the struggle and unrest of natures of the intense or ideal type, to whom life is fateful tragedy or sorrowful disillusioning. I think of her ruling always a realm of peace and love.

Under her gentle rule is a young brother who is a more baffling study in his mercurial moods. He can be delightful in his graceful gallantry; and then his delicate, finely featured face is mobile and charming. But he has moods of withdrawal, when he wraps his small personality in defiant gloom and glowers at us across impassable gulfs.

Again he chooses cynicism as his prevailing expression, and is severely critical in tone and sardonic in smile. At other times he is contentious, and fully equipped for skirmishes on the croquet ground with feminine foes, with taunts of ridicule and terrorism of tyranny. There was abject subordination to his lordly self-assertion until Dorothy appeared; dowered with a temper of her own, and not trained to acceptance of "the one man power." Then came rebellion and declared antagonism. But after a pitched battle over balls and mallets, in an hour will come a change, with such graciousness of courtesy that Dorothy is disarmed and there is a friendly truce.

Saint Cecilia and myself, who watch with mingled amusement and anxiety this waging of war and the signing of peace, rejoice always when the white flags are flying. The play of these two natures upon each other, the ready resentment, the fierce warfare, the battling of pride with desire for peace, and then the full-hearted reconciliation, with real underlying sympathy, is a perfect little comedy. It is a case of intellectual sympathy and temperamental antagonism. Such touch of nature upon nature in later life would give possibilities of tragedy. With them, this morning, was a compatriot, a life long friend of the father; a Prussian officer retired from the service, tall and elegant. He has the perfect manners of a man of the world, and a cynical grace in the indifference of his intellectual attitude towards all social and public questions. I studied him as an exceptional and interesting specimen, a bit of exquisite mechanism, without the disturbing influence of a human heart, or the surging tide of human blood. He was positively restful to one surcharged with emotion, from his polished coldness, his statuesque immobility. I thought that I had mastered him by my silent, critical scrutiny, and found a type of man new in my world; but he is spoiled for me as a character study. For the other day when his old friend grew pale with sudden faintness, and the shadow on his face was like that of death, I saw in the cold grey eyes of my unemotional type, hot, human tears.

In an invalid resort, there is always the creeping

of that familiar, yet ever strange shadow over some loved life; while watching group by their untiring devotion, their futile hope, claim our tender sympathy, or happily, our helpful service. The sunlit valley would fail in human meaning, if here also tired lives did not rest, and loving hearts break with the pain of parting. Can love be as tender elsewhere, where there is no shadow of possible loss?

Dorothy has a friend among the new guests, so naturally I have been drawn into the companionship. He is individual and therefore interesting. He bears a Spanish name, but claims England as his birthplace and an English mother. London is his home so far as bachelor membership of good clubs can give a home. He is familiar with the art world, holds as friends many men of literary fame, but is strangely un-English, unrooted, migratory in habit and experimental in intellect. He has spent many years in South America and is now on his way to New Zealand for investment in the promising mines of that colony. Dorothy has a deep sense of resentment underlying her enjoyment of the new friend. For in their first evening talk, he took the conservative side on many subjects; especially defending the institution of slavery. Dorothy blazed upon him with her fierce indignation. I was talking with a group across the room, but noticed the flush in her cheeks, the flame in her eyes. When I called her to go upstairs, she was in an absolute fever of excitement, and I could not quiet her. Again and again she burst forth in her defence of liberty and popular rights; then recounted the arguments of her adversary in favour of slavery, of aristocracy, of monarchical forms of government, as opposed to democracy and a republic.

When I came to know her antagonist I found him an advanced liberal; and he confessed that he had taken his conservative line of argument to inflame the feeling and quicken the eloquence of the young advocate of the people.

Dorothy approves of his liberalism, but can scarcely forgive the indignity and injustice she suffered in that mock battle. Her foe of the evening, her constant friend, offers a wide field as a social study. I have touched him lightly, with the exception of one long talk when the mid afternoon light paled into faint twilight as we discussed forms of government, creeds and social theories.

His mind offers positively no walls, he holds no forms. He abjures all systems of faith, all forms of government, all social traditions as partial, incomplete and out-worn; and is a believer in individualism as the one absolute power. He is a dark, handsome man, but with a shrouded look in his eyes and with an atmosphere of mystery about him. He is most kind to Dorothy, most courteous to me. I enjoy with a kind of daring pleasure, touching a mind so unfettered by the thought of others, so fully individual; but I feel in the absoluteness of his independence, something almost de-humanising, as if lives and hearts were pawns in some fascinating game, to be played with dispassionate impersonal interest. In his dark-eyed fascination I discern something akin to the flaming presence of Mephistopheles.

In sharp contrast with him is the figure of a frail, delicate girl, touched by the shadow of early death. She is last of a race, on both sides swept away by consumption. She is facing the foe with a gay defiance, suffers from a hemorrhage, disappears for a few days, then flashes back among us in charming costume, and takes her part in the evening dance. One day I heard her say that she was tired of the dullness of this life, that she would like to go to a ball or her own funeral. Poor child, with all the instincts and ambitions of girlhood; with the sadness of an unmothered and homeless life and the creeping chill of this sure shadow. I think her nature heroic to meet the lonely, unsmiling fate with this stoical gaiety. What more utter loss than to be disinherited of the hopes of youth? Later we learn the boundaries of our world, the stern hills that shut us in, the cold, salt sea which holds our little island life in its cruel clasp. But the world of the young life should be calm, sunny and unhorizoned save by the sweep of its own hope.

A charming group among late arrivals has given me much pleasant study, and an hour or two of enjoyable companionship. The gentleman is a Colonel in the U.S. Army, but with Boston culture stamping him more visibly even than military training. I see him always in a glamour of reflected glory; for he is brother to one of the heroes of my girlhood, one of the immortal heroes of all our hearts, the first, I believe, on the Northern side to fall upon battle-field, giving to his historic name and fair youth proud place on the roll-call of our Nation, and leaving as legacy to the world two wonderful novels. One is the breeziest, broadest sketch of the ungirdled breadth of western plains, the unpierced heart of the Rockies; the other is a deep, psychological study of the good and evil in human nature, the hereditary taint of impurity in a soul incarnate in fair woman form. The last is strangely profound and philosophical for the creation of a young mind; suggesting familiarity with the long, fierce struggle of light and purity against principalities and powers.

The Colonel, also with honourable war record, is unlike my ideal of the brother; whom I picture fair and daring as young viking, dashing fearlessly through life, as with impulse of leadership he dashed fearlessly to his death. But the present representative of the name is dark, with hair and beard touched now to iron grey; with quiet movement, low cultivated voice, and expression of perfect social repose. His conversation is lucid, clear-cut, incisive, and with quiet grace of utterance however keen-edged the critical words. His wife is the fairest of blondes, with almost infantile sweetness and charm. She is an invalid; suggesting by the delicate fairness of her complexion, the faint, low tones of her musical voice, the utmost fragility. And here my love of beauty rules me. The purely white, perfectly formed hands of the fair invalid, with their softness of outline, their dimplement of beauty (such as only babies have), hold me in willing thraldom. I have been guilty at times of carefully choosing my place in the reading-room, where I could watch their graceful play. My heroine of the beautiful hands is wearily homesick for the Washington home and life, and feels keenly the change to a *Presidio* on the Pacific. Shall I confess it? She has christened the Golden State, "Califorlornia."

Two new-comers are the bearers of a name familiar in English History, and wear the old, proud name with easy grace. They are father and son, and so inseparable and devoted that they can only be known together. This charms me; the genial sweetness of nature with which they study American life and ways. They came to us with a warmth about their hearts, as of those claiming welcome from near, but unknown kindred. Coming with that expectant smile, naturally they have been met with answering smiles; and with a responsive throb of English hearts, warmed only by two or three generations in our brighter sunlight, so quickened into fuller, freer expression, than the reserved nature of the Mother Land.

We are in national youth; like all young things sensitive to warmth of touch, to glow of smile. So I believe our English friends, when they tell me that the American welcome met them on ship board, made them at home before they touched our soil, and has flashed for them a track of brightness from sea to sea. When English natures give recognition of our true kinship to themselves, it is English blood that thrills in our veins, English memories that stir in our hearts.

But when we are met with a disowning, disinheriting stare of irrecognition, as curious specimens for foreign study, or interesting fossils disinterred from the old Colonial life by shock of eruptive republicanism, then we are the rebels of '76, natural aliens and possible foes. So these two English guests, speaking in the rich, mellow tones I love so well, will tell by and by in their London home pleasant stories of their kin across the sea; and we shall hold their memory as part of our true heritage, our right to the fulness and richness of English life, the lights and shadows of English history, the undimmed greenness of English fields, the deep-rooted steadfastness of English homes and the outer strength and inner warmth of English hearts.

Another Englishman, broad-shouldered, young, with the fair complexion, light moustache and close cropped hair, so familiar to all who know young England in drawing-room and hunting-field, wears his forehead knit into protesting frown against the fate which sent him into exile; and deepens his voice into thunderous growl, as he criticises, condemns, curses, this crude American life. Self-elected exile, we shall keep him exile however long he stay. We have a fairly-ripened sunny side for those who choose to be gladdened by our young, quick growth, but we have doubtless sharp poignant flavour for those who choose to set their teeth on edge with green, immature fruit.

One slender, delicate invalid, I have watched at safe distance; for I see in his weakness there is resentful indignation against posing as invalid; the natural protest of youth and manhood against the passive, suffering fate. I see in his extreme sensitiveness, hear in the keen, nervous tones of his voice, the pain of a strong nature, unnerved and unstrung. I must watch, for sake of the wife and boy. The wife is beautiful with the fair, sweet Madonna-like beauty, and moves about him with tender ministering grace. But I do not wait to see the wifely devotion, but for the rare shining of her smile. When it comes, oftenest as the child brings his hands full of flowers to her, or marches in his masterful way across the piazza, it is so glad, so bright, so tender, that I feel warmth stir about the roots of all pleasant things in my own heart. The boy, about four or five, is broad-shouldered and stalwart, with long, fair curls, and a face boldly freckled as he wears his sailor hat always pushed back halo fashion about his head. His face is broad and strong; and his whole air one of complete self-possession and easy mastery. He has a full, deep ring in his young voice, and an expression of natural authority. I love to talk with him; he gives his ideas with no uncertain, childish vagueness, but clear, positive, absolute.

Sometimes he brings me a flower, and once, when I had been ill two or three days, I asked the young knight why he had not brought me a flower as he promised. "Did you forget me?" I asked.

"No," he answered with charming assurance, "one day I picked a rose for you, but I met another lady on the way, I like her too, so I gave your rose to her. She was right here on the porch, so I thought I would not climb the stairs to take it to you." I thought his artless confession the most perfect, prophetic masculine creed.

You will say, perhaps, that my picture lacks shadow. Doubtless, but Santa Barbara is a world flooded with sunlight. This blue sky shows scarcely the faintest film of a cloud; so with loyal light trancing always a golden world, what wonder that I miss the shadows? One familiar figure I shall introduce to you as the Public Conscience. He is a gentleman strictly honourable, severely upright, but entirely unsympathetic. He is not only "a law unto himself," but a rigorous, relentless law to all others.

He sees in life no delicate gradations of circumstance, by which right and wrong so nearly touch; no subtle, temperamental differences which affect moral judgment and its outward expression; no lifelong strife of opposing powers of light and darkness in the same nature, through which there can be no clear triumph of the right, but at best only rallying of spirit force against the invading evil. To him, the division has already taken place between the sheep and the goats; and woe to the stray goat which he finds among the sheep, and scarcely more mercy to the sheep caught wandering once where only the goats should be. Under finite conditions there is always injustice in absolutism; so our friend of unwavering conscience, of unfaltering judgment, is sometimes cruel in condemnation. But such cruelty is always in the name of justice. No one would more fairly judge, more fully approve those of consistent strength, of outward integrity of life. But to the faltering of will, the uncertain of step, to the daring to whom comes the temptation to reckless leap; to those of subtle, questioning mind, who doubt the accepted forms of good and evil, and to those of broad sympathy to whom all human must needs be human, he is merciless in criticism. Outwardly he is most thoughtful and kind in social courtesies to those within his accepted circle, but absolutely blank and irresponsive to the excluded. Often he passes as I read on the porch, always with courteous greeting, and often with kind suggestion that I allow him to choose me a sunnier place, or move my chair to a corner better sheltered from the wind. I smilingly acquiesce, but think how significant of his nature that he should feel the presence of sun or absence of wind which pleases him, must be the rightful adjustment of light and air to all others. I see in him a dislocation of fate. Instead of cynic on the sunny porch of the Esperanza, he should with scientific training have been a surgeon, for which he is fitted by microscopic eye and mind like true, keen blade. But now he chooses us as subjects, and I feel sometimes when facing his inferential smile and uplifted eye-brow, the pangs of possible, future vivisection. I know well that his severity of judgment, his cruelty of social execution, rest upon recognition of honour and purity; but he has not reached even a bowing acquaintance with charity and sympathy.

Many groups come and pass with kaleidoscopic rapidity and play of colour. Yesterday, a party of ladies left, Southerners travelling by carriage through California. That is my ideal of travel, and I suppressed a sigh of envy as in comfortable open carriage, with drapery of becoming wraps they dashed off with span of spirited grey horses. To-day a four-in-hand arrived, bringing back a party of young men from the Yosemite, brown-faced, gay-voiced and with suggestions of camp life in their picturesque flannel shirts and broad hats. One bronzed young face I greeted with joy, thinking of the sweet-faced mother, following with wistful eyes her boy's slow return to health and strength. There are some queer characters among us; one a Dragon, who devours children on the croquet ground and picks their mothers' bones in the seclusion of an upstairs den. This Dragon, so tradition says, was once defeated in single combat by the Fairy Prince. But I shall leave such natures undescribed; as these are human studies and this is no place for abnormal developments, which come through hereditary strain of bitter blood, or by pressure of personal pain.

Think of these moving about among the creepers or the roses, sitting in big rockers in groups, swinging lazily in hammocks, or with books in shadowy corners and you have my picture of porch life.

CHAPTER XIII

ON FINCH'S HILL

I THINK the most ardent home lovers are those fated to life-long wandering. With me the longing for a home is a deep abiding pain, only comforted by the kindly illusions of the coming resting-place, which lures me on like some fair desert mirage of cool, palm-shadowed spring. Now I think that I have found my fate. Such love as mine for Santa Barbara must be so powerful, so persuasive, that adverse circumstances will be won into smiling compliance. So sitting at my windows, I face often my future home on the hills, and on our rides I see what others miss; visions as we pass of gables and dormer windows, of broad piazza and red-tiled roof, the calm green lawn and the glad rose-garden of the home which waits me. On the broad, sunlit porch, I watch groups of those beloved by me, and see above the hearts where I love best to dwell, my own roses worn. Does such joy await me?

Meanwhile, we chance sojourners here talk with the wistful tones of those long in exile, of homes in Santa Barbara valley; sometimes of the broad fruitfulness of ranches, oftener of homes upon the foot-hills, in the leafiness of Montecito, or upon the Mesa, facing the full grandeur of the mountains. Only Themis, who is never deluded by false dreams or flitting visions, disdains all thought of home here; content, justly content with the bay-windowed amplitude, the porch pleasantness of the Esperanza. But I long for home with the intensity of desire of those to whom fate has said, " Ye shall dwell in tents." Sometimes I feel that life is utter, absolute loss, without the rest, the deep-rootedness of home. But I know that such view is material and sceptical; it is a worship of brick and mortar, a glorification of the temple, not of the spirit which the temple shrines. For the possession or non-possession of the outward symbol of life can never be the measure of life itself.

Home life is doubtless helpful to a calm, strong development of character; with its routine of positive duties, its growth of associations, its restful companionship and its possibility of social life. But fortunately, the unfolding of life in thought and feeling is not dependent upon the ownership of eaves and gables. Because the home is the finite condition, but the home-longing the expression of the immortal need of harmony between the life and its environment, the longing must be grander possession than the home itself. Still, the desire to be fitly tabernacled is part of life's full experience, an expression of its creative instinct.

In home life is manifested woman's plastic art, her inspiring and moulding touch, by which a home is sometimes evolved fairer than its fairest inmate. A home should be, I think, a larger, looser self, worn with the ease and grace of drapery, with folds so ample, and lines so sweeping that it reveals individuality yet veils the unloveliness of personal idiosyncracies. The hereditary homes, which come to us shaped by other lives, significant of other experiences, are like the stately brocades, the rare laces of our grand-mothers, in their antique charm. Then the touch of the owner must be not that of creation but of reconcilement; bringing into harmony the softened shadows of the past, with the individual lines of the new life. But in America, most homes are homes of creation, and though the abode of many, should be the incarnation of one spirit. A woman's life should be written in her home; her past with its warmth of sunlight, its shadows of memory; her present with its strength of service, its grace of sympathy; and her future with its calmness of coming twilight, its restfulness of hope beyond the night. No woman's life has full, visible expression without a home. Homeless women are denied their natural language, and speak with conscious effort, with sense of loss, a language less vital and human; like deaf mutes by sign and gesture. But emotion is more than utterance, life more than its utmost expression. We may miss the insignia of our rightful rank, but we cannot be disinherited. Those, whose spirits are at home in the truth, the faith, the love, which are immortal, have built for themselves, not tabernacles on the Mount of Transfiguration, but eternal homes.

I have sometimes strange dreams, when in a state of physical exhaustion and brain excitement. Let me tell this one. I was wandering through space, drifting, it seemed, upon some broad sea of light, still on and on; at first with delightful sense of freedom and movement, then with awakening consciousness of boundless, homeless eternity. I passed angels in groups, who made no pause in their swift, winged flight; and with increasing speed, whirled past luminous planets and flaming meteors. A sense of finite weariness came over me, an unutterable longing for rest. I was an exile, an alien on this unshored sea of space. At last, I uttered a hopeless, lost cry. Then came floating towards me a figure majestic in outline, with outspread wings of yearning tenderness. I was comforted, companioned, as it swept towards me in its flight; but as it neared me the strange glory paled, the wings grew faint and shadowy, the heroic figure lessened into human likeness, and I recognised a dark-eyed, wan face I knew; but with the light of peace where had been the shadow of suffering. It was a poor woman of Santa Barbara, loyal-hearted and long-suffering. I had wept with her above her dying baby, and kissed the sweet cold face on which her hot tears fell. "Mother Mary," she cried, "my heart shall be her home, the heart so lonely when the baby died, and which she filled with love in the days when I wept and she comforted." Then, looking where her eyes were turned, I saw the Virgin Mother, with the Holy Child cradled in her arms, and as I watched about her came my loved ones, those of far dim memory, and those for whose loss, life had been one long, passionate pain. Not exile and not alien, I was at home in spirit life. That human touch had given me my place with the loved and loving in Eternity. My home, I found in space, the tender, loving heart of that wistful-eyed Spanish mother.

I wakened from this dream with a strange thrill as of tearful joy. I felt freed from the transitory shadows which we call loss and gain, and resting in the consciousness of the eternal verity of love. I had touched the immortal secret, found the everlasting home. Still I long for the assured ownership, the outward stability and the inner beauty of a real, earthly home; and I would have it stand on these near foot-hills, with outlook to the sea, and close to the sunlit glory, the solemn shadows of the Santa Ynez Mountains.

Our ride to-day was to my favourite site for home, where two points of beauty tempt to inconstancy and lead to endless arguments between the Spectator and Dorothy on one side, and the Crusader and myself on the other. The day was warm (not with scorching glare which those on the Atlantic coast know as heat), but with sunlight a little more fervid and sea breeze somewhat fainter than is usual. It justified white dresses and delicate lawns, and made the piazza as gay as the garden in its out-blossoming of colour. We waited until after three to miss the midday heat and have the soft sunset light upon the hills on our homeward ride. We were only four, and all heart-sick wanderers, with thought of possible home in this valley, where (whatever outward fate may decree) all our hearts shall dwell. We had planned to ride to Finch's Hill, loiter along its crest, study the finest points of view, and make ourselves happy with ideal homes. Dorothy was the gayest; for talk of home wakened in her heart no memories of other homes, and faces which will shine henceforth in no home of earthly building.

The Spectator holds life always with a smiling grace which I have learned to know is not gaiety of heart, but resolute courage; the acceptance of the present good, with no disloyalty to the dearer joys of the past, no distrust of the shadowed future. The Crusader touches all that relates to his own life with cynical lightness, as critic at a drama failing in the unities; but I know that under that gay indifference is knightly loyalty of heart and soldierly sternness of soul. With the same smile, with which to-day he offers a rose from Santa Barbara garden; he offered his strong young life to our land in those days when men were called to swords and women called to tears.

We followed the trail up the foot-hills to a side slope, broken into three plateaux. The highest gives near, solemn view of the mountains, Santa Barbara peaceful and panoramic in the valley, and distant out-look of the sea, but missing the curve of the coast line. The two lower terraces have scattering groups of live oaks, which soften the foreground, and looking inland is the sweep of the valley golden with grain, and the rounding lines of swelling hills. Behind, the mountains are rugged in sharp, stern greyness, but melt in that valley view into softness of outline, as if some great sea had crystalised its rolling surge and lifting wave into these vague billowy lines.

This crest, only a few hundred feet above the Valley, gives an impression of uplifting, a sense of space which suggests the illimitable. There, with an unbroken sweep of horizon, embracing sea and hills, the companionship of the solemn, steadfast mountains, and the sweet human nearness of the valley and town at our feet, I would build a broad, sunny home, Italian in architecture, with broad terrace and uplifted tower, all light and strength and calm. The highest plateau should be glad with roses, the second green and restful with lawn and trees, and the lowest fruitful with vineyards, and orange and almond groves. The Spectator says that the view is too extended and panoramic, lacks tenderness of foreground, and is merciless in its unbroken breadth, its unveiled fulness. The Crusader draws a deep breath, looks with quick gladdened gaze from the near, stern mountains to faintest blue of the far sea line, and exclaims. "Everything is here: the sweep of sea, the strength of mountains and the space of sky."

"Everything but water," quickly corrected the Spectator (who is a student of the California water supply), "and foreground. It is like an eye without a lid."

"No," answered Ultimata, "it is like an eye uplifted in rapture or worship. The sweep of the lid, the fringe of shadow is for the drooping, downcast eye."

"There is a lack here," persisted the Spectator, "there is nothing hidden, no mystery, no promise, no new unfoldings."

"There is infinite variety of expression," asserted Ultimata, "in the play of light and deepening of shadow. Even now the mood of the day is changing, the lines softening, and the distance dimming into subtle sweetness."

"A narrow view," added the Crusader, "has always a definiteness of outline, a persistency of expression. The glory of this is its possibility of response to varying moods. It is like the gracious hospitality of a large nature. One is so conscious in most persons, as in most views, of the walls, the fate of hard stern limitations."

"But," laughed Ultimata, "the Spectator as an Englishman glories in walls. I remember well all the green loveliness of my first impressions of England in my drives on the banks of the Mersey. I was asked on my return from an afternoon trip, what most impressed me in England, and I answered, 'The walls.' I meant only the obtrusive selfishness of walls, which excluded parks and home gardens from the eyes of passers-by, but after long residence in England I often recalled as rather philosophical, that first discovery of mine; that England with all its rare lovableness, was chiefly noticeable for its walls. The walls it throws about its gardens are most significant of the reserve which will not share lightly its joy, its exclusiveness of ownership, the sacredness of the home domain. But can I ever forget the shelter and delight, the unshadowed pleasantness of being guest within English walls? So much depends on the standpoint of observation, whether one belongs to the included few or the excluded many."

"The earth belongs to the excluded many," answered the Crusader, "and the walls must fall."

"But I hope," said the Spectator, "that England will not soon lose her glorious parks, and her greenness of home lawns; and only behind walls can such culture be reached and maintained. I do not care for my fractional part of the unowned, unloved earth of Henry George and his theorists."

"The new truth looks always rough and aggressive to the old traditions," responded the Crusader, "but the battle must be fought between class privileges and popular rights in the older lands, as in our own more distinctly between capital and labour; but everywhere between the walled-in and the walled-out."

Dorothy returned from an independent exploration just in time to catch some of the talk about walls, and added her wisdom by saying, "I like walls if they are not too high, and are easy to climb. This led us back from social discussion to personal talk.

We rode through the eucalyptus avenues and the home gardens of the Finch place to the rival point of outlook. This is literally a point; heavily wooded with live oaks and picturesque with great boulders. Dorothy, with a cry of delight, was off her horse, scrambling over the rocks and up the trees; which, with their low, spreading branches are as pleasant for climbing as the delight of my childhood, the gnarled old apple trees. The view here is quite changed in character. There are glimpses of the valley seen through the trees, exquisite bits framed in the foliage, a narrowed mountain view; not the sweep of the range but a bold group of peaks. The charm of the billowy valley is lost by the higher crest of the Finch place; but there is gain in winning the lovely curve of the bay, and the lines of the hills as they dip towards the beach. The view loses in grandeur but gains in loveliness; it is less broad but more charming.

The Spectator affirmed, "Here you have more elements of beauty. This view is inexhaustible, always revealing itself; with every change of position you get new vistas, it is all glimpses and gleams. It has a charming wooded foreground, and is full of suggestiveness. It is not a panorama, but a series of pictures."

The Crusader said, "Yes, it has a charm of its own, is full of covert beauty and hidden meanings.

It lures and wins, but it would never uplift and inspire. It is the loveliness of the finite, the other has a thought of the Infinite."

"This is a siren," added Ultimata, "with veiled glances and subtle smile, the other is a sibyl with prophet power and unveiled vision."

"For daily life," answered the Spectator, "I should like better the reserved charm of such a siren, than the full, fierce shining of the sibyl's eye. These heights of vision should reward our best, bravest climbing; but for home I should choose a more restful, tender outlook, just such hints and suggestions of perfect beauty, as you gain here through the green, shadowy foreground."

"You would not marry your perfect ideal then," asked Ultimata, "but choose some maiden of lesser loveliness for home life, reserving the right to occasional climb and exceptional inspiration in your ideal's presence?"

"I would marry my ideal," replied the Spectator, "but my type of womanhood would not be the strong, brave, fully-outlined woman in whom you glory; but the woman of folded meanings and of veiled tenderness. I should wish her to be like this view, full of possibilities, never fully revealed, known by hints and suggestions, but softened always by mystery."

"I am true also to my ideal," said the Crusader; "I should love the sibyl with power by one rapturous glance to lift the soul, and broaden its horizon with clearness of spiritual vision. Better than any folded meanings, the sudden flash of the Infinite thought across the human."

"Let us leave ideal women and come down to houses and architecture," said Ultimata. "In place of broad, sunlit spaciousness of home, here I should choose a house of early Gothic, like some of those in the old villages along the Rhine; all quaint gables, with heavy cross beams through the grey stone. Set on this hill shining through the live oaks, I should wish a house of grey stone with red-wood beams. Which would be lovelier; the simple breadth of sunny wall of my Italian villa on the terrace, or the broken lines of Gothic quaintness here?"

"Oh, Mamma!" exclaimed Dorothy, dropping down from a tree among us, "the Gothic house, all gables and queer corners, full of hiding-places and sure to have a ghost!"

"The question is growing complicated," said the Crusader, "between space and peace as against shadow and mystery. I think a group of houses on this hill might meet all our needs, give by contrast charming effects, and allow us to work out some social and psychological problems. There should be an English home, 'four square to every wind that blows,' solid, ample, generous, set in lawns and gardens, with grey stone walls where grapes would ripen, but where, unfortunately, ivy could not cling. This should have Spectator's view, all gleams and glimpses with the expression always of veiled reserve. Dorothy should have the Gothic house, as quaint and unknowable as her queer little self, with shadowy corners and ghostly passages. Ultimata should have her Italian villa imported from her beloved San Miniato hills, with a southern garden, graceful fountains, olive and fig trees, and the shining of scarlet poppies as in the Tuscan fields; and I would defy all schools of architecture, and build a house after my own fancy, to suit my love of space and the southern climate. It should have a great central hall two stories in height, like an enclosed court, with easy chairs, couches, low book-cases and writing tables, with windows towards the mountains and windows towards the sea. On the one side should open from it a shadowy library and a sunny, artistic drawing-room; on the other a large dining-room with rose vines framing the windows, and a glimpse into a moist, cool fernery. There should be breadth of piazza for out-of-door companionship and for moonlight walks; and surmounting the house a great turreted tower, giving that glorious view, full sweep of horizon with the slumbrous valley and shadowed mountains, sunlit Santa Barbara and the far, luminous sea. And I would have acres of roses for the children and the fairies."

"I like your house best," said Dorothy, "but I think I will give up the gables and the ghost and live with Mamma. I do not care to go to housekeeping alone with a ghost."

"Then why not live with me and the fairies among the roses?" asked the Crusader.

"Because a Mamma to tell fairy stories is more important than the fairies themselves," Dorothy made loyal answer.

"I have always liked Gothic architecture in everything," said Ultimata, "from cottage to cathedral, but in the South it seems unreal and fantastic. Gothic houses need long twilights, winter evenings, snow on the eaves, a weird shadowiness in the landscape, and the sough of wind through pine trees."

"The pine trees are not lacking in California," answered the Crusader, "and I have seen nothing on all my travel so Gothic in grandeur, as the stateliness of the red-wood forests."

"California is strangely inconsistent," replied Ultimata, "with southern sunlight on bare brown hills, on vineyards and olives, true Italy, in light and beauty; then the dark green solemnity of pines and red-woods and the wildness of a rocky coast. Santa Cruz is nearer kin to Norway than to Italy; Southern California and the northern coast are worlds apart in climate, production and expression. Northern California I have seen only as a tourist, and hold vivid memories of its beauty, but I have not the stirring of one wistful longing when I recall it. But I do not like to think of the day when I cannot look on these brown hills and dream in this sunlight."

The Spectator questioned, "Why should you be so fascinated? To those of sensitive lungs this climate gives release from suffering, the blessedness of soft air, and the promise of life. But I can hardly understand its charm to you. You lack books and pictures, you miss the excitement of varied social life. In your case, it seems the choice of sleep with the delight of dreaming, instead of life with its waking activities."

"I choose it," responded Ultimata, "because I am by nature a dreamer. Here dreaming is natural, rightful, with no dread of sudden shock of wakening. In New York, with my love for seclusion and solitude, I feel the jar of the active life about me, without power to become part of its activity. My dreams are broken, and yet I never waken into full working vigour. There conscience and temperament are at strife. Here there is sweet unity in life."

The Crusader said, "I think before those houses stand material facts upon the hillsides, we shall all waken some day to the consciousness that we have dropped asleep and had a pleasant dream in Santa Barbara Valley, but that we are rested and eager again for the stir of life."

"You doubtless will," retorted Ultimata, "for a man when most in love can analyse his emotions, sound their depths, or their shallows, and make a psychological study of the effect of the tender passion upon himself; but when a woman loves, it is with the abandon of her whole nature. Her intellect has no power of calm withdrawals to take measure of the high tide, and watch for its subsidence. I love Santa Barbara so well that I cannot picture life elsewhere. I even doubt memory when it recalls life before Santa Barbara was known to me. My intellect is in love, my imagination, my whole power of emotion. But Santa Barbara is with you a passing fancy, the subject of a summer's flirtation. With women love is a growth from a living root; with most men it is a flower worn as a *boutonnière*, to be replaced when faded."

The Spectator observed, "If you are beginning one of your interminable arguments upon sex in intellect and sex in soul, Dorothy and I will have a race with a fair start, to decide for ourselves our respective merits." For by this time we were down the hill, and nearing the beach for a dash on the sands before our return.

The word was given and we started on a good run. If there is a perfect pleasure on earth, it is a lope on these white sands, with sunset light upon the hills and sea, and the consciousness of true comradeship, though no breath is spent in spoken word. It is escape from limitations; power of flight, and companionship loosened from the needs of usual utterance. The look of challenge, the swift glance, the smile of triumph as one dashes by, or the acquiescent smile of defeat if one fails in the race, and at the end the glad, sudden recognition of each other's freer, larger selves. One hour of that true companionship gives fuller revelation, than a season of drawing-room masquerading. Out of breath, and tired with our run, we slackened our speed and came up State Street on a gentle, easy canter, turning into the Esperanza just as six o'clock struck. We said hurried farewells and parted to dress for dinner.

When we met at table with quiet greeting, I wondered which were our true selves, those of the free, wild dash, or those of low-voiced conventionality; or how many selves, strangely folded and involved, we each possessed.—*Quien sabe?*

CHAPTER XIV

"THE GREATEST OF THESE"

I HAVE had a few days' imprisonment, but with gift of roses, with notes every day, books and papers sent to fill the leisure, and Dorothy's most unprofessional nursing, I have been very happy. Then yesterday, Themis came, and I always enjoy true, dual companionship, eye to eye, soul to soul. My ideal of society is a series of tête-à-têtes. She flashed in upon me with her unshadowed brightness; forever unshadowed, since it is shining of the spirit, not any surface reflection. I cannot picture her life under eclipse. We chatted of our friends, of the latest Esperanza news, of the glorious sunlight; then talk turned into realms of shadow, for we spoke of a life once known to both, fair with youth, fair with beauty, but later touched with loss; that subtle yet absolute loss to woman of social whiteness, the loss not of recognised sin, but of questioned virtue; then the drifting out on the dark river by act of conscious despair. The thought of this wrecked and submerged life, and of the many broken lives, floating out at last, loose, unclaimed drift-wood on the cruel tide, led to tender, earnest thought upon the possible harmonising of social integrity with Christian charity.

Themis, as habitual with her, took the larger view in defence of social purity and truth. Ultimata in her weak-minded or strong-hearted fashion, throbbed with the pain, and fainted with the loss of the weak, and often wronged subjects of social condemnation.

Ultimata said fiercely, "When I read of that suicide, knowing her proud, brave fight for life and social recognition, and the averted faces and unseeing eyes which met her, I hated the whole structure of society and the Christian Church. Say that she had sinned, which neither you nor I could know, nor critic of keenest eye: is there practically in this world of incompleteness, and in the Church of confessed sinners, no place for penitence, no power of forgiveness? Has Christ not yet found a resting-place upon earth, that his teaching of charity is defied by His Church, and denied by us all? We are braver than the Jews, for we dare to face His wistful questioning eyes, and yet throw the first stone as those 'without sin.' I believe in charity as the heart of Christianity, and the spirit of philosophy."

"And I," answered Themis, "with the utmost tenderness for the sinner (or the one suffering from the shadow of possible sin), believe in justice even where it leads to condemnation; in the absolute rightfulness of keeping society pure by the exclusion of the stained—yes, even of those suspected of stain."

"What loss to social purity," retorted Ultimata, "that the severe-eyed law of Sinai was ever supplemented by the evangel of love. It leads only to moral bewilderment, to spiritual untruth, to holding a creed of charity and forgiveness, yet withholding its hope and helpfulness from weak and wavering lives."

"We can at our highest only approximate the ideal society outlined in Church teaching," responded Themis. "With our present social structure, mercy and justice are often absolutely antagonistic. As human laws strive only to attain to justice untempered by mercy, so I think society has only the right to absolute decision between right and wrong. Any compromise is an unsettling of the foundations on which rest the stability of our homes and the safety of society itself. You are an ardent republican, though you know that this form of government represents the wisdom and thought of the majority, and that the minority must yield to the dominant will of the many. So, society exists for the greatest good of the greatest number, and there is weakness and treason in sympathy with sin."

"I admit," answered Ultimata, "that legislation can only aim at strict justice, or such approximation to justice as can be reached by outward devotion to truth; but as its aim is absolute, so its penalties are definite, and there is some rightful proportion between the wrong and its results. But society is manifestly unjust in its processes of thought, its methods of judgment. It summons the suspected before an invisible tribunal, gives no audible hearing, makes no clear charges; then utters by its silence or its scorn a condemnation unto death. There is no open trial, no authoritative judge, no court of appeal. I think no sin forbidden by the decalogue is more cruel in its far-reaching wrong, than the faint breath of blame which unjustly dims the whiteness of a woman's life; or the unchristian scorn, which forbids a woman's life once sullied the right to forgiveness, and the hope of spiritual purification and social redemption. A man may always rebuild his fallen life, but we ruthlessly write 'ruined' upon a woman's life, if its walls have once swerved from the perfect line. There is no ruin in God's world as there is no death. Science has given us some blessed spiritual watchwords. 'Conservation of Energy,' is one of these. Under the life we call 'ruined' there is vital flame, power of growth and possibility of fuller, final development."

"That I would neither be so unscientific nor so uncharitable as to deny," answered Themis, "but the spiritual development need not come by social recognition. There can be striving after purity, true repentance, and doubtless high development, even after open sin; but social re-habilitation is fraught with perils to the many, greater than the gain of forgiveness to the individual. If the same conventional drapery is to disguise saint and sinner, the purity of life would be sacrificed and young lives suffer taint from contact with accepted evil, against which there is no social protection. Christ recognised the value of the outward symbol of inner purity, when he demands in the parable that guests at the feast should not fail of the wedding garments, and when he bids the waiting virgins have store of oil and lighted lamps."

"Yes," replied Ultimata, "but Christ did not demand absolute purity from those who wore wedding garments, but that such robe should testify the soul's desire to be clothed in white; neither that waiting virgins should carry lamp never quenched in sudden darkness, but that the kindled light should confess the spirit's watching for the clear shining of the truth. But we deny the garments to those who long for the white robing, and forbid lamps once darkened all hope of future lighting."

"But," asked Themis, "practically, how would you change the usages of society? You would not include Magdalen asylums among the homes for social recognition?"

"No," answered Ultimata, "but I would make it more possible by charity of judgment, by spirit of forgiveness, to keep tempted lives out of such asylum, and in the ranks of life's rightful workers, life's honoured guests. I do not deny the existence of a class known as 'lost women,' but I think Christ will question why with lighted lamp, we did not make kindlier search for each lost life. I know society must recognise such class as a source of loss and evil, a danger to its own well-being. My protest is against the earlier judgment of society, the careless acceptance of thoughtless gossip, which deepens in the telling into fatal scandal, the social irrecognition of those in slippery paths, to whom hand of greeting might be salvation in the critical hour. There are many unmet, unloved lives to whom the admiration and proffered friendship of men of honest seeming, offer perils unknown to lives wrapped in love and sheltered in true homes. We should be merciful in judgment when love is the tempter, for love is the natural right of every soul, and many sin through long, unjust denial of that blessed birth-right. That any fail of honourable love is one of the results of imperfect social organisation, of hereditary wrong. By the sovereignty of love, by the sacredness of wifehood, and the higher sanctity of motherhood, I would plead for the sorrowful, defrauded lives, who know only the passion of love, but miss its uplifting into the blessed relations of home."

"But," argued Themis, "the very purity of home and sacredness of marriage, by which you plead for mercy, would be sacrificed by careless, irresponsible recognition of illicit love and would lead finally to social acceptance of 'Free Love.'"

"I am not so startled as many by the name, 'Free Love,'" answered Ultimata. "While for social stability, for the welfare of children, for the loyalty of those accepting solemn vows, and for the development of character which comes through a life of duty even when joy fails, I am a believer in the rightful permanency of the marriage relation; still I think a rebellion, political or social, is usually the precursor of a genuine reformation, and that name, 'Free Love,' is very significant. Can it be by the utterance of outward vows without heart response, by a sacrament at which the spirit fails, that we have fettered love? Love should be free, but not for disloyalty of change, not for light renunciation of duty; but free for spiritual right of choice, for fulness of expression. Because we have made marriage without love a thraldom, where marriage with love should be freedom, 'Free Love' has risen as a righteous protest.

"The outward form of marriage must abide, but we must recognise as more sacred than its form, the true oneness which comes not by utterance of vow, but by experience of love. Marriage is both a spiritual union and a legal recognition of such union. I would not lessen its value as a social contract, but I would question whether two living in loyal love without religious rite or legal contract, sin as deeply against true purity as those living in legalised marriage without love. For the good of society, I know, the outward marriage, though loveless, is safer than the most absolute unity of love without such form; but I am trying to penetrate to the secrets of the individual lives, and to discover whether love or the legal recognition of love is most needful to spiritual unity. For social reasons, because of human weakness, the outward form is a finite necessity. But we are told in the spirit world 'they neither marry nor are given in marriage;' but by all science unfolds, all that our spirits can comprehend, the duality of sex is eternal. Love then must be the law which eternally holds spirit to spirit. But in a condition of perfect harmony, of spiritual truth, there will be no need of outward service, of uttered vow. That riveting of the tie by legal contract, that symbolism of a ring to bind, is protection against the temptation to disloyalty, the possibility of wrong, which marks an imperfect condition. In the higher life, love, with clear vision to recognise its mate, with spiritual right to claim such soul, will need neither ring nor vow. Love will be eternally free and eternally loyal. I have scarcely been talking, Themis, but trying to outline my thought to myself. I know you will not misinterpret my spirit, though my words may shock you."

"No," answered Themis, "I know that you regard law as the accepted social order, and duty as the law of the individual life. As long as you accept their recognised limitations as needful and right for human development upon earth, I shall not deny you the right to perplex yourself with the eternal mysteries. I feel strongly that now the only safety is in the established and recognised order of life, in law, in social traditions, and in church creeds. As long as human nature is imperfect and human language incomplete, there will be discrepancy between our highest ideal of right, and right as embodied in the law of the land, the dogma of the Church and in the unwritten social code. But I think all these expressions of human thought are at each age, the world's best approximation to absolute truth, its best incarnation of justice; so I dread light unfolding of vague theories, which would seem to justify rebellion, and unsettle social foundations."

"You are always wise and just, Themis," admitted Ultimata, "I should prefer for safety and comfort to live in a kingdom ruled by your justice, rather than one ruled by my own sympathy. I am at heart not less reverent than yourself, but less charitable in my judgment of society, because so pitiful towards the sufferers, exiled and disinherited by that unwritten social code. Practically I shall continue to recognise socially a woman under the ban of popular condemnation, unless I am convinced of flagrant wrong-doing, and always outreach my hand to one who having sinned, is striving to regain the right to honourable, pure living. I should like to organise a new Crusade against slander, and stir the hearts of women with zeal for charity of judgment, tenderness of love, towards the suffering and the sinning. The badge should be a white cross to typify the power of forgiveness and the promise of ultimate purity."

"You are an enthusiast, Ultimata," answered Themis, "and many bold theories and daring acts would be forgiven you, when women of calmer judgment and slower word would suffer condemnation for similar thought and deed. So do not blame others for cruelty or cowardice, who are more fettered by custom and conventionality."

"I understand," said Ultimata, "that one of my temperament gives her friends glorious opportunity for the divine virtue of forgiveness, and her foes the easy triumph of exultation over her erratic and uncertain course. For two things I earnestly strive, to be true to the conviction of to-day, though I cannot reconcile it with the thought of yesterday; and to discern spiritual and eternal truth, underlying all phases of faith, all forms of development."

"Your ambition is lofty," laughingly rejoined Themis, "but it was the philosopher who steadfastly gazed at the stars, who fell into the well; and I think your life would be safer, calmer, more consistent, if you looked more carefully at the paths of usual human treading, and less at nebulous, celestial truth. I will take an illustration from your riding. Keep to the high road or follow well-defined trails, or some time you will get lost on the hills. I am glad that your 'alter ego' is, as you describe him, calm in temperament, conservative in thought. I think you need his touch always upon your eager, excited life. Be quiet now, read an old-fashioned love story, and get a good night's sleep. We want you on the porch, there is a drowsy air of acquiescent amiability which is oppressive. We need your ready, fierce challenge to a controversy. I shall report you as convalescent and in your characteristic, combative mood."

"I am conscious to-day of having indulged in a free lance kind of attack, but I have had three quiet, dreamy days," pleaded Ultimata, "and your presence stirs me always like high mountain air. Santa Barbara will never lure you to lotus eating and lassitude. You have the clear outlines, the invigorating atmosphere of the North. Your presence is a protest against the softness and languor of this southern world. Do not desert me, for I have no moral power of resistance to the charm of this sunshine, the breath of these roses, the mystic light upon these hills and the slumberous calm of the Pacific."

"You ought to go East," said Themis with a good-bye kiss, "yours is a case of love at first sight, and absence and diversion are the best remedies. We will go together in the late autumn, winter in New York or Boston near the theatres, art galleries and book stores; then next summer you shall introduce me to your other love, Mount Desert."

So she left me, and I lay on the sofa with that sense of rest which comes from companionship with a nature strong and self-controlled. I wondered once again at that mystery of temperament which gives to one mind the sure, firm, outward step, and to another the power only of broken and uncertain flight. This assured strength, this rightness of mental movement is manifest in the physique as well.

In our occasional evening walks upon the porch

with the Crusader, Themis keeps step and swings upon her heel in turning, with military precision; while I keep time with eager beat, or loitering movement of my own thoughts, and am constantly called to order for being out of step. I think my failure in life might best be described as being always out of step. I do not work well under organisation, do not keep my thought in ordered movement with the thought of others. I am in theory a flaming herald daring to outrun the popular thought; but in practice a tired straggler from the well-trained ranks. But one comfort there is in all forms of failure, as in that of invalidism. It was the family invalidism, Dorothy's occasional cough and my general worthlessness, which justified pilgrimage to this coast, and loitering months in this Valley of enchantment. To you, in strict confidence, I will confess that I am conscious of a greater gain in this seeming defeat. It explains my broken fragmentary life, and saves me from condemnation by ordinary standards of weight and measure. I know there is in me an inherent fragmentariness, which under changed conditions, must still have made life a failure. So invalidism is not only outward weakness, but merciful disguise for weakness which is organic and individual. It was a relenting of fate to save me from recognisable ruin. Instead of an absolute, historic failure, I have a place among the possibilities and potentialities of life.

My friends speak of me with that lingering tenderness, which wins for me gentle judgment as among "the might have beens" of happier destiny. There is one nature, always uncertain of aim, faltering of step, that carries on forever an argument within itself, which is its own field of warfare. For success, a nature must have assured unity, otherwise it loses in intellectual civil war the strength it needs for outward conflict. That explains the inadequacy of many minds to meet the needs of life, the fatal lack of grasp.

There is now much scientific study of heredity, with the purpose of throwing light upon the leading types and countless variations of humanity. I think one subtle point remains still untouched by light: the power which blends, or the weakness which fails to blend, these inherited temperaments and faculties into absolute oneness. In the study of the relation of children to parents, there is not only the question of the transmission of two sets of powers, but how far through flame of love, through spiritual affinity, or through reciprocal magnetic influence, the two can be made one. Until this unifying power, or its lack, can be determined, there can be no positive result predicated from knowledge of the parents, or study even of generations of ancestors. Some characters carry forever unharmonised, or in direct antagonism, the natures of father and mother: some more complicated in organisation bear in themselves multitudinous foregoing natures in inevitable unrest. Where two natures or temperaments struggle in one person, life is long warfare; where the heritage of many natures or temperaments meet unreconciled in one, the result is chaos, and one short human life cannot evolve order from such elements, though their varied and conflicting powers give promise of ultimate fulness and richness of endowment. For any true judgment of an individual, we should see backward through all ancestral elements and forward to the eternal harmony.

CHAPTER XV

KNIGHTS ERRANT

DOROTHY has missed of late her riding companion Mae, who has returned to her St. Louis home. So she rejoiced greatly at meeting at the races (whither she went with the Spectator) Harold, who is now the possessor of Irony.

I found this horse of military pretensions but unheroic performance, unsuited to Dorothy, who had set her affections upon Brownie; so I was very glad to transfer the big proportions, uncertain ways, and future possibilities of the handsome colt into hands where he would have bountiful stable, kind guardianship and a course of wise training.

I am rather proud of my first sale of horse flesh, as I had been often smilingly assured that I had paid twice the real value for the colt. I told the presumptive purchaser that my only justification for asking, after familiar acquaintance with Irony, his original price, was his fine blending of martial aspect with Christian virtue. He had, with warrior bearing, the spirit of humility; and showed no selfish pride in wishing to be first in a race, or to dim by his achievements the glory of others. I thought his moral influence over an ambitious boy would be admirable. But I left with the purchaser, who was a judge of horses, the decision as to his real value. I received the cheque for the original price of one hundred dollars; but how much was due to Irony's virtue, and how much to my skill in managing the sale, I have never been able to determine. But I felt some justifiable pride at gaining this experience in horse flesh and mustang morals, without financial loss.

Dorothy came back from the races with plans of riding with Harold, whose quiet grace of manner, love of horses, and kingly name won her admiration; and I think one element in her prospective pleasure was the thought of companionship with the colt, for she never forgets the thrill of her first ownership of a horse, and the triumph of those first rides. Since that day of meeting at the races some weeks ago, there has been much good comradeship. It is no infrequent sight to see the big, grey colt dash up to the hotel porch, where he is greeted by an old time whinnying by Brownie, and his rider with out-spoken enthusiasm by Dorothy, who in Scotch suit swings herself cavalier fashion into the saddle. Harold has a noble head, broad brow and large, full dark eyes. His great charm is his grace of manner, his courtesy of bearing, so unusual in a boy of that age; generally painfully self-conscious or aggressively rude. Dorothy thinks him the incarnation of chivalry, and gives him not the passive admiration of loyal lady behind castle window waiting the fame of his daring deeds, or watching his triumphant return; but the fealty of knight to brother knight, for on all their rides they are Harold and Donald. These children, as I call them, these companion knights as they deem themselves, do not climb foot-hills and explore cañons only, but penetrate the depths of enchanted forests, seek the shore of golden sands, cross unknown rivers into fairy land, wage warfare with invisible foes, and return flushed with triumph from perilous adventures and fierce encounters. They both carry "real swords", and when antagonists fail them, they dismount for friendly tilt upon hillside or beach; and evolve from their own gleaming and clashing weapons the glories of full tournament with helmeted knights, caparisoned steeds and fair watching women, with Queen of Beauty holding crown for the victor. I like their mediæval play, for they ride always in spirit in the cause of right, with loyalty of unspoken vow to truth and justice against wrong and evil. They hold high ideal of knightly honour, its rightful devotion even unto death to the oppressed who need helper, the imprisoned who claim deliverer; in faithful allegiance to warrior king as brave and invincible as Arthur when he wore Excalibur, and the unbroken circle of the Round Table reflected his valour and his purity.

One afternoon last week, I watched them dash towards the beach, but waited long and late for their return. The sunset light faded into short twilight and the evening shadows fell before, through the dusky night, I discerned two phantom-like little figures pause before the gate; but I was re-assured when I heard the gay parting words. I met Dorothy, brimmed with the day's gladness and the morrow's hope, with face of stern reproach, which relented as I listened to their story: how the tide was low, and after passing Castle Rock and the ravine leading to Hope Ranch, they thought they might venture on a long, dashing ride to Moore's Landing.

There was, I know, an exulting sense of freedom in this resolve, as they had asked no leave, a thought of possible peril as the tide might rise, and a thrill of delight at facing the unknown. So on they went; but as they rode homeward the tide rose, the shadows fell, and they had a wild, heroic dash through water surging about their horses' flanks, and sea fog which rolled in upon them in cold, grey clouds. Rising sea, foam of waves, and the weird fantastic shapes of mist about them, were all foes to be met by cavalry dash and knightly daring. So they rode against time and tide, and reached home wet and weary, but victors still.

Another day lately, they returned after starting on the morning ride, to beg that they might take lunch and spend the day on the hills. The plan was to follow the trail, lunch in some spot of the day's discovery, and leave no trace by which to be followed. But I insisted upon definite choice of place; that in the early afternoon some of us might ride to meet them and have a lope together as part of the day's pleasure. They compromised by the acceptance of adult additions to the party for the afternoon, but their pleasure in our society did not take the form of inviting us to lunch. I found most of our set already engaged for an afternoon ride to Cathedral Oaks, but the Crusader volunteered to be of the party of rescue, and seek with me the children on the hill. Finch's Hill had been the place chosen, the wooded point with its grove of live oaks and its grand, grey boulders. So we two started, but to us it was only an afternoon ride, with lengthening shadows of the dimming day: to them the glory of the morning, the prophecy of joy, the full day's gladness, the vision of valorous deed and the shining of the hero's crown.

Reaching the crest of the hill, we looked in vain for climbing figures, for tethered horses. No trace of our knights errant, no answer to our call; but soon they came in wild dash towards us, having finished lunch, and mounted for an independent ride, before our coming.

The view was perfect; of Santa Barbara in the valley, of hills swathed in yellow light, of mountains in this near view, stern and grand, and over the silvery foliage of the oaks the shining of the calm, blue sea.

The children chose Sycamore Cañon for the ride. Naturally we yielded: how should we maintain independence against their allied forces? The beauty of the Cañon justified their choice. The delicate leaves in fair greenness, many touched with golden light (the faint prophecy of the Autumn's fading), gave tender, cool shadow beneath which we rode, two in merry ringing talk, two in thoughtful silence. For the presence of the children with their world of ideal joy around them, impressed us, I think, with sense of the sadness of real life, with its limitations of fate, its inglorious strife, its frequent defeats, its uncertain triumphs. They rode, as those who ride with hope; we rode with memory. We parted in the twilight. Dorothy and I will never ride with knights of nobler bearing, or of finer spirit.

One of Dorothy's great joys is to visit Harold's home, where there are grand live oaks to climb, and a generous barn with hay loft for favourite retreat, and corn cobs which furnish artillery in their frequent battles. Then there are five horses to pet; all with special points of attraction, and histories of their own.

It was certainly a startling rise in the world for the colt Irony to be transferred from the routine life and miscellaneous society of a "Livery" to the space and elegance of this æsthetic stable, which with its fancy clap-boarding and contrasting colours is as lovely in its way as the quaint Dutch house to which it belongs. Sometimes, while Dorothy climbs the trees or visits the horses, I am happy guest within doors. The drawing-room is spacious, many-cornered and large-windowed, with view of the hills and near groups of noble trees. It has restful couches and shadowy portières, the latest books and lovely bits of colour, and best of all the clear light of an individual mind. For the Theorist, as I love to call her, is always flashing with brightness, electric with spirit. She has a face as changeful as an April day, with play of sunshine, sweep of sudden shadow. She has lived a free, out-of-door life, and carries with her the spirit of the hills, the breath of the sea. This freedom of life characterises her nature also. She likes a broad horizon, heights to climb, dim, shadowy regions to explore. She is broadly humanitarian in her sympathies, and daring in her acceptance of new social theories and latest scientific discoveries. She is broadly, bravely, truly a woman: expressing in her own home life her many-sided individuality; but claiming all fields of thought for woman's heritage, all space for woman's sphere. She is a daring horse-woman, and eager lover of science; with a tender feeling for art, and fine, critical appreciation of literature. I like her for her varying moods and her quick response to the thought of others.

There is a fine, original bit of girlhood in the house, known to me only as "Baby", with honest eyes and ways of her own. Baby is now the owner of a donkey, so the place will have a new attraction and congenial friend for Dorothy. Sometimes, while we loiter, Santa Barbara's solitary bicycle spins up the path to the Gothic porch and we have the pleasure of a chat with the host of the home; in liberality of thought the peer of his wife, but touched with a shadow of melancholy. From companionship with him, we learn where Harold wins his chivalrous grace of manner and his dark, earnest eyes.

I enjoy a home hospitable to ideas as well as to individuals; where theories, experiments and discoveries find a wayside inn for transient rest, if not deemed worthy of longer shelter. But I have one conservative side to my nature; the need of a deep, unstirred religious faith, in which the spirit may dwell, while the free intellect sweeps the seas for new worlds to make its own. I know many think that a hold upon spiritual faith must fetter the intellect. I cannot think that; since by faith in immortality we broaden the finite horizon to the Infinite, and give to mortal thought, immortal wings.

I can meet with feeling of kinship all who hold to faith in a hereafter, all who hold spirit to be the eternal verity, matter the transient form. But all phases of materialism, whether of scientific hypothesis, or unspiritual social ethics, are to me impossible of acceptance since impossible of conception. By thought I cannot apprehend the cessation of thought; by spirit I cannot conceive the annihilation of spirit. By the conscious thrill of that inner self, apart from throb of heart and pulsing of the blood, one feels immortality. By the impassioned beating of the prisoned spirit against the finite walls, one knows that the falling of the walls must be, not loss of life, but larger life.

Harold and Dorothy have their metaphysical moods; for one day not long since, she came home with a tired, shadowed look in her face, unlike the glad, breezy expression which she brings generally from companionship with her chosen comrade. I asked about her visit. She answered, "Harold and I have been sitting on the hay, and talking about the beginnings and ends of things until our heads grew dizzy." I advised the most reckless race, the most perilous climb as safer for them than an afternoon of metaphysics in the barn.

They had one charming adventure lately; when Dorothy was perforce the rescued lady, and Harold the knight of her deliverance. They dismounted for a play, and left their horses as is their custom free to browse under the trees. But some wilful spirit tempted Brownie, and she dashed up the slope and over the crest of the hill.

Harold mounted quickly and started in pursuit; while Dorothy had a prospective experience of the feminine destiny (someone has lately described or classified woman as "a waiting animal").

Brownie gave Irony a good run of two or three miles, and was caught then, because, like some others of her sex, she intended all the time to be caught. Harold led her proudly back, for the captive to receive from Dorothy a severe lecture upon the duties of ladyhood; some of it, she said, quoted from sermons delivered to herself, to show that she remembered their wisdom and was generous enough to share her good things with others. Then, when the culprit drooped her head, either in contrition or in search of a green spot to nibble, she was given a kiss, mounted, and they started on the homeward way.

I have been leading a very quiet life for weeks, as Dorothy has been much away from me on these long trips. I have been perplexing my mind with subtleties of the Spanish Subjunctive; and delighting my heart with a robe de chambre, on which flowers are growing under the touch of my own hand. I can hardly realise the fact, that I, always supposed unequal to the threading of a needle, should be entranced with embroidery; that having escaped the Kensington fever in its first epidemic form in London, and the more violent and popular outbreak in New York, I should fall victim to the contagion in Santa Barbara. My friends' artistic work captivated me, and I timidly hinted at a faint desire to learn the mysteries of the art myself. The frank opinion of an observer (who had witnessed the original style and erratic workmanship of my attempts at doll dress-making), that I positively could never master it, was like throwing down the gauntlet, which naturally I picked up. Strange that the hands treated always with distrust and disdain, should have shown a ready deftness of touch in this delightful flower culture.

It is such a joy to watch the blossoms grow with truth of outline, delicacy of shading, and a certain instinctive individuality in the turn of the petals, or the heart of the chalice. Then this womanly work gives me a sweet sense of being at home in the woman world; that world where so many heart throbs have been quieted, so many wistful longings expressed, so many poetic fancies inwrought in the meshes of feminine handiwork, from the weariness of waiting in Penelope's web, the pride of queenly heart in the tapestry of Bayeux, the patience of cloistered nuns in the broidery of altar cloths, to the mother hope in shaping of christening robes to-day.

Then I feel a tender, quickened sense of kinship to the dear mother (whose girlish, unshadowed memory seems more child of my love than mother to my woman years). For I recall the flitting grace of her slender fingers as they wrought out some artistic fancy of her own. Pale, phantom outlines of her warm, living flowers I cherish still in the exquisite embroidery of my own christening robe and cap.

Much glow of feeling, much prophecy of joy, has found expression in my work—fields of buttercups, daisies and clover upon soft fabric of pale blue—for the little sister in her beauty as bride, in her dignity as wife, will give grace to its falling folds and feel about her heart some warmth, not of its drapery, some gladness, not alone of its summer blossoms.

I have finished this masterpiece and given a formal opening, so many wished to see my art work. It won many praiseful comments, but when the Spectator smiled with genuine pleasure at my field of wild flowers I was content, for my Kensington wears like medal of honour, the approval of this true artist. I dare say that I shall never create another flower, the joy was in feeling my power to create.

I am not definitely ambitious myself, but I dislike to have positive limitations assigned by others to my possible power. So I am longing now for opportunity to take drawing lessons. I think my sense of colour is good, but my power of form weak. I never see broad field of grain or space of sunset sky, without a passionate desire to grasp and hold the glory; but I am consciously so weak in outline that I dare not venture. Think of the awfulness of this experience, when before some sketch of his own, warm with sunset light, I gasped my longing to express myself in art, and the Spectator in his quiet, dispassionate way remarked, "I doubt your ability ever to draw a straight line."

Why should he doubt? Was it an unconscious condemnation of the uncertain, indeterminate lines of my thought; a covert criticism upon my mental mistiness, my spiritual vagueness?

I have pondered that doubt deeply; and I am fired by the desire to disprove it, by presenting the Spectator some time with a drawing of my own, of astounding accuracy, and unrelenting firmness of line. Only my thought of triumph is dashed by the dread (owing to a habit of his of quite forgetting his own words), that I might labour for years to attain to this fidelity of touch, only to find that he had no remembrance of the remark which was challenge to my proud spirit. He would never know that he was crushed.

Dorothy has art advantages beyond myself, as she is often invited by the Spectator to go upon his sketching trips. He is temptation in an irresistible form, so lessons always give way before the charm of these artistic mornings. He is wise friend as well as delightful companion to a child; as he never hesitates to give criticism with simple directness, or even condemnation in an unmodified form. I like this, as Dorothy (in spite of her mother's stern régime) is slightly spoiled by the delicate flattery of older companionship, and the smiling toleration of her original ways. So my mornings are happy when I see Daisy, laden with art symbols, and Brownie, carry off the sketching party. Several days they have spent on a hillside near the Mission, and Dorothy feels personal pride in this picture with the grand old church set in golden fields, with the sweep of the brown hills beyond. Dorothy's gain in art must be by power of presence, by sympathy only: for though the Spectator has often kindly offered her paper and pencil for experiment, she is doubtless conscious of the lack of straight line potentiality in the family, for she remains faithful to the book chosen as her morning companion.

While the Spectator paints, she reads aloud Shakespeare, Sir Walter Scott, "Prince and Pauper," or Aytoun's Scotch ballads. The last she no doubt renders with dramatic intensity to an English auditor, for she is yet unreconciled to Scotland's loss of independent crown and flag defiant:

"With the Ruddy Lion ramping
In its field of tressured gold."

Not of Scotch lineage myself, I tried to effect a diversion of her sympathies by unfolding the heroism of Dutch history. But all in vain: windmills and canals could never rival stormy loch and heathery mountain, nor siege of Haarlem or Leyden stir her blood like the fatal fields of Flodden and Culloden. She will pass all the roses of Santa Barbara, to pluck with reverent heart and wounded hand one stray Scotch Thistle, with its bodyguard of thorns, its heart of royal purple.

CHAPTER XVI

A SPIRITUAL SYMPOSIUM

LAST evening was cool and breezy, and the breath of chill in the air made hearth-light and social companionship a real joy. I generally spend the evening with lessons, or reading aloud to Dorothy; except when Themis and I join the Crusader for an hour's military training on the porch. But last night Dorothy begged to be of the party already planning and posing for tableaux in the Rubys' room; Elinor, May, Nellie and Grace, with the neighbours Bertha and Mabel. Theirs is a spacious sitting-room, with alcove and bay window so well adapted to preliminaries and presentations of groups, romantic, historic and dramatic.

Kings, queens, princes, pages, ladies-in-waiting, knights and lovers they represent; while the docile and patient children in their mimic life are admirably rendered by Barbara Esperanza, a New York arrival in the doll world, and the two comfortable and pliable rag babies, Prue and Priscilla. I gave a conscience-smitten thought to the letters I had planned to write this quiet evening and to-morrow's Spanish lesson, but weakly walked with Themis into the drawing-room. Except when lighted and decorated for dances, this is a solemn, depressing room, and generally deserted for the light cheery reading room. But my head likes better the solitude and shadow, than strong light and a gay crowd.

We took two large easy chairs drawn up near the blazing wood fire, and were just planning a confidential tête-à-tête, when the Crusader and Spectator came in from dinner. As the Spectator has taken to evil ways in joining a nightly whist party, it was a pleasure to win him back to the path of virtue by a good talk. So I compromised with my conscience, settled back in my chair, and put up my feet with an air of decision on the fender. The best this world gives socially is the informal talk of real friends; the companionship which comes by accident, not appointment.

To chance to find the waiting chairs by the open fire, with just the right ones to fill them, is a means of grace I never neglect. I know that duties can rightfully wait upon the spirit of such an hour. I do not believe in too severe a plan of life, which maps out present and future with unchanging topography: I like ease of movement, response to the mood of the hour, freedom of impulse, and faith always in the possible inspiration which awaits us.

Earth's divinest teaching was by the wayside,

upon quiet hill, with familiar talk, and with the breaking of bread. And in all our lives, truth is revealed oftenest in unstudied and unguarded hours. The clear shining of spiritual light may be in sunset flame, in mountain glory or in fire upon the home hearth, in friends' faces at our side, or in a child's uplifted eyes.

The Spectator said, looking at Ultimata, "I wish that I could yield to the spirit of the hour with your perfect abandon. I am always haunted by innumerable duties and desires, which give a ghostly unreality to the pleasure which I wish to enjoy. I ought to join the whist party, who depend upon me to make up the table. I ought to go out and take the record of the thermometers and barometers for to-day. I ought to write home letters and I ought to finish a borrowed book."

"With so many claimants," answered Ultimata, "you ought to yield to the one with which your wish makes alliance. For the fulness of power in any hour must be developed in harmony with the mood which controls it. If you feel like lingering here for a talk, that is duty."

"Is that a safe interpretation of duty," questioned the Spectator. "I thought duty was oftenest the denial of self."

"Ultimata is a dangerous sophist," said Themis. "She always finds an argument to justify the caprice of the hour. If she is in love with Kensington, it becomes for the time her religion."

"I yield to the law which governs my own

nature," was Ultimata's defence. "I can only work when the spirit moves. I use the expression honestly and reverently. I cannot define what I mean by the spirit, how far it is my own and how far some controlling influence foreign to myself, but it rules my life. I read, write, teach, think, and talk with my friends, according to its guidance. The spirit moves me to-night to sit by the fire and enjoy your companionship. If any of you leave you miss the revelation of the hour, perhaps make the hour barren of revelation to others. For an element might fail needful to the unfolding of its spiritual meaning."

"Rather than make myself a rebel against Ultimata's ruling spirit," said the Spectator, "I shall yield to the temptation of the evening's talk, the easy chair and the fire; and I think her philosophy admirable which relieves me of the responsibility of decision."

"Why do you so unchivalrously leave me alone in my defence of the true spiritual significance of moods? Are you assuming masculine superiority to their recognition and their rule?" asked Ultimata, turning to the Crusader. "I have no doubt your stronger, grander character is severely ruled by law; and when the laws which govern wind, currents, thunderstorms, and volcanic eruptions are fully elucidated, I am going to give myself to the scientific study of the laws which control your nature."

"I accept your classification," answered the Crusader, "for, without doubt, the laws which govern these phenomena must be as true, as harmonious, as those already discovered and accepted which explain changes of seasons, ocean tides and the movement of the planets. I find the phenomena more interesting which are still untamed, unharnessed to known laws."

"I believe that," responded Ultimata. "For your finest poem is the revelation of a comet's soul. I always wished to ask you if the story was autobiographical."

"No," retorted the Crusader, "it was written since my companionship with you, and recognised as a speaking likeness by all your friends."

"Well," answered Ultimata, when the laugh at her expense had subsided, "I honestly believe in moods. I find nothing so unnatural, so unscientific, as the denial of their legitimate place and power in life. The most unaccountable caprice, the wildest vagary, as well as the most subtle spiritual impression must be the perfect result of recognisable causes. Heredity, temperament, circumstance must produce as unvarying and inevitable result as sun and cloud and mountain conformation, in weaving the apparently fantastic, but absolutely truthful outlines of passing shadows. I do my part towards the higher education of the age, by offering the phenomena of moods. Let some master-mind discover the underlying law."

The Crusader responded, "I do not claim to be that happy mind, with power to unravel the mystery and reveal the law; but I have taken some interesting notes of your whims and vagaries for the good of science."

"This plea for the validity of moods as a true scientific revelation of the mind," said Themis, "would relegate social criticism and moral judgment of others to a place among the lost arts, for who could command the full data?"

"No one could, no one can," answered Ultimata fiercely. "There is nothing so unjust in this world of injustice, as judgment of others. It is always partial, incomplete, and therefore false. The wisest words ever written (and I positively will not listen in refutation of my statement to any quotations from Shakespeare or Bacon, or both in one), are those by George Eliot, 'There is a great deal of unmapped country in us, which would have to be taken into account in an explanation of our gusts and storms.' Since reading that, I have enjoyed my own outbreaks of temper. I no longer repent or apologise, but make a scientific note of the fact."

"You commenced the talk," said the Crusader, "by the statement that you act only when the spirit moves. Did you ever attempt by a study of Spiritualism to learn whether this sense of a controlling power is only the result of natural law acting in yourself, or a spiritual presence giving personal influence through some subtle relationship with your own spirit? That question opens up a whole new world for inquiry."

"I know Spiritualism," answered Ultimata, "only

by the recorded experience of others. It opens a realm fascinating to my mind, for I am by nature a mystic. But as revealed in its own literature it is as yet so imperfectly developed, so vaguely lighted, so peopled with shadows, that it gives no steadfast light for guidance; but startling, uncertain, phosphorescent gleams, neither akin to the sure stars of heaven, nor the safe lamps of home."

"I think," said Themis, "one might more safely follow Will-o'-the wisp or Jack-o'-lanthorn across salt marshes than trust to the so-called revelation of Spiritualism. It leads lives from the safety of Church and from the shelter of home, to leave them unhoused and bewildered. Spiritualism has no form or outline. It is a temple without roof or walls, and with no God for its altar. It is destitute of law and order. It seems to me not a system, but the denial of existing systems of faith. It gives spiritual truth into the keeping of the illiterate, often the insane and the impure. What can we think of the revelation, when we know the ignorance and immorality of so many of its professional mediums? I do not believe in a search for truth, which leads into conditions so unfavourable to intelligence and culture. I shall not seek light in darkened séances."

"You do not belong to this planet," answered the Crusader, "you are so impatient with the beginnings of things. You recognise truth only when it is fully grown and becomingly draped. But all growth in this world is from small, unpromising seed. A grain harvest in embryonic form a man can hold in his hand."

"Yes," said the Spectator, "but Spiritualism has been growing a generation now. We can judge by its harvest as well as by its seed. Is it not in its development like tares among the wheat?"

"You are a patient student in other fields," replied the Crusader. "Have you given to the whole subject of Spiritualism one tithe of the interest and observation which you have to the variations in the Santa Barbara climate? You do not expect to reach meteorological laws without long familiarity with the physical facts resulting from such laws. You meet with apparent contradiction, with much discouragement; but you never doubt the existence of a law, you never allow yourself to be defeated in your search after truth. Have you studied Spiritualism?"

"No," frankly confessed the Spectator, "I have felt very much as Themis does, but with less intensity of conviction that it was an unsatisfactory field for study, an abnormal development."

"Everything is seemingly abnormal in its embryonic condition," replied the Crusader, "but nothing is really abnormal if we could sweep the whole field of cause and effect. Spiritualism is now an historic fact, an undoubted development, an accepted revelation."

"But," said Ultimata, "from much reading of spiritualistic literature and companionship with those who hold the faith, I find the truth as held by them so vague, so nebulous that it eludes my touch. I long unutterably for the clear shining of light from the spirit world. I wait with a sense of wistful expectancy a fuller revelation. I believe that the veils between this life and the Beyond are sometimes withdrawn, and that to some is given the clairvoyant vision, which penetrates the shrouding of the senses. I liked Bunsen's answer, when some sceptic confronted with the marvels of clairvoyance asked, 'Then what are our eyes for?' 'To limit our power of seeing,' replied the philosopher. To accept the evidences of our senses in this finite condition as the utmost boundary to all possible knowledge, is to avow materialism as our creed. For the senses are only material avenues by which we reach the truth. I have never believed the testimony of the senses to be final and absolute regarding spiritual truth. But when asked to distrust their evidence, or to accept phenomena which transcend their limits, I wish the gain of larger, fuller truth than that revealed by usual human process. I am not sceptical regarding the reality of Spiritualism, but dissatisfied with its message."

"Let me ask you one question," interrupted the Crusader, "what do you think is the prevailing peril of this day to spiritual truth?"

"Scientific materialism," answered Ultimata.

"Then Spiritualism has delivered with clear voice its message," replied the Crusader, "for through all the mists of uncertain revelation, one truth shines with undimmed clearness, the fact of individual immortality."

"Then," remarked the Spectator, "it has its value to those who have doubted immortality; but to those who hold the truth of the Christian revelation, such testimony is superfluous."

"Yes," added Ultimata, "as proof of immortality: but if Spiritualism by control of the requisite conditions could assure us companionship with our own loved ones passed beyond, it would flood with light the valley of the shadow of death, and fold in warmth and blessedness, lives cold through loss, and pallid with loneliness."

"What warmth and blessedness could there be," asked Themis scornfully, "in companionship so frigid as that given in raps, in darkened, dubious messages through strangers; or even if materialisation could be reached, by the faint phantoms of those we love? Better our hearts' memories and our power of pain proving our own loyalty."

"I also feel," said the Spectator, "that the sacredness of love is sacrificed by this medium of communication. One may better wait to give the personal touch, and the living clasp to his own after the finite years shall have passed, than desecrate his love by its expression through an unknown and material 'medium'."

"That is to me the fatal limitation of Spiritualism," confessed Ultimata, "that by no longing, no up-reaching can we touch our own. I think that I have a kind of spiritual pride which withholds me from circle and séance, I feel of spirit friends, as of those still on earth, that love will make its way. If with the larger power of the immortal life they long towards me, as I towards them, they would surely wing their way through space, as here on earth they could always find strength to reach me by weariness of earthly road. With one dear friend, *the friend* of earthly years, the friend I fully believe of future eternal companionship, I had most subtle spiritual communion, and both gave the promise if the earthly gulf could be bridged the freed soul would find its way back to the unlighted life of the lonely friend. Once, Douglas, known to you as the Professor, was called suddenly to England. I made him the bearer of tender messages, of loving gifts to the dear friend, and day by day as he neared the English coast, I thrilled with the thought that he would touch her hand, look into her unfathomable eyes. I was content to reach her through him; for he held her in tender reverence not less loving than my own. With smiling expectancy I waited for his letter, which should bring warm thought of her, the very grace of her own words, the light of her welcoming smile. The letter came. The day before he reached England the beloved friend had passed away. To me no message as she left the earthly life; no message when she touched the eternal shore. Through those first days of deathly separation I had waited with the gladness of the old smile on my lips, when I went unannounced guest, sure of welcome, to her Durham home. I felt the warmth of her greeting, the grace of her hospitality, when Douglas should sit beside her fire, and both would speak of me. No sense of loss when she left me; no thrill of broadened, deeper life to me when she became immortal. Those who know the spiritual tenderness of her 'Two Friends,' can faintly feel what it is to be Dora Greenwell's friend, lonely upon earth, with no faintest whisper of love, no consciousness of her presence across the valley through which she passed. She was to me, poet to entranced listener, saint to heart of Catholic, priestess to worshipper at lighted altar, and friend of fuller power, of grander soul to my reverent, up-looking life. She was sibyl on earth, but fails of voice in the spirit world."

"You will not seek truth," said the Crusader, "in scientific spirit, with dispassionate calm, but demand with unreasoning intensity that it should give the single message for which you wait. Her nature had touched yours strongly on earth, but with changed conditions after death, there may not be between you the relation favourable to communion, and yet spiritual truth might come to you through other spirits if you would but listen."

"It is not unreasonable to love our own," protested Ultimate, "to wait loyal-hearted for them; not seek the companionship of strange spirits. I do not like general society on earth, and I do not expect to like it in heaven. I long for my own, for conscious touch of their natures upon mine, for the eternal unfolding of the earthly promise given in our love and spiritual nearness."

"But," argued the Crusader, "you do not refuse contact with new natures here upon earth; you submit to certain laws which govern social conditions here; you accept new experiences, even those partial and imperfect. Why not study the new revelation, with the same willingness to gain truth and light with which you watch the unfolding of the earthly story?"

"Because I am tired of limitations and imperfections," answered Ultimata impatiently. "If I seek companionship with those passed into fuller, broader life, I expect a clearer, grander message, not echoes of earthly knowledge, nor faint suggestions of uncertain wisdom. You talk of the intellectual protest with which you touch the positive walls of finite natures, but in most spiritual communion there seem even narrower limits."

"I make a distinction," said the Crusader, "between the truth to be given, and the language in which it is uttered. The medium of communication between the spirit world and our own is yet imperfect; but even through this new and unmastered mode of expression, there have flashed messages of clear recognition from friends beyond to those waiting in loneliness of heart and unfaith of spirit for the deathly solution of life's mystery. Only one waiting in the twilight with no promise but of the falling night, can know the thrill of joy with which a message comes, bearing in itself proof of the individual immortality of the beloved and lost, and the assurance of love and loyalty beyond the grave.

Thousands through this new revelation walk with uplifted eyes of faith, who saw in earthly love before only its end of 'dust to dust, ashes to ashes'. And the whole world is stronger, steadier in this transitory experience, because of the ever clearer proof of immortality."

"But this need of strange mediums, of mystic circles and mysterious séances, seems so unworthy of spiritual truth," rejoined the Spectator. "It jars upon the nerves, offends the taste and insults the intelligence of those seeking light."

"You forget," answered the Crusader, "in your devotion to the established forms and elaborate ritual of the Church of England, how undignified, how unnatural seemed the early development of Christianity to those who judged from the sacred shadows of the Jewish Temple, or by the classic spirit of Greek mythology. The gathering of fishermen and publicans in an upper room, was a trivial theatre for the unfolding of the world's new faith. The very personality of the Master, with the home in Nazareth and the carpenter's shop as the scene of his early life; and later, the spiritual claim with the power of miracle to attest His divine power, must have seemed an inharmonious and impossible blending, to those who watched for a Messiah of royal lineage and royal destiny. The tongues of flame upon the heads of those who waited for the coming of the promised Spirit must have seemed an unmeaning and material symbol; and the speaking in many tongues a confusion, perilous to law and order. We cannot create a faith, nor control the conditions under which a spiritual revelation is given; but by study of these conditions, by acceptance of any modes of communication which promise enlightenment, we may eventually learn the laws which govern the communion of mind with mind, without personal contact or material presence. I watch reverently for the fuller unfolding of the new faith."

"I have always felt," said Ultimata, "that there is no antagonism between Christianity and Spiritualism; since Christianity attests the reality of all that is claimed by Spiritualism, wonders and miracles transcending known human laws, messages from the dead, and the materialisation of the spirit—or I suppose more correctly speaking—the mystical power of vision to discern the spiritual or astral body. Since Christianity rests its own claim as a divine revelation upon so-called supernatural manifestations, it can never reasonably deny the evidence of such power; and if once and again in the past, spiritual force has manifested itself in ways refuting usual human experience, and contradicting the evidence of the senses, there can be no impossibility in similar revelation in the future, except on the part of those who hold that God's relation with the race is limited to the acts of Jewish record, and the dogmas of Christian creed. But to those believing in the natural and inevitable relation of the Infinite mind to human nature, and in the recognition of that relation in all forms of faith, there can be no absolute irrecognition of the claims of a new revelation."

"I am glad," answered the Crusader, "that you use the expression, 'so-called supernatural law'. We narrow our own horizon when we decide that known laws only are natural. Supermundane these higher laws are, but supernatural they can never be, since nature must be governed by law. I think that you are just in your feeling that Christianity is not rightfully antagonistic to Spiritualism. Robert Dale Owen has called attention to the fact, that the Catholic Church has always accepted and taught the possibility of miracles and spiritual manifestations in all ages, only it has limited the power of such manifestation to the Church itself. This author feels that much of the vitality of the Catholic Church, and its hold upon the human heart, results from this recognition of the spiritual force, and that Protestantism has chilled and impoverished its own life by denial of such power, and by scepticism regarding its present manifestations. Spiritualism is only bringing to a focus the world's universal faith in the unity of this life with the spirit world as confessed in myth, legend and tradition. When I say the world's universal faith, I mean of course the world of seers; for each nation and age has those of clairvoyant vision and mediumistic power. Spiritualism so far from plunging the world into mysticism, is lifting it from mysticism into some clear, calm understanding of its relation to the Life Universal."

"Why, if there is no natural antagonism between Christianity and Spiritualism," asked Themis, "should most believers in this new revelation withdraw themselves from the Church, deny its creed, and assume an attitude defiant of law and order? There can be no denial of the fact that many spiritualists hold a belief subversive of established morality, and inimical to the stability and purity of home life."

"The temptation of a new faith," answered the Crusader, "is always towards enthusiasm, which endangers for the time the settled foundations of society. It is not peculiar to Spiritualism. Christian martyrs and the early Fathers were very uncomfortable to deal with, as social factors. Even the Master brought a sword, not peace, and taught a faith which led transiently to the disintegration of homes, and threatened social revolution. A new faith is intense, absorbing, and does not always work well with established forms. But there is nothing inherent in Spiritualism which should lead to disorder; on the contrary, the recognition of spirit as the one verity, must lead to higher and more enduring forms of culture and development, though there may be a state of transition which will be disturbed and unrestful."

"You think then from your close study of Spiritualism," inquired the Spectator, "that it would leave undisturbed social morality and the sanctities of home?"

"I believe that a full development of the truth as revealed by Spiritualism, would give more loyal

A SPIRITUAL SYMPOSIUM

adherence to duty, more patient acceptance of life's burdens, from the conscious nearness and the eternal compensations of the spirit world," responded the Crusader, "but a partial understanding of its truth, in minds unaccustomed to thought and impatient of restraint, may lead to reckless disregard of social duties and home ties. Some minds only assimilate enough of a new truth to lead them to irrecognition and denial of the old; and neither the individual life, nor society can be built upon negations."

"I think that I understand," said Ultimata, "how to a mind like mine, Spiritualism might result in a life unsteady and unnerved for practical ends. I long so for communion with the spirit world, for the breadth of its horizon, the freedom of its development, that I think the discovery of mediumistic power in myself, would lead me into such eagerness of spiritual vision, that my whole life would be ecstatic moods of uplifting when such communion was possible, or the reaction of depression when I suffered from the withdrawal of the power. I think the moral foundations would never be imperilled, but the power of action would be lessened, the sense of duty in homely and familiar ways would be deadened by clairvoyant vision to discern that larger, grander life."

"I do not think," said the Spectator, "that practical power of action as developed in you, could safely suffer diminution. And as our talk to-night commenced with your defence of the mood of the hour as controlling influence, I should not like you to accept Spiritualism as your gospel; for, with your desire for communion and your faith in the rightful authority of a longing to determine duty, Dorothy and your friends would be deserted for tables, slates and other mediumistic symbols."

"Yes," added Themis, "you have not the calmness of judgment, the dispassionate powers of observation, which would fit you safely to study spiritual manifestations. Your mysticism and power of longing would make you victim to the deception and delusions now linked with Spiritualism."

"But," interposed the Crusader, "that same mysticism and power of longing would, if you developed as a medium, give clearer vision and higher sweep of wing. I should like to see you a medium. You are sensitive and impressionable, and have the true mediumistic organisation."

"The practical duty of the hour conquers," said Ultimata, "or the changed mood of the hour gives a new interpretation to duty. I must recall Dorothy to herself and take her to bed. She always acts a boy's part in the tableaux, because of her short hair, she says; but I fear from an enjoyment also in the dreams of daring of the boy's life. Riding cavalier fashion in a Highland suit has given her a kind of dual life. She is as truly Donald with thought of dash across the border, or fierce foray, as the dreamy, poetical Dorothy. (She proudly disdains the fact that Highlanders fought on foot, and feared most the mounted foe.) I must try to convert her to simple, consistent girlhood. I intend

A SPIRITUAL SYMPOSIUM

for her twelfth birthday a lovely side-saddle and riding habit, to see if the prospective instincts of young ladyhood will stir in response to my bribe."

"You will lose your money," observed the Spectator, "spoil her pleasure, and take a familiar, picturesque little figure from Santa Barbara. I love to watch her fearless dashing horsemanship."

"And I think," said the Crusader, "that you should insist now upon a side-saddle for her. She must temper her freedom with grace, and modify her bold spirit by the acceptance of conventionalities, or she will be a failure as a woman."

"I shall not break her spirit, be sure," answered Ultimata, "to make her a womanly success judged by a man's standard. Let her develop fearlessly. A generation of such girls will change the standard by which women are judged."

"But I do think," Themis ventured to remark, "that there is strength of self-control as well as self-assertion. Dorothy is so fearless in spirit, that you need not give her opportunities for the development of independence. But life will teach her harshly, if you do not gently, the need of social compliance, of gracious submission to the limitations of circumstance."

"Poor Dorothy," sighed Ultimata, "whatever I plan, Fate is after all the controlling power. Fancy that child by unkind destiny, doomed to fashionable life in a conservative circle."

"I pity the circle," laughed the Spectator, "it would suffer frequent electric shocks."

"I believe in the power of individual electricity to quicken into life even the most formalised society," said the Crusader. "Dorothy in such a world would first shock its inmates, then become the fashion."

CHAPTER XVII

EARTHQUAKE AT DAWN

WE have had a week of interesting experience, universal and individual. The universal was our fractional, infinitesimal share in an earthquake shock. I wished this experience as a chapter in our California story; chapter I can hardly call it, it was so transient, so instantaneous—but thrilling paragraph, or strange, suggestive line with hidden meanings and deep infoldings. It was at dawn, when through the darkness there is a sense of coming light, not yet the earliest penetrating ray; a premonition of day, but no brooding of warmth through the nightly chill. I wakened with a conscious thrill, as of expectancy. In an instant I felt the cause; a strange, solemn vibration, it seemed not of walls or house, but universal, all embracing, as if the earth tottered on its foundation. I did not think definitely of danger, nor of swift ruin and deadly downfall. The sensation was of freedom, as if life were being loosed from finite limitations; of uplifting as if the earth were winged, and fluttering with power of infinite flight. I felt a broadening and deepening of the individual life, as if already it were merging into the calm and vagueness of the universal. But the personal fibre was still there, for I longed to clasp Dorothy's hand, to feel still the human warmth of my own, and to wrap about her in this solemn, strange awakening, the familiar mother-love. I thought not of death, but of life, broad, blessed, unhorizoned. Then came two or three lesser vibrations, like the drawing of quiet breath when peril is past, and then calm and silence. I can never forget that supreme uplifting, that spiritual elation followed by a tired, spent feeling of utter weariness. I was like one wakened from some grand dream, withdrawn from some cloud-like vision of the immortal, to feel the narrowness of near, earthly walls, but the steadfastness and comfort too of home roof and shelter. I felt that I had touched, then missed my hold upon the Eternal; but in the morning there would be Dorothy's kiss and the love-light in her glad young eyes. I could not sleep. I thought of my own longing, felt since earliest childhood to have death come to me in sudden form; not the slow lessening of power and dimming of home light, but a quick ecstatic breath; not the conscious loss of earth, but the swift, keen rapture of spirit-flight through eternal space. I do not dread death, but yearn unutterably for its fulness of life, its infinite fulfilment of all finite longing. But I should not like in the slow, conscious experience of approaching death, to watch the faces that I love grow faint of outline, misty of meaning, as if already I were to them but phantom and memory. Better the quick flash of the immortal light upon the faces that wait me there; the swift consciousness that the tearful memories of earth are the waiting smiles of the Beyond. Then I rose and wrote a little poem on the earthquake; so real as an expression of my own feeling, but so mystical, that I fear not nearest friend will penetrate its spiritual meaning. But it will be to me like a pressed flower held in love and memory, infolding a world of rapture and of loss.

I waited eagerly for the morning to hear Dorothy's experience. I had crossed to her room, as soon as calm for thought and movement after the shock had passed, but found her sleeping tranquilly. Early, as is her custom, she flitted across the hall to me; the little Aurora of my day, in rosy dressing gown, with cloud-like lines of white lace. I looked at her face to see if there were any deepening of shadow in the changeful eyes, but she looked quite calm and unstirred.

"Did you waken in the night, Dorothy?" I asked.

"Once, Mamma; but I had such a strange dream. someone was swinging me very high. It was dark, but I felt that I was above the trees, far over the houses, and seemed almost to touch the stars. I like swinging, but it was strange and solemn swinging so high in the night. I was cold and lonely, and wished the swing would stop that I could find you. It stopped suddenly, and I saw, outlined in light, an angel fly past me. It was the angel who had swung me so high. It was almost like having wings, to have been so far in space. The jar of stopping wakened me. There was not even a gleam of light, so I knew that I must not disturb you. But I thought that I would be contented in this world after that strange dream, and not let my fancies fly away with me. I think I like better to sit in your lap and be rocked by the open fire, than to have an angel swing me to the stars."

I told her of the earthquake, and that its vibrations must have been the strong angel touch upon her dream swing. She felt so wronged, so uncomforted, that she had missed the full consciousness of the shock; but her dreams were evidently rocked by the earthquake.

In the morning the talk was all of that experience. Many confessed definite fear, others vague alarm, and all seemed to have longed with instinctive quickness for human companionship. Was that longing the expression of love, or the need of steadying the vibratory human life by its own familiar world?

Oc's description I thought good, "House velly sick, much shakee." He seemed to think the Esperanza had suffered from a congestive chill.

Who knows but his diagnosis is right; and that poor mother earth has through her great dumb frame some quiver of pain, some thrill of feeling, when she shivers with earthquake shock, or flames through her fevered veins with volcanic fire.

CHAPTER XVIII

ON THE SANDS

I GO less often to the beach for long, loitering hours than is usual with me at the Eastern sea-side resorts. For there the heat make sea breeze and surf bathing almost a condition of life itself. But in this equable climate there is less temptation to the daily dash, the exhilarating delight of rising with the wave, or dipping under the foam-crested breaker. Then horseback exercise lures one somewhat from the sea, to win new surprises always in the windings of the cañons, the grouping of the mountains; or to follow trails across the hills, giving ever-changing views of the Valley with its gateway to the sea. Though, after all, the finest ride is a lope at low tide along the firm, white sands. This we often take; all, I believe, with the sense of immortal youth, as the sand spins beneath our horses' hoofs and the beach looks a far, smooth sweep for our winged flight. But simply sitting on the sand for long, dreamy hours is a pleasure infrequent in my life. The power of light is merciless to head and eyes longing for shadow. Then I think one's heart needs to be at rest, for close, intimate companionship with the sea. I love it in its moods; its storm of fury or its surge of unrest, when it seems human in its passion of protest against the unyielding shores which are the limitations of fate to its infinite longings. But in tranquil, continued communion with the sea, I feel in a strange, sorrowful way, the hopelessness of life, the pitilessness of nature. In that constant ebb and flow, that steadiness of its mighty heart-beat, there seems a controlled power, which makes human life so unresting beside its broad calm, so alien to the perfect sway of accepted law. Children love it, who miss the sense of the sea's mystery in sheltered play upon warm, yellow sands: and lovers seek its shore, for only that sweep and space are as broad as their unhorizoned hope. But to those who have missed both calm and breadth in their own lives, its illimitable blue is too like that lost ideal world; and a meadow path leading to human home has warmer comfort.

The Pacific as seen from this southern coast is so unchanging in its calm, so luminous in its blue, that it misses the stern majesty, the storm colouring of the Atlantic. It is akin to the Mediterranean, which holds in its heart the smile of an Italian sky; or the Adriatic where it clasps with lover's rapture its jewelled bride Venetia. Its tide is gentle and caressing in its slow, measured movement. It speaks with no thunderous surge, prophetic of storm and loss, but in a love song of low, musical rhythm.

I thought that I should dream whole days away upon the warm sands, looking across its space of light. But I cannot: my heart will not sleep and be part of this dream of peace, but stirs in a wistful, wakening way, with its own unrest. But the other morning I was tempted to make one of a large party, filling the car: some bent upon bathing, others to form a watching group upon the sands. I so seldom lose myself in the usual gay life of pleasure seekers, that I was thrilled with a pleasant, mild excitement, from the glad voices, the playful thrusts and quick repartees. The central figure of the party, indeed the leading spirit, whose habitual and enthusiastic bathing (does the *spirit* bathe?) had tempted others into sharing the pleasure, was a San Francisco lady; handsome, portly, with a gaiety of nature, a graciousness of social culture, which made her a universal favourite.

The sunbeam baby of the house was of the party, with father of quiet reserve, and girlish mother. With them was Saint Cecilia, seldom won from the shadows of the sick room into out-of-door life, but to-day brimmed with natural girlish fun. I went, carried away by the enthusiasm of the San Francisco lady, whose eagerness overcame my inertia. Several young people, late arrivals, were of the party. The Crusader responded to a playful challenge of the young mother, and went as her escort. Just now he is her home missionary field; and if he dies a heretic it will not be from lack of the subtle logic and the spiritual persuasiveness of Father Newman, with whose books he is liberally provided. Dorothy and her little friend were to meet us on the beach, having started earlier for a horse-back ride, and Themis had promised to join our ranks, but as an aristocrat in her own phaeton. Having reached the beach we divided into the two prevailing classes, doers and critics. I was of the passive group. Soon Dorothy and Blanche came dashing past the pier and along the beach, then dismounted for a play in the sands and a talk with us. Themis soon appeared and gave me a seat in her phaeton for the half hour which she could stay, as she had an engagement to take an invalid friend to drive in the warm midday hours. From our comfortable uplifted seat we had a fine view of the beach and the bathers. Santa Barbara is chiefly recognised as a winter resort, so by most natural but imperfect logic, the public decides against its claims as a summer watering-place. I do not wish a crowd in the summer. The Esperanza is so delightful with only sufficient guests to form one social, familiar household: with such space of halls, such amplitude of porch, with unclaimed rocking chairs in the reading-room, and dim, shadowy corners for quiet talk in the cool drawing-room. But with a lofty disregard of self, for humanity's good, I must bear my testimony, that there is only one spot on earth more delightful than Santa Barbara in winter, and that is Santa Barbara in summer. But its irrecognition as a watering-place is evident from the quiet upon the beach. Only four or five outsiders, with the Esperanza group, about twenty-five in all, made up the bathing party; and about an equal number were sitting on the sands, some leaning against two old fishing boats—for the beach is guileless of the atrocity of a pavilion. The ladies, as they flitted across the sands to the rope were very picturesque in gay suits, and many with red turbans, belts and stockings. Then came the dash, the ejaculations, the submerging and the re-appearing of drenched mermen or dripping mermaids. The baby was given a dip, which she took first with a gasp of apprehension, and then a gurgle of delight. I think there is no such release from social activities and from all assumed disguises, as in a change of element. I always notice the greater naturalness and individuality of people during a long sea voyage. They escape their conventional selves and find their underlying natures. And a dash in the surf gives such joyousness of freedom, such exultation of spirit, that one could scarcely recognise under the riotous fun, the usual gentle-voiced, quiet-mannered Esperanza acquaintances. Those of wildest antics, were Saint Cecilia, with scarlet turban and kerchief, transformed into a handsome peasant, and her friends, the gentleman of courtly dignity, and the devoted wife. They plunged and dived, swam and floated and played pranks upon each other; looking most unlike themselves in their fantastic fun.

After a little gay chat about the bathers, and sympathetic laughter with their glee, Themis left to keep the engagement, and I looked for Dorothy on the sands. I found her and Blanche with flushed faces and eager eyes following the movement of the Crusader's pencil, as he wrote in his note-book. I was warned off imperiously as a trespasser upon private property; with the information that Crusader was writing charades, and that I must not interrupt. It was evidently thought that my presence would not be inspirational, so for a time I quietly watched the group. Blanche looked very charming. She has fair complexion with no colour: her paleness making more brilliant her merry, laughing eyes, and the face framed in warm, chestnut curls. There is an expression of daring and dash about the child, from the light in her eyes, the rebellious freedom in her tangled curls, to the springing little foot which she places in the stirrup as she leaps to Dick's back. Dick is both wild and obstinate, but Blanche saddles and bridles him herself. Sometimes he will not take the Spanish bit, but throws up his head suddenly, and lifts his little owner quite off her feet into the air: she holds on till he lowers her, when she makes another attempt to adjust the obnoxious bit; when again he lifts her high, as she clings to his head. But in the end he takes the bit, and Blanche triumphantly mounts him. She is as reckless a rider as Dorothy; and when the two race there is a look of spirit even to the wild floating of Dorothy's shoulder scarf, and the tossing of Blanche's brown curls. But Blanche has another side, as she is full of tender, housewifely ways, a helpful little daughter in the home. When I speak of this in reproachful tone, Dorothy replies defiantly, "The best housekeeper needs a house to keep. If we had a home, with a kitchen stove of our own, I should astonish the world by my practical power, and people would say, 'How like her mother!'" This daughterly satire silences me.

The Crusader is to me a baffling study, as he sits there in the sands, writing charades faster than the children can guess them; then convulsing them with laughter, when he reveals the secret hidden under the clever, rhythmic verses. For the most careless, impromptu line has his perfect sense of form, his touch of literary art. One would need longer study than the passing companionship of these summer days to know him truly; for he offers constant temptation to misinterpretation from his many-sidedness. As I watched him in the first days at the Esperanza, so chivalrous in manner to all women, but delighting most in graceful gallantries and charming compliments to the fair maiden sisterhood, I thought him only a fascinating man of the world, a social dilettante. But how reconcile that with his heroic war record, to which I was no stranger? I waited for light. He won the children by his sparkling wit, his inexhaustible fund of stories, and his real tenderness of heart towards them. They decorated him so lavishly with *boutonnières*, that he was obliged to make a rule to take their flowers in regular succession; not to break by neglect any embryonic woman heart, or elate with prospective triumph some belle of the future. While observing him as a social meteor flashing across our sky, I heard him a few times in discussion upon political measures, or questions of finance; and felt the power of a master-mind in his original thought, his daring acceptance of startling theories. For a month I only knew him by sight, by sympathetic observation or silent criticism. I thought him brilliant, but baffling, and a most unprofitable social study. At last, through a condescending literary comradeship established with Dorothy, I came to know him. I think it rather too much in the way of problems and pleasure, to have California and the Crusader to study the same season. He is, in irreconcilable moods and seeming miracle, not unlike the State: with its wealth of ripening harvests, its fruitfulness of southern trees, the almond and the olive, its luxuriance of tropical flora, its broad sweep of pastoral calm, its unrevealed riches still beneath its golden soil, its strength of solemn mountains, its space of sunny sea.

I smile sometimes at his graceful compliments and distrust his integrity and strength. Then in an hour I am electrified by his power of thought, his passion of utterance, when he assails a wrong however strongly entrenched behind law or custom, or defends a right though unrecognised by State or Constitution. Then I thrill with thought of the old cavalry charges, and forgive him his social flatteries. By birth, taste and the habits of life, he is an aristocrat; but when I dare to think him selfish or exclusive in some critical mood, he shames my narrowness of judgment by his fierce advocacy of the rights of the working classes, his sympathy with labour in its struggle against capital. He is a vehement anti-monopolist. When he talks of public questions I think he has missed his destiny in not giving his life to politics; but when I read his poems, I think literature has sustained a loss in missing him from its men of letters.

I cannot refute the popular accusation that he is a "squire of dames", for he has given much ardent friendship to women and won full measure from their responsive natures; but in my heart I believe him capable of stern loyalty and eternal faith. He has been much studied and criticised, as he is a man of brilliant power and magnetic presence.

I was never good at guessing riddles. This I do feel, that to have been less he would have attained more. His versatility has been his loss: for he has displayed his brilliancy in many fields, but exerted his full strength in none. Though a man of recognised power; judged by his possibilities he is a failure. With concentration of purpose he would have been a greater outward power; but a less complete and sympathetic man. Perhaps, by this many-sided contact with life, this unmeasured lavishness in the expenditure of self, this social unfolding and personal magnetism he may have touched the age as deeply, though less visibly than by continuity of effort, economy of force.

Speaking of him in loving tone, Dorothy once said, "His motto should be, 'I flutter in all ways, but fly in none.'"

But the Crusader's flutterings out-sweep the flight of others.

Soon the bathers joined us with fresh, glad faces and a resumption of ordinary manners with civilised garb. The Crusader's circle broadened to take us in; and we all exhausted ourselves in vain endeavours to read the hidden meanings of the children's charades, which when once revealed shone with such dazzling clearness. Then we enjoyed a paper of figs which Saint Cecilia produced in a mysterious, gracious manner, befitting the saintship. There is no earthly experience so perfect to me, but that figs would be an added element of enjoyment. Then we buried each other's hands and feet in the dry, warm sand, and talked with smooth streams of sand pouring through our fingers as if we were all animate hour glasses (which I suppose we are, measuring every hour with golden grains or desert sand).

CHAPTER XIX

LOST ON THE HILLS

DOROTHY and I had quite an adventure the other day, though not of the heroic kind, nor of deathly peril. We started about three for a horseback ride, having stated at lunch that we were going to Mission Cañon. To that cañon we went: but as we know its charms by many rides and are less familiar with the others, we decided to take a road which leads out of Mission Cañon to that most unjustly known as Rattlesnake Cañon. This gives, I think, the most magnificent mountain views of any of the valley roads. We threaded our way between its narrow walls; sometimes with stretch of road, which gives opportunity for a good lope, but often climbing steep bits or dropping into ravines. We halted often in the shadow, and stopped upon the high crests, to wonder at the unfamiliar grandeur of the mountains, taking new groupings with every turn of the road. We are accustomed to talk of the steadfastness of the mountains; but I have been much more struck by their change of base, and their migratory habits.

One summer we spent at that most home-like spot, the Mount Adams House, near Jefferson, facing the White Mountains. The view is superbly fine; and night after night we had sunset effects which I have never seen elsewhere, perhaps from the direction in which the mountains looked, or the way in which the sunset light struck and was reflected by their surface. I do not know; but they were translucent in the sunset, like masses of amethystine or rose quartz. In their stately, processional range, I knew those mountains; whether lighted with sunshine, or draped with cloud shadows. But in our drives my bewilderment was complete. In our trips, Mr. John, brother of our host, liked to drive me, apparently from pure politeness; but I suspect for the fun of reviewing me in my geography lessons. We would give two or three turns, I with my eyes fixed upon the mountains in mute appeal, lest they should take advantage of any diversion on my part to change their places. Then Mr. John would say with external suavity, " Tell me their names, now."

I failed every time. I was not to blame for the pranks of the Presidential peaks. They had left their solemn historic line, and crowded and pushed, looking over each other's shoulders like a group of surprised schoolboys.

All summer I studied their vagaries, and when in the leafless November days the Family Head arrived, unfailing in locality, unerring in topography; I invited him to the upper piazza, and said in triumph, "I can introduce you to the White Mountains by name, but never in our drives expect me to recognise them. Now they are in reception state and I pay them my loyal respects; but I shall not chase them, when they choose to play childish games of hide-and-seek." His moustache twitched in a way known to me, when his easy superiority needs no proving and meets with no refuting evidence.

Nature did not include a compass in the faculties with which she endowed me.

Dorothy and I wandered on, until the lingering shadows suggested our turning homeward. It was later than I thought, as I found by looking at my watch, so we took a good steady canter (though Dorothy rebukes me for using the word canter or gallop, as a confession of my eastern origin which should be ignored in full California naturalisation). Suddenly an inspiration seized me: I seemed to see that by following a steep trail which I discovered leading up the side hill, we could cross its crest and, I felt sure, drop down into Mission Cañon, thereby shortening our ride home. We took the trail which led up the hill, but it brought us face to face with unkind fate in the form of a rail fence. We left the path, to seek for gate or bars. We were on what seemed a grassy plateau, and we wandered on and on in search of an opening. At last, discouraged and chill, I thought that we would abandon the attempt, and follow the trail back to Rattlesnake Cañon. But the trail eluded us: we kept on and finally reached a slope which we followed, thinking from the summit we could discern house or road. We seemed to have wandered far from the Santa Barbara world of light and warmth. The air was penetrating in its chill, familiar flowers and weeds had disappeared; and on the bleak ridge was only a tall shrub with thick, grey leaves, growing among huge boulders, which made it difficult to find a way for our tired horses. It looked not like the home-like foot-hills; but like some stern spur of the mountain in its greyness and its gloom. Back and forward we rode among the boulders taking fantastic shape in the dimming light, among the grey, ghostly shrubs.

I talked gaily to keep up my own courage. Dorothy showed a brave heart, but looked pale and cold. We had no wraps. The hill seemed far, the night cold to be alone and unhoused. I considered whether the folds of my riding habit could keep Dorothy from deathly chill through the long night hours. I felt tremulous, yet nerved by that inner courage which dares not fail when a young life turns towards us in perfect faith and in full assurance of our strength. At last, I appealed to my own voice for help. Strange, that through years of weakness, it should have kept its range of power, from deep chest notes to vibratory treble. Its compass is beyond all need of good society. I have often wished under intensity of feeling, that I were an actress: that under the mask of assumed character, I might sweep the full octave of my own being, and utter forth in thunderous tone or shrillest note, the depths of unrest, the height of desire, forever unexpressed. I gave my voice its utmost power on that lonely height. Again and again I uttered loud, ringing call, which reverberated in the stillness. At last I thought that I heard a faint answering voice. I gave another hopeful outcry, and surely there came a far-off response. We followed its direction and soon came to the edge of the ridge, where we looked down upon a little adobe house far beneath us. There seemed, looking down, only a sheer, steep ledge. An old Mexican, two or three women and a boy were gathered in the little vegetable garden about the house, all with lifted heads, scanning the crest for sight of the wanderer. I called still, motioned, and waved my handkerchief as signal of distress.

Soon we saw the boy catch and mount barebacked a white horse, and disappear in the trees near the house. We waited long, it seemed, before he came in sight on the ridge. He knew no English; so I aired my feeble Spanish phrases, and followed him down a steep trail to the house. There, I begged the old Mexican to let the boy go with us to the Esperanza, though now in sight of a travelled road; as I explained that I had no money with me to pay for this great service. With bright smile and native grace, he disdained all thought of money, still yielded to our solicitations to have the boy act as our escort. We stopped at a neighbouring adobe, where our cavalier borrowed a saddle of massive Mexican make, which was soon adjusted and he mounted for the evening ride. Now it was quite dark by this time, and his white horse looked like a pale phantom as he kept the road just before us. For we were really tired and spiritless, with the reaction after intense excitement; so even the old plough horse made better time than our steeds on the weary, homeward way.

Just as it struck nine, we entered the hotel grounds. The house was gleaming with lights, and the hum of voices from office and reading-room sounded like welcome back to the human world. The boy showed glittering teeth in the darkness of his face at receiving a reward which looked large to him for a few miles ride to town, but small to us remembering the loneliness and chill of that ghostly crest.

We saw none of our own friends, but went to the dining-room, dark and locked. After much vigorous knocking it was opened and we asked for Ivan, our own waiter. Any sketch of the Esperanza would be incomplete without him. He is a Russian, was a soldier in the Crimean War; but has wandered so many years that he says he cannot speak Russian, though he understands it. He prides himself on his wide travel and his accomplishments as a linguist. He speaks in a thick muffled tone, which reduces one's mother tongue to an unknown language. He is lame from chronic rheumatism, but even so looks young for a Crimean veteran. He has sharp features and a prominent nose, which gives him a severe expression; but he is our favourite waiter. He has ideas on all subjects, which he never hesitates to give when topics which interest him are under discussion. He speaks to me generally in English; but if he is out of temper and has a grievance to disclose he is confidential in German; and if he is in a facetious mood he essays the graceful sprightliness of the French. He impresses me as taking an accurate measure of persons and things; and I am sure, but for the limitations of my own education, he would be poetic in Italian, chivalrous in Spanish, and insurrectionary in Polish. Ivan met our timid appeal for dinner with an unmoved countenance, listened to our narrative with the nonchalance which befits a man of the world in dealing with an afternoon adventure upon the hills of Santa Barbara, refused in plain English, growled in German, swore under his breath a few Russian oaths retained from Sebastopol, then relented in French and gave us a just dinner; not too varied and tempting, for that would lead to recklessness and late hours in the future; not too meagre, for that would lessen our absolute faith in him; but a dinner in which our own short-comings and his magnanimity were both apparent. Very grateful for the mercy vouchsafed us, and much refreshed, we climbed to our rooms. It seemed so strange to come back after such excitement and anxiety, such danger and deliverance, and find ourselves not even missed. How very atomic we felt ourselves in the Esperanza world.

Dorothy begged to sleep with me, and I was glad

to have her that night within the warmth of my clasping arms: for I had suffered more than she knew, to feel that during a night upon the hills, mother-love could not keep her warm, nor guard her from the possible perils of exposure. We made a fire upon the hearth: feeling so truly, blessedly at home, as the light brought out golden glints on the wall, and depth of colour in the rich curtains. About ten o'clock there came a tap at the door and Saint Cecilia flashed in for a moment. She had missed us at dinner, but thought we might have chanced to be later than usual: remembering, however, that we had started for a ride she was haunted by an apprehensive thought, so came to see if we were safely at home before going to her father's room for nightly vigil. How lovely her sympathetic face looked as she listened to our perils; with full comprehension of the weird loneliness of night upon the hills. How charming to have a saint in one's human circle, with such light in her eyes, such tenderness upon her lips. Dorothy slept well: but my dreams were chill and wan, with night shadows, grey shrubs, uncanny boulders and phantom horses.

I rather dread a confession to the Family Compass; I have borne so much smiling sarcasm on the subject of my erratic wanderings. He once complimented me by saying, "There could be no question of the culture of a lady who had been lost in every city of Europe." He should remember that I never went astray in London; I knew it by intuition, and it opened to me the hidden recesses of its mighty heart. In fact, I lose myself most in the modern right-angled cities where there is no individuality in the straight avenues, no peculiarity of obtuse or acute angles in the corners. I learn much sooner the quaint crookedness of Nuremberg, or the oriental picturesqueness of Prague. I hope you will not be so unkind as to think this a confession of my spiritual affinity for dark and devious ways.

After this we shall ride with wraps strapped on our saddles, sandwiches in our pockets, and compasses on our watch chains. I shall, I think, resign all hope of original discovery and exploration, and follow beaten tracks. But it is very trying to have an exploring spirit, with an uncertain head. If only the cardinal points had been more strongly marked in my organisation I might have been an honorary member of the Royal Geographical Society.

We had a very charming ride the other day to see Dorothy's little friend Blanche, who, with her family and friends, was in camp in Dinsmore Cañon.

It was my first glimpse of camping, which is so characteristic a feature of California life. We found them in a grove of live oaks, near a running stream. The tents in the shadow, the gay dresses of the children and the moving groups made a very picturesque scene. We only stayed for a little chat as we found that they were about to break camp and move to a cañon a few miles beyond. I know how imperfect my California experience is, unless I visit its quartz and placer mines, and have a summer's camping. But I have no longing for life in tents. I have a real respect for the camp life of pioneers, the explorers, surveyors, geologists, the vanguard of the army of progress; who upon unmapped mountain crests, on unmeasured deserts, or in vastness of primitive forests, build camp fires which are true beacon lights, and set tent poles as forerunners of the home roofs which shall follow. I have always longed for physical strength for a really rough experience; to share in the hardships of emigrant life, or adventures of explorers. But failing in that, I do not care for camp life as a summer play. I understand its charm to those of settled, conventional life; who escape the tyranny of city fashion or the thraldom of village pettiness, in this breath of the freedom of nature in forest solitude or upon mountain height. But in my own wandering life I wish rather to find rest, in sense of stability, in the semblance of permanency. I seek the hotels which most approximate home life in appointments, in big easy chairs, restful couches, and grace of drapery. I like, if only resting for a few days in a wayside inn, to create the illusion of a home; with my own books, a few sketches on the walls, and touches of colour in gay table scarfs and sofa rugs.

California is the paradise of campers; with its long, dry summer, its glorious climate and its diversity of scenery. Then in many of the wilder regions it offers great temptation to fishermen and sportsmen. The one question of moment in locating a camp is the water supply. So the cañons having running streams or being near the rivers are the favourite spots for these cities of tents. For some of the camps assume community proportions! Indeed, in this climate the shelter of a tent is scarcely needed; many travelling with only blankets for protection.

We met, early in the summer here, a Boston gentleman and his wife who have lived for the sake of his health an out-of-door life almost entirely, for six years. They possess a waggon with the most perfect camp equipage, of chest holding supplies, dishes of granite ware, and delicate cooking utensils. This chest in its economy of space, its ingenious folding and fitting of article within article suggested a conjuror's trick box, it was capable of such expansion and surprises. Under the seat were the rolled mattresses of wool, with linen and blankets in the form of bags. There was a place for fodder for the spirited black horses, and they carried light saddles, constructed after an idea of the inventive host of this house upon wheels. They always rest long enough at midday to build camp fire and cook a comfortable dinner from soup to pudding. The seat lifts out, and at night the box of the waggon becomes their sleeping room, as they do not like close contact with mother earth. Earlier they had a tent, which with light support fastened on to the end of the waggon, gave them an upstairs dining-room. But they have dispensed with the extra luxury and now dine on the ground floor. With only a valise for luggage, in addition to camp appointments, they are equipped, with the exception of a fine dog, that must not be forgotten, who runs under the waggon, or when tired or at the word of command leaps to the shaft, which is his special apartment.

This life has been entrancing to both in its constant change, and its opportunities to study fully the beauties of this marvellous state. But at last the longing for anchorage has come, and I grieve to say, owing to some defect in their organs of vision, or some inexplicable idiosyncrasy, they have chosen San Gabriel, not Santa Barbara as their mooring place. I am sure the wonderful waggon will expand into a home, original in plan and complete in appointments. That camp equipage should have a place in Arabian Nights, with its wonder working possibilities, its power of transmutations. Dorothy's ideal home was found when she saw that waggon, and I rejoiced that the peregrinating Pater was not here to be charmed, or I should have been a feeble, protesting minority, ruled by the ruthless, reckless majority; doomed to a life on wheels, camp fires for my only hearthstone, and wool mattresses for my lares and penates.

Several houses in Santa Barbara have tent rooms in the form of broad porches with canvas roof and curtains. The first originated with a young lady after a summer in camp in the Yo Semite, whose lungs refused to be reconciled to the atmosphere of rooms, walled and roofed, after that deep breathing of mountain air. Once I was hospitably offered this tent room. It commands a fine mountain view, so I drew back the curtains and watched the familiar

Santa Ynez range grow majestic and mystical in the light of the full moon. It was a rapturous experience, but not restful; as I could not for hours quiet myself in the glamour of that flooding light upon the glorified night world. Then I had a continuous serenade: for California chanticleers know that ordinary bursts of exultation at dawn could never express their superiority of fate in breaking shell in the Golden State, so they crow all night long. Then came that stir of the wakening world: first an inarticulate hum, then the myriad sounds of quickening life from bird notes to the milkman's call. I enjoyed the night as an exceptional experience, but was glad to leave the space and glory of so bewildering a bed-chamber, for my own bay-windowed room, with exclusive walls and darkening shades.

I like at night a positive protective wall between myself and the immensity of space. Moonlight, stars and mountains are too vastly suggestive for night companionship. We seem able only fully to know ourselves and control our own lives, by withdrawing them from the mastery of nature. The first step in civilisation is from the nomadic life with flocks and tents, to the rude hut with tilled fields. When sweeping breadth of plain, crossing mountain chains, and fording streams, men are held in a kind of communal life with nature; one of her forces, with winds and storms and tides, in changing the physical features of the earth by their torrent-like movements of hordes, or convulsive eruption of scattered races.

To assume his true mastery over nature man must withdraw from its breadth and fulness, to cope patiently and slowly within narrow limits with forces adverse to growth and culture. He must wrestle with the thorns, not sweep desert and wilderness for such gain as can be won from soil left to its curse and fate. In youth we are all Arabs, with eye for brave, broad sweep; feeling no need, in our exultant strength, of any rest beyond the white tent on the sands, under the shadow of the palms and open to the stars; and with thoughts eager to outrace the speed of Arab horse, with head alert and quivering nostril.

CHAPTER XX

"OUR SKETCH"

I HAVE had a new revelation of Santa Barbara. I knew it in its effulgent sunshine, in its infrequent rains and with its soft veiling of fog; but yesterday it had a mood of gloom. There was a stormy sky with high wild wind. In the east it would have portended rain. But here there was no massing of heavy clouds against the horizon, or moving in sombre ranks across the sky with shadow procession following over the darkened mountains. The sky was sullen grey; the mountains, solemn and unlighted by the passing of faintest sunlit smile, had withdrawn from my familiar caressing touch, and stood stern and estranged. They neither glowed with sunshine, nor purpled with shadow; but in the revelation of this new mood of gloom showed harsh, sharp outlines, and stony-hearted irresponsiveness. Even the low, familiar foot-hills showed neither golden lights nor warm brown shadows; but a cold, uniform bleakness of colour. The near fields, not transfigured by the idealising sunshine, looked only reaped and bare—fields past the summer's glory and the autumn's ingathering; and the live oaks and the eucalypti showed in the wind their silvery sides, and the peppers swayed like graceful green plumes. The ground was strewn with rose petals; and the garden had a sad, wind-swept look, as if with sudden apprehension of autumn breath and winter chill. All the morning I sat in my bay window, facing the mountains grown so strange in this shrouding of sudden gloom. I felt as one who watches the first look of alienation upon a face known only in the glamour of love's young dream. The mountains called mine; and known, I thought, in every caprice of sunshine, in every mystery of shadow stood cold and aloof. I felt strangely solemnised by nature's unfolding of her soul of gloom, as I watched the darkened day and listened to the wild music of the wind. I love a high wind in the day: I respond to its every note, from its long-drawn, sorrowful soughing through the pines, to its tragic shriek over the maddened sea. But a wind at night is weird, and makes me a frightened, tremulous child. I think always of hopeless ships with rent sails and shivered masts; of graves yet warm with the hot, human tears of love; of the sadder, cold, forgotten graves across which the wind alone makes moan; of desolated lives and deathly partings. I am swept in an hour by all life's tide of awfulness and loss. I suffer from the chill touch of ghostly memories, and from the darkening wings of strange forebodings. Once, when the wind wailed through the pines and Scotch firs of Cluny Hill, in Morayshire, I wakened my companion of tranquil mind and quiet sleep, who suffers from no hauntings of the past, no presentiments of the future. I moaned out my melancholy impression that there was sorrow, or the shadow of death at home; that I should never see the glad light in the dear young sisters' faces, or should miss forever my father's repressed but deep-hearted greeting. The sleepy, unsympathetic answer came, "Do stop thinking and go to sleep; you always bury all your family when the wind blows at night." I felt much aggrieved; but I think since then I have refrained from the old pastime of digging graves because the wind blows.

But wind in the day excites and elates me. It is like some grand bugle blast calling to heroic conflict. I feel the stirring within me of power which only waits the battle-call. I feel the warrior heat about my woman heart, the warrior strength in my woman arm.

I am sure the inspiration came to Joan of Arc; not when the pastures were tranced in sunlight, and the sheep browsing in pastoral calm; but when some mighty storm darkened the hills, and marshalled clouds swept in hurrying ranks across the sky's grey field.

While I watched the mountains Dorothy read aloud in her strange, vibratory tones. Jean Ingelow's "High Tide", Kingsley's "Three Fishers", and "Call the Cattle Home across the Sands of Dee"; Buchanan's "Ballad of Judas Iscariot", and Mrs. Browning's

"Rhyme of the Duchess May". Its last lines were our morning's benediction:—

"And I smiled to think God's greatness flowed around our incomplete-
[ness,—
Round our restlessness, His rest."

After luncheon, I stepped out on the porch to feel the breath of that strong salt air, and to watch for a moment the shaking of the trees, and the swaying of the vines in the strong wind. The Spectator proposed a party to the pier to watch the grandeur of the storm over the sea. There was a stir of excitement, an expression of approval; so I equipped myself in close walking hat and long redingote, to face the force of the wind, as I thought, with a goodly company. But one and another drew their shawls around them and retreated to the glow of the reading-room fire. Dorothy posed as martyr; for I felt that I dare not subject her sensitive lungs to this fierce wind. But her wistful eyes pleaded so strongly, that arrayed in long rough ulster, scarlet Tam O'Shanter pulled well down over her forehead, and a veil against which she protested with smothered indignation, and her Scotch zebra shawl for further protection on the pier, I allowed her to be of the party. The Crusader, Dorothy, and I went down ignominiously in the shelter of the car; while the Spectator, armed with portfolio and paint box, walked that he might call for an artist friend. When we reached the pier, Dorothy, and I were glad to cling to the Crusader's proffered arms; as we were like vessels facing a head wind under full sail, with our drapery so blown about us; but by dipping and tacking we reached the end of the pier, and Dorothy and I were somewhat sheltered in its solitary seat against the protecting walls of the steamboat office. Soon the Spectator and his friend appeared; somewhat short as to breath, but triumphant as to expression. We had a little general talk before the Spectator settled to his work. His friend has been to me a familiar figure for months in Santa Barbara; though I have only lately had the pleasure of studying him, except as he passed on horseback, or I stole a look at him upon the beach or on some side hill, where, under the shelter of his artist umbrella, he was busy at his easel. He rides a fine powerful horse (I have dropped into Dorothy's fashion of giving precedence to the horse). He is very tall and slender, with eyes of Scandinavian blue and fair pointed beard: from the style of his beard, and his broad-brimmed picturesque felt, Dorothy and I long ago christened him Van Dyck. We spent, not long since, a party of us, a pleasant morning in his studio. There were many interesting water-colour drawings, sketches made during his summer in camp in the Santa Ynez Mountains, and several strong portrait heads in crayon. But two pictures interested me deeply. One was a sketch of a graceful girl mounted on a powerful black horse. Her habit was tossing in the wind or with the motion of her fearless dash; her broad-brimmed, plumed hat blown back from the young, bright face. Under the horse's feet was the firm whiteness of Santa Barbara sands; beyond, broad sweep of the sea, and graceful lines of the hills as they curve round the bay, completed the characteristic, breezy sketch. Around the margin were the most exquisite little studies of California life; a view of the Mission, a glimpse of the hills, the bold outlines of Castle Rock, the head of a *vaquero* with bearded face and battered hat, a darkbrowed Mexican woman with pointed kerchief tied over the gipsy locks, the figure of a comfortable, hooded monk, and most irresistible—a patient little donkey with laden panniers, so realistic in its charms that Dorothy gave greeting in braying which would have won response from any well-bred donkey. There was so much of California in this picture: its sweep of sands, its space of sea, its rocky coast and sunny hills, its dash and freedom, its incarnation of American spirit in the bold, daring rider. The other was a study in oil of a young Mexican head; I think, of a sheep herder. It was so warm, so brown, with such depths in the southern eyes and such picturesqueness of costume in the faded flannel shirt, and customary bright handkerchief knotted about the bronzed neck. It suggested a Murillo.

I know the artist too slightly for social judgment; but his clear, far-seeing artist eyes, his musical voice, and his apparent unconsciousness of self, make up a pleasant personality. The Crusader fell into conversation with him on subjects of art, and Dorothy listened entranced. I saw that the Spectator had seated himself on the pier with his back against the wall, and had taken out paper and opened his paint box. It occurred to me, that I had never seen a sketch really made from its first line, out of doors: so I spread down a shawl beside him and proffered all my powers of inspiration and sympathy, if he would allow me to have part in the sketch— that subtle, spiritual part with which women must content themselves in most forms of intellectual creation and earthly ownership. The Spectator said that he liked to be talked to when he was sketching but never troubled himself to answer: so I dropped into place beside him and watched the quick, firm strokes with which he outlined the end of the pier, and the group of brown, water-soaked posts; then a faint line suggested the distant islands. But the mood of the day had relented. The sea was cool grey with green light breaking through the lifted waves, with broken white caps flecking its surface, and long line of foam as it touched the shore. There was no wild unrest of waters; no shrouding darkness of the heavens. The dark, purpling grey of the sky had paled into almost a luminous pearl tint; and the Islands lay like faint, white clouds on the horizon. The scene was no more the sternness of suppressed storm, the grandeur of controlled gloom; but the breathless, solemn hush which follows intensity of feeling, mood of uplifting. I watched with keen, ecstatic delight, akin to the joy of the creative power itself, the grey waters sweep under his hand, with the green light prisoned in breaking wave. Then a little fishing boat with spread sails, came skimming into the picture, and, with a few touches, a flock of sea gulls poised on lifted wing. The islands revealed themselves as pale phantoms across the cold, grey sea; and the sweeping curves of the beach, and the lines of the hills as they dipped to the sea, completed the sketch. In two hours the scene was there, a visible memory; the mood of the hour caught in tone of sea, in tint of sky; and the weathered brown pier as familiar foreground.

I talked rather exultingly of *our sketch*, and had quite a god-mother's pride in its true, clear effects. Then we rallied forces, gathered our wraps and started homeward: I with the delightful sense of having had a new experience in the birth and completed growth of the picture; though the Spectator said it needed finishing touches, which it should have the next morning in the studio. But I thought it the perfect expression of that hour; and begged him to leave its truthfulness unmodified by later revising touch.

But this morning I suffered some humiliation though feeling much pleasure, when coming up from lunch I found a thin large package slipped under my door. Opening it, there was the sketch in its cool grey and green of sea, its brooding mystery of sky, its dreamy Islands, and faint, shadowy hills sweeping to the beach. With it was a characteristic deed of gift—a card with the words:—" Our Sketch, from one of our to the other of our, with kind regards." I felt my face flush at the thought that in jest I had laid claim to part ownership of the sketch: but its own beauty and the humorous words which made it mine, won my own forgiveness for my own audacity, and I found only my friend's fine touch as artist, and still finer touch as friend, in the gift and its quaint words of bestowal.

In all my years of wandering I have never before lost my habit of seclusion, and freed myself so far from the thraldom of my own reserve as to become part of the general society life of a hotel. I have always felt that I should breathe an atmosphere less pleasant to me than the silence and shadow of my own invalid room. But here I have enjoyed to the utmost the gay, changing life. Its gaiety, in truth, I only enjoy in a disinterested, spectacular way; but the companionship of the inner circle given to chat upon the porch, longer talks in the dim drawing-room, or broken argument in the quiet pauses of a horseback ride, have been to me both rest and inspiration.

It is singular how unlike, the touch of different friends upon the life. With one there is a power of harmony: and in such presence the tangled threads seem deftly straightened, the pattern shines out in the half woven web, and one is content to wait the unfolding of the fabric of fate, sure of bright lights and tender shadows in its folds. With another there is an electric power, from which the faculties, dull and unlighted a moment before, the life with white ash settling upon its embers, kindle and glow in full-hearted radiance. Still another has the gift of exquisite sympathy, which tempts to fullest unfolding of the nature; revealing depths of emotion and hidden roots of feeling unknown to ourselves until that warmth of touch gave sudden quickening into full flower. I think the miracles of achievement in life are wrought less from one's own consciousness of power, than from the high ideal faith of friend or lover; which is spiritual shield in the conflict, cool laurel leaves in the heat of the race, and lifted wings in the hour of possible failure. Because of such faith one dare not fail: because of such love one cannot fail.

Still other friends have a charm of calm, which lulls life to sleep, and gives the grace of blissful dreams. Blessed in the long weariness, the merciless strain of life, the natures with gift of rest; in whose presence there are always cool shadows, hushed voices and a sense of twilight peace. I think socially people should be divided into opiates, irritants, and stimulants; or perhaps better into the mesmeric, electric, and magnetic.

Here comes my magnet, Dorothy. She has achieved dinner dress—happy child!—by a long, soft white lawn pinafore with a crimson sash. But my favourite trailing black gown meets with disapproval:—" Mamma, why are you all in black—you must be in a mood, and I shall feel chills creeping over me. Let me warm you, I shall put on your great amber beads...."

Was it their electricity, or the daughter touch,

which gave me a feeling of sudden warmth about the heart? After dinner Dorothy told me stories of the amber fairies; yellow-robed, sunny-haired fairies by the Baltic Sea; and all their pranks of bewitchment which stupid, scientific men profess to understand and explain by the laws of electricity. The talk of amber and the sea led naturally to *Undine*, and Dorothy read in German the glad chapter where the fair maiden, through love, first found the true human heart; and the sad chapter where through love's disloyalty she lost the warm, human life, to clasp the false, unworthy knight in her mermaid arms, by the flowing of pure, constant stream about the grave of his faithlessness.

Dorothy said with a sigh, "What a mistake to get a human heart only to suffer with: and yet how much dearer the broken-hearted, human *Undine* is, than the water-nixie with all her wild ways. Why are sad things always sweetest, and why should *Undine* be lovelier than Cinderella who married the Prince, or Sleeping Beauty, wakened by the touch of her lover's kiss?"

CHAPTER XXI

MY "CARCASSONNE"

I OFTEN, in this valley of fulfilled hopes, recall the pathos of the poem which sings of the peasant's defeated hope, as he dies on the hillward road leading to Carcassonne.

Towards the roofs and spires of that city, gilded by sunlight or mystic in shadow, he had longed through all the weary years of his working life; to fall by the wayside with the vision still luring like a fair mirage.

Though denied to dying eyes, still Carcassonne had been a power in his life. Perhaps the uplifted city of his dreams had been in truth more to him than the fields he tilled or the harvests he ingathered. The uplooking towards its glory, the thoughts won by that far height from the valley's narrowness and the familiar soil, had been his city of refuge, his ideal world.

If I were to write an autobiography as life confession, or seek to reveal the secrets of another's nature, I think that I should study the character more by its losses than its gains; tell the story of what it missed and where it failed, rather than number its visible achievements. For the outward acts, the material possessions, the recognised relationships of a human life are clearly written in its history, legible in common sunlight. But its inner dreams, its disillusions, its undimmed ideals, are the invisible, subtle influence which give the spiritual atmosphere of grey doubt or radiant faith:—

> "In the pleasant orchard closes
> 'God bless all our gains,' say we,
> But 'May God bless all our losses,'
> Better suiteth our degree."

The real germ from which the growth of life upsprings into gracious fruitage or ungenerous barrenness, is oftenest a hidden root of pain or loss; an ambition or passion buried as deep as the well-spring of tears.

This prelude means that our valley has not given itself unreservedly to my love: that in a human way it hides its secrets and so enhances its charms. The full revelation of a nature, a place, a truth, is materialisation. Spiritual grace comes always from suggestions beyond our ken; like the enfolding of shadows which veil a far, faint hill, until "in a light not of sun or star", it lifts in some transcendent hour, a Mount of Transfiguration. So Santa Barbara does not wrong me by its reserve; by my renunciation. It gives me dreams as well as memories; broadens its valley fairness into the unknown, the unexplored, the illimitable world of fancy. Day after day it unfolds its loveliness; in cañon exploration, in foot-hill climbs, in inland rides through fruitful fields. We have scaled the rocky road to the Hot Springs: giving in its high, narrow cañon a wonderful glimpse of mountain, valley and sea, with Point Outlook on the crest sweeping the golden world and blue Pacific in a glory of space and light. We have ridden through the fragrant bean fields and fruit orchards of Carpinteria, have dashed past the generous ranches and whitening fields of pampas plumes of Goleta, and abandoning saddle horses for a four-in-hand have wound through the narrow defiles, then swept out upon the high roads of Casitas Pass with new groupings of the mountains and a fair chain of valleys until we reach the wooded, hill-girt Ojai. But Hope Ranch eludes me. My failure to reach it after many plans and horse-back parties organised for the special ride has led one friend to christen it my " Hopeless Ranch ". But I think it is more truly Hope Ranch to me than to those who have threaded its ravines, climbed its hills, loitered under its tree shadows, then dashed homeward by the beach in the evening light. I imagine the breadth and beauty of this ranch only by passing it on the San Francisco road, with its border line of low, undulating hills crowned by magnificent live oaks. But I know only by narration, by anticipation, by envy (shall I confess it?) of the happier equestrians who return gay and exultant from the ride through its loveliness, the charms of this elusive spot. I am sorry to miss it: more sorry to miss the companionship which in sunlit hours, or sudden grey of gloaming, is part of the memory of its fairness to those friends who crossed its hills, then swept through the ravine which opens to the sands with space of sea aflame in sunset light, and the Islands like some ideal shore to tempt longings beyond the horizon line of our own world. I refuse to be tempted except in longings. For California, which refutes many preconceived opinions, contradicts many accepted facts, is conservative in this inexorable condition its islands also are surrounded by water.

The Fairy Prince, who is an enthusiastic fisherman and ardent sailor, often tempts victims to take this island trip in Captain Larco's little craft. Then groups return looking like "old salts" in blue yachting shirts, with bronzed faces and bearing strings of glistening, finny trophies, and marvellous stories of the unknown world. We hear of the bold hill ranges of Santa Cruz and Santa Rosa, where thousands of sheep find pasturage on the picturesque slopes: of the rugged coast line fringed with kelp, holding wealth of fish, treasures of iridescent abalones, and seal rookeries. But our thoughts voyage most wistfully to Anacapa, in seeming only a bare, grey rock—but in truth a wonder world of dim fantastic caves.

In the prose epics of the returned adventurers from the shores of the larger islands, we listen to descriptions of tropical ferns, of rare shells, of curious fossils and of Indian remains.

But no botany, geology, conchology, archæology, ethnology, and all allied scientific powers could win us to dare our fate on the unstirred, smiling Pacific. So the Mediterranean smiled to lure us, one summer day, long years ago, to that fair, fateful island of destiny and exile, Elba.

But the smile was treacherous, and the "true inwardness" of the southern sea was bitterness and unrest. So we distrust the fair seeming of the Pacific smile. I listen undisturbed to the stories of the aquatic richness, the scientific treasures, and the possible acreage of pasture land in these Islands; and know that they uplift from the Pacific, not for sheep ranches, for fisheries or scientific exploration, but to give a fair distance for our dreams, to faint into vaporous white in midday light, then glow with spiritual effulgence in the sunset flame like celestial hills across the deathly sea.

CHAPTER XXII

THE WINGED HOUR

I HAVE had one charming ride this week, thanks to Dorothy's indulgence and generosity. She came running up one morning and called out in wildest glee, "The Crusader has asked me to take a long beach ride. It will be a good afternoon for it, as the tide is just right, so we can go and come back on the sands. He has ordered Bolton, and we are going to have a cavalry dash. You need not put on that aggrieved air, Mamma. Your daughter, you know, never forgets or neglects you; so we shall allow you to go, but only on condition of good behaviour."

"And what is good behaviour in this case, Dorothy?"

"To be modest and retiring," was the explanatory answer, "to remember that it is my ride with the Crusader, and that you are only third party, not to interfere with our racing, and not to look at your watch in that suggestive manner when the sun is still quite high: you often give me cold by taking out your watch in that thoughtless way; it strikes me with a sudden chill, for I think at once that it is growing late. I wish my own watch was a little steadier in its habits."

For Dorothy is the possessor of a watch as queer and uncertain as herself. She was so often late at lunch, and sometimes in the afternoon rides stayed until the short, chill twilight fell; and she met my rebukes by saying that if I had no compass in my head, neither had she a watch. I thought that I would wait for Santa Claus' coming, or for the impending twelfth birthday to give the coveted treasure. But remembering Dorothy's fondness for "an unbirthday present", and feeling that I should be relieved of much tiresome waiting and anxious watching by supplying this lack of a time-piece in her head, I appealed, not to the fairy godmother—who should appear on such occasions—but to a grey-bearded conjuror, who works many wonders in Dorothy's behalf.

So, in an obscure corner of a box lately received from New York, there lurked a small leather case, which when opened revealed an exquisite little silver chatelaine watch. It was the latest style, stem winder, with partly enclosed dial; and on the chatelaine in bold relief were two armed figures with helmets and shields, recognised by Dorothy as undoubtedly Achilles and Hector. Well, the watch has sustained perils and faced adventures, unequalled, I am sure, in the siege of Troy. The result is, that after three months' service it is a scarred, maimed veteran on the retired list. So Dorothy again rides without any visible, ticking conscience in the shape of an inexorable watch.

I consented to the conditions of obscurity and abasement in the invitation for the afternoon. For I am timid about taking Dorothy myself long rides on the beach, for fear of being caught by the incoming tide beneath some of the bold pathless cliffs. Then I have had experience as "third party", and should fill to perfection that subordinate rôle—for Sundays at home (not the home which consists of taxable brown stone, or substantial suburban villa, but the home of being all together)—Dorothy always claims as her own special victim for the day, the Emancipated Expert; and keeps him in thraldom to her whims, which makes Monday's return to the office quite a mild and restful fate. They take long walks, spend afternoons in the park, go to the seaside and enjoy Sunday in the liberalised spirit of the advanced age. Occasionally, I am formally invited, after a whispered consultation between the two, to go with them. I seldom accept: for any protest of mine against stopping to give buns to the bears, or cake to the swans upon the lake, or against lingering with sense of loving relationship in the monkey house, or, if the beach is chosen, a feeble, old-fashioned objection to being seen *on Sunday* with pail, shovel, and obtrusive lunch basket, is met by the reproachful remark from Dorothy, "Whenever we ask third party, she spoils the day with her unreasonable whims. The idea of wearing gloves to the beach, or of refusing to lend her parasol to stick into the cages with buns and cakes! It has just a good point on purpose!"

I generally watch them start with a reasonable reconciliation to my lonely lot. But I have taken part in their outings often enough to know the shadowy subservience which befits the role of "third party".

I must say if Dorothy is careless in other respects, that she is continuous and indefatigable in her efforts for my mental improvement and moral discipline.

If I am not a sweet-spirited, mild-mannered mater, it is not from any failure on her part to teach me the most approved creed and catechism as to the becoming Christian graces of humility and unselfishness in a mother's character. She does not limit herself to creed and catechism, but makes me the subject of stories with painfully pointed morals; and has even been so dominated by her own system of filial ethics, as to transform a fairy tale into a scientific chart of the rocks and reefs which might dash mothers to fatal wreck of their future peace of mind, but for the skilful seamanship, the unfailing steadiness of the daughter's hand upon the helm. I enjoy Dorothy's stories, and often lead her by my intent listening, to their full elucidation: but I have a way still of sometimes daring fate, by standing at the wheel myself.

At luncheon I received from the Crusader a formal invitation given with his stateliest grace, his most martial bearing, to accompany Dorothy and himself on the afternoon ride. I smilingly accepted, but felt through all the fun a chill, faint foreboding of a possible far-off future, as mother-in-law. Could it ever be—will it ever be—that Dorothy will really make me third party in her life's fulness and joy? In anticipation of the loneliness and awfulness of such a fate, I resolve inwardly to learn to knit silk stockings, play solitaire and otherwise prepare for my depressing destiny.

I suggested to Dorothy that it would be a compliment to the Crusader, if she should order a side-saddle from the stable, and ride as a lady in response to his invitation: I also thought, in giving this delicate hint, that Dorothy mounted in that unfamiliar way, would be less reckless in challenging her escort to races. But Dorothy quickly responded, "Yes, it would be a charming compliment, as he would win in every run. But I have been carefully educated, you know, Mamma, never voluntarily to pay any man the compliment of being second myself, if by any daring dash I can be first. I am really unselfish in wishing to be first: it is so much better for men to be second, they are not so tempted by pride and conceit and all those evil spirits. I have great hopes for men, Mamma. I think a few centuries of being second would make them quite lovable: I see a missionary field opening for me. I should like no convert better than the Crusader. Wouldn't you like to see him really tame and tractable? Talk of tame lions! I think nothing would equal the charm of seeing him quite mild and tethered. I would feed him with the fattest, plummiest buns, and I am sure you would lend me your parasol to stick through the cage. I think that I should never trust him to eat out of my hand."

At three o'clock Bolton, Brownie and Pacer were waiting us, and we mounted in a glad-hearted way, for Dorothy's gaiety was infectious. We started slowly, always insisted upon, as good cavalry form, by the Crusader. So we walked down State Street, stopping for me to get a new whip by way of helpful influence in the coming race; for Pacer is easy gaited and delightful to ride, but not with spirit stirred by youthful zeal. The day was sunny and glad and the village street had quite a stir of life. We met Themis in her phaeton, and stopped to upbraid her for not being mounted on "Royal" instead, to complete our party. She alluded, with a gay laugh, to the greater appropriateness of a phaeton for grey hairs; but was assured by the Crusader, that the fastest saddle horse in town would be in harmony with her eyes (which have the glad defiance of youth).

Later we were passed on our walk by the Spectator and Van Dyck, who only greeted us as they dashed past. Just at the pier we were tempted to another pause, for there we met Artista in her village cart and Perdita with her. They look well together, both dark, Artista with a statuesque regularity of feature, and Perdita with nose slightly retroussé, flashing brightness of face, laughing eyes and lips quivering with repartee. Only the eyes in her quiet moods, give revelation of her deeper, stronger self: those eyes which under their surface light have that strange, shadowy wistfulness. Artista was in severely plain, tailor-cut dress of golden brown with high plumed hat to match, driving gauntlets of the same warm colour; and held reins and whip with easy mastery. Perdita was in black, with cardinal shawl as light wrap about her shoulders, and warm light of a cardinal parasol touched her face with a faint flush. They made a pretty picture upon the broad sands, now dark and wet from the outgoing tide, and beyond the slumberous sea with its sunlit dreams. The Crusader said (will he never attain to the moral strength of passing a woman without a compliment? Here were two, both young and pretty, so of course the temptation was irresistible), "I am sure that you two never appear at the table, or drive together, without some preconceived plan of costume; otherwise there could not be always such charm of harmony, or such flash of contrast."

"How much more poetic," quietly retorted Perdita, "to believe that we could not be discordant; that by some grace in ourselves we must be a charming colour chord. Now you only compliment our modistes and milliners and Artista's tailor. I am not bold enough yet to patronise a tailor, and perhaps I know that I have not the stateliness of form which would justify those severe lines."

"You mean," said Artista (for they are given to a mild warfare of words), "that you lack the dignity and reserve which suits the plain style of dress. You would never forego fluttering ribbons, softness of lace, and a touch of coquetry generally."

"Perhaps," replied Perdita, "my coquetry may be of the guileless kind: but the dangerous coquetry is the sheathed, subtle spirit, veiled and hidden. Is it not so?" appealing to the Crusader.

"The danger is," answered the Crusader, "when a man encounters both types in full sunlight, on the Santa Barbara sands. The only true courage is in flight."

"I am so glad to hear you talk of flight," exclaimed Dorothy, "for so far it has been every lady's ride except mine. You are not to pay another compliment, or give another smile this afternoon. You are to be funny all the time, except when we are racing."

"Dorothy, you are a most unreasonable little autocrat," answered the Crusader, "you demand rain in the dry season, when you ask a man to be funny who has spent over fifty years of his life in being serious. If I could indulge in pride at all, it would be in my uniform solemnity of aspect: I am a living rebuke to frivolous children and fast young horsewomen. Now I have a sermon for you. Why didn't you ride like a lady on a side-saddle, with an appealing little air of helplessness which would touch a man's chivalry, not ride beside him with that air of easy assurance? Have you no reverence in your nature, that you respect neither my seriousness of spirit, nor my superiority of sex?"

"You know that I hate to wear those glasses of mine," retorted Dorothy, "but I must put them on or borrow Papa's big magnifying glass, to see your seriousness and that superiority of sex. I do not blame men, though, when riding in their own fashion, for feeling superior to ladies mounted on side-saddles. But I shall not ride in that unsafe, one-sided way, just to have you patronise me by helping me to mount and dismount, with my feet all entangled in a long habit. Helplessness may be very appealing; but I like to dash about, jump down and open the gates, and take a leap into the saddle again. I like a good run and a fair race better than compliments and symphonies and the kind of nonsense you keep for those proper young ladies."

"Well, Dorothy," said the Crusader, "you will never be a proper young lady. I have a vigorous imagination, accustomed to daring flights; but I cannot picture you a listless, languid young lady in ball-room train, with corsage bouquet and fan, accomplished in the language of flirtation. Neither can I fancy you walking down Fifth Avenue, with an irreproachable Easter bonnet, and an ivory Prayer Book, on your way to a ritualistic church. I tremble for your future, when I look at this dashing Highland suit, that defiant freckled nose, and those ungloved, tanned hands. You will be harder to train into civilised ways, than to make a proper park trotter out of that daring, dancing little devil of a mustang which you ride."

"Is swearing at Brownie the way to civilise me?" asked Dorothy. "She is a perfect little lady with the tiniest hoofs and the daintiest ways: she takes her steps as if she had been at dancing school, but you criticise her because she is not ladylike enough to be slow and stupid. I know that she can beat Bolton."

Without another word they were skimming over the sands, in the most dizzying way. For a time, with touch of the whip and swinging it in full sight, I kept abreast of them; but the dash was too much for Pacer's middle-aged moderation and I dropped behind, but in breathless, eager sympathy with the race. I did not wish Dorothy to be reckless. I am always cautioning her against it; but I did not wish her to lose the race. Far on they sped, then drew rein suddenly and turned their horses' heads, walking back to meet me. Dorothy had won, though only by a horse's length as they came to a rocky bit, which ended the race. Dorothy was quietly exultant, for she never doubted Brownie's spirit and speed. The Crusader assumed an air of hopeless chagrin, as he said, "Get Dorothy another horse. That little imp of hers will bewitch the child. She calls it Brownie rightfully, for I really think that it is one of those unearthly, uncanny Scotch sprites. If she rides that streak of lightning now, as an old woman she will ride the traditional broomstick through the air. With a high hat and a hooded cloak, you will look very well, riding astride, Dorothy."

"You will not be there to see how well I look," answered Dorothy, "unless you happen to be visiting the Man in the Moon. I think you do go there sometimes, to get new ideas for your moonlight songs and sonnets for proper young ladies. I heard you reciting some of them to Artista the other evening; and I knew that you had been spurring in your old cavalry way that Pegasus you are so fond of riding, and had taken a high leap."

"Now, Dorothy, you are not satisfied with being a witch on a broomstick, you are jealous of the Man in the Moon, for fear he may swing in his orbit beyond your broom. Will you race with him?"

"Oh, no," said Dorothy with an air of indifference, "I should not be contented with a slow old moon who just goes at one pace round the earth. My broom will chase the comets and dash with the meteors. So even by visiting your chum, the Man in the Moon, you could never keep me in sight."

"Now," said Ultimata, "let us have a good, steady lope and leave this questionable society of witches and comets. How can I manage Dorothy if you will encourage her in such nonsense? You talk of ladyhood and repose, yet you fill her head with the most absurd vagaries. What is the use of my trying to make her domestic and practical, when you challenge her to such flights?"

"I would not try," calmly replied the Crusader. "It is only fighting against fate to have such ambitions for her. There is a missing link between the conventional, controlled type of womanhood and Dorothy."

"What link," asked Ultimata eagerly.

"The link of a calm, well-poised, unemotional mother," was the daring response. "With another mother, I could fancy Dorothy a good, quiet girl, in a dark blue riding habit, with a row of precise military little brass buttons up the front, with long gloves drawn with perfect correctness over the faultless, tight sleeves, and a stiff little hat with a modest brim. Such a prim, proper, prudent little puritan of a Dorothy! How I should admire her!"

"Another mother indeed!" cried Dorothy. "You are jealous yourself to talk so of my mother; you know very well that she is my kind. I like a mother who dashes and dares: who can tell fairy stories in the twilight, or who can look like a tragedy queen when she is angry. You should see her then, she doesn't need stupid cavalry oaths. She swears with her eyes."

"Dorothy!" Ultimata interrupted, quite shocked, "How dare you talk so! You know that I am always quiet and controlled. In fact I have been called the Sphinx from my expression of unstirred calm."

"I did not think that the Sphinx was the embodiment of perfect, unperturbed calm," remarked the Crusader, "but the symbol of hopeless unrest and baffling mystery: you are unfortunate in your illustration."

"What a funny riding party," laughed Dorothy, "the Man in the Moon, the witch on a broomstick, and the Sphinx. The group should be photographed on the beach."

Then we touched our horses and swept along the smooth, wide beach. There can be no greater joy than that swift, glad dash all abreast; with the sand flying beneath our horses' spinning hoofs, the salt breath in our faces, and the space of sea and sky about us. We swept past the road leading to Hope Ranch, past the high, steep cliffs which gradually lowered and dipped into a gentle slope as we reached Moore's Landing. I had refrained from giving Dorothy cold by taking out my watch; but the sun admonished us to keep to a steady, swinging lope on our homeward way. The exultant sunlight had hushed itself into the soft, gentle tints of the waning day, and a change came over our mood as we turned our horses' heads and faced the mountains warm with sunset glow. The sky was thrilling with the ineffable evening light, and the sea tremulous with its quick response to the changeful glory of that rapturous colour.

"Oh! look at that wing!" cried Dorothy; and we all stopped by sudden impulse to draw a deep, ecstatic breath, as we caught that clear outline of a great, lifted pinion sweeping across the sky.

Against the pale blue, just touched with pink light, the wing lay pure white with feathery edge touched with deep, glowing crimson. It was a solemn spiritual symbol. What could it mean to our unwinged, finite lives?

Dorothy repeated in low, tender tones a favourite verse from St. Nicholas:

> "There is a great white cloud like a wing
>   Across the heavens lying,
> It must be one of the Day's great wings,
>   For they say that the hours are flying."

"Why does a wing,—from tiny swallow against the blue, to celestial vision like this of the Day's great wing—stir such longing?" asked Ultimata. "Is it some faint, fluttering prophecy of our own future flight? I never see a bird cleave the air without that swift uplifting of spirit, as towards some finer element, some freer, broader sweep of space. Is it the result of the teaching of all mythologies and faiths of the higher winged hierarchies; or is it our own intuitive upreaching towards a larger life?"

"It is, I think," answered the Crusader, "both hereditary legacy of the spiritual conception of the ages, and individual consciousness of a life prisoned in finite conditions. The very teaching which has given us this winged symbol of angel and goddess was the early expression of the spirit's protest against the physical limitations of this life. So we inherit the symbolical creed of the ages, while we feel with individual longing the fulness and freedom typified in power of flight."

"I do not like Spiritualism," said Dorothy, "because

the spirits come without wings: they just float through space. That must be too calm. I should like to feel the beat of my wings against the air; I should like to poise and dip and mount, as I have watched the flocks of wild pigeons across the country, or the sea gulls over these sands."

"You see, Dorothy has unconsciously confessed to sharing my feeling," remarked Ultimata, "that all life is conscious of effort. She wishes the sense of resistance in the air, the triumph of cleaving her way. That parting and pressure of the element through which motion is made must be part of the thrill of flight. Why in Spiritualism does this blessed symbol fail?"

"I think, though I have never had the enquiry suggested before," answered the Crusader, "that the strongest lesson of Spiritualism, its underlying truth, is the full identity of this life with the future, its absolute oneness; and this is symbolised in the unchanged features, the familiar smile, the very garments worn and known on earth. To see a dear friend radiant with spiritual light and with lifted wings, would suggest changed conditions, strangeness of environment, perhaps wider space between that soul and ours. But to see the friend, or have through clairvoyant, the friend pictured to us in the dress on which the home firelight played, or the morning robe which trailed across the lawn and through the garden paths, thrills us with the old tender love, the loyalty of earth, of which the friend seems unchanged part. It seemed the teaching of all faith to lift earth heavenward, then wings typified our larger, fuller possibilities: but the new faith teaches the closeness of Heaven to earth, so spirits unwinged walk our human ways."

"Well," said Dorothy, "if I should die, Mamma, and come to see you, I shall come with wings; you shall hear them flap, and see how high I can fly, and then how gently, how softly, I can hover over your head, until I touch your hair lightly and shadow you with my wings. I should not be an earthly little girl, but a real true angel, but not all in white, that looks dead and cold: I should like iridescent colours on my wings, like the beautiful shining of the dove's throat."

"Don't talk so, Dorothy, you know that I love better to have the little human girl, who teases for stories and is so very unspiritual that I ache with her weight, when she will sit in my lap so long for the twilight talk in the firelight."

"Yes," said the Crusader, "and if you missed her here, you would care more for the folds of the old Highland dress, the floating of the scarf, and the Scotch cap on the short brown hair; than for the unfamiliar vision of her glorified winged spirit. The time was that the earth needed uplifting by spiritual symbolism: but it needs now the sense of harmony with the Hereafter, the feeling that our own here are our own there, that the human form and face—yes, even the lines of familiar earthly drapery have place in the spirit world, that death is not alienating but reconciling in its touch, that those passed away are not exiles in space but our recognisable, beloved friends. Still I confess to the same feeling about the symbolism of wings. I never think of fuller, freer life, without the imaginary ecstasy of flight; and I unconsciously classify people by their length of spirit wing and their power of future flight."

Slowly the wing faded from the heavens, growing pale and shadowy, then melted into the deepening red of the evening sky. I have never seen so glorious a sunset in Santa Barbara, where the evening tints are delicate and evanescent. The faint pink deepened into rose, the rose burned and glowed like a sea of flame; while beneath, the Pacific caught like a sympathetic soul the strange, intense glory and yearned in lambent, lustrous waves towards the warm, waiting shore. The mountains were tranced in tender, roseate light, which deepened in the distance into purple shadows. We rode on in silence, as if part of some solemn, hushed service. Then the red fainted into warm grey, etherealized near the horizon into that mystic aqua-marine, as if the sky caught its tint from the watching sea. The water was of the same delicate colour, with just a glow of red across its coolness as if it held in memory the sunset glow. Then slowly a dull grey crept over sea and sky. We touched up our horses to escape the falling shadows, and soon reached the pier, looking like a dark shaft across the waters.

"Dorothy," the Crusader said, "you must never forget this sunset ride, with the wing coming to lift all our thoughts. If there had been a pair of wings I think we should all have taken flight, and perhaps not found our way back to earth."

"Then I am glad there was only one wing," answered Dorothy, with an evident effort to throw off the solemn, brooding spirit of the hour. "It looks cold and dark up there, I shall be glad of the open fire when we get home."

"Let us have a run to warm us, Dorothy," Ultimata suggested, fearing the late hour for her. So we dashed up State Street to the clear, ringing music of our horses' hoofs on the adobe road. Soon we were dismounting at the porch; Dorothy down and Brownie free before the Crusader lifted me to the ground, feeling a little chill and stiff.

"If your fire is not lighted, come for a few minutes to the reading-room," begged the Crusader. "You are both cold." It was six, that inexorable hour, but we were both tired and tempted by that quiet room, the flaring logs on the hearth and the waiting chairs. How homelike and blessed the warmth and light. The room was deserted as the guests were at dinner, or dressing for that high festival; so we lingered in quiet, familiar chat, as if our spirits had not flamed with the sunset or lifted with the wing. Then we toiled wearily up to our home corner, where the lamp was lighted and the fire ready laid for the kindling match.

"Mamma," said Dorothy, "I shall put on my cardinal dress to feel bright and warm; and you must wear that olive green, with the red light shining through—the dress I call 'gloom and glory'. For this ride was 'gloom and glory', only the glory came first, and the gloom was so very grey and chill: I think the end should always be glory." In the child's solemn voice I heard the music of "Gloria in Excelsis".

CHAPTER XXIII

LORELEI

I HAVE, between mornings on the sands, beach rides, and porch studies, many interludes of solitude. So for a few days again I have had only the constant companionship of the mountains, and the inconstant companionship of Dorothy, who flashes in upon me, whip in hand, to narrate the latest equestrian exploit. Dorothy has a tender home side, and would brood over me lovingly hours at a time in these days of imprisonment; but her nature is too sympathetic to bear shadow without showing its chill in a pallid, plaintive look, which I cannot bear on her little face: so I banish her from the sunless north room and the shadowed mother life. But evenings she charms me with a sketch of the day's doings, or reads aloud with her finely modulated voice which vibrates to every chord of pathos or humour which she touches. She is never more bewitching to me, than when we sit together in lamplight with just a suggestion of fire on the hearth, and she yields her sensitive spirit to be played upon with master touch by the poets. Then her little brown face is transfigured; and I see the true sibyl light shine in her eyes, and irradiate the tremulous lips and the undimmed child brow. Mother eyes even do not find her beautiful in repose, with sunburned face, rebellious nose and freckles (though of the dainty infantile kind). But her face has that charm of quick responsiveness to every change of feeling: can twinkle with humour, flash with lyric light, lift with defiant daring, or dim into twilight tenderness.

Shadows on the mountains do not respond with more changefulness of outline, more variations of light to sky and clouds, than Dorothy's face to the sky and clouds of her spirit world. Long ago, in a charming valentine, her eyes were called "mountain pools", and I in mother talk had earlier named them my mountain brooks. They are like those brown New England streams, showing through clear, rippling waters the flashing colours of their pebbly bed. Through the hazel grey of her eyes there are touches of green light, golden glints, and still brown shadows. In losing many joys and missing many hopes, I comfort myself with being mother to those eyes, with their changeful light and their unchanging love. Perhaps it needs the mother heart or clairvoyant vision to see all this in the little, round, brown face, looking so childish above the simplicity of the favourite white pinafore. I am so fond of these fine lawn pinafores, hanging in long loose folds from the yoke, just touched at the throat with soft, caressing lace. I always think boy choristers and acolytes so charming in their surplices: and Dorothy, in cathedral shadows against golden background of organ pipes, could seem the one, or with swinging censer in solemn procession between dark-robed priests and stately cardinals, could personate the other.

Last night she dashed up from dinner with eager delight, and cried, "Oh Mamma! it is too charming; a real Lorelei has come! She is tall and slender, very fair, with waves of golden hair; and when she lifts her eyes it is like sunlight shining through water. She is truly Lorelei: she wears a sea-green dress, all shimmering, with white lace like curling foam. I know that she combs her hair with a golden comb, and she will sit on a rock in the sea and lure someone with her sweet, strange voice. I think the Crusader knows her, for he sat at her table to-night and they talked like old friends. I hope she will not bewitch him. He would forget human little girls if the siren should charm him with her songs."

Her picture of the new-comer gave me a feeling of eager interest in her personality and her possible influence on the general social life and our own closer circle. In the morning, I received a graceful little note from the Crusader, to say that he had been delighted among the new guests to be greeted by an old school friend of his daughter; one whom he had known in her fair girlhood, but whom he found touched with a more spiritual loveliness, from the light of her happy wifehood, and the shadow of her early widowhood. He felt almost the joy of welcoming his own daughter in meeting the dear friend, who recalled so vividly their merry maidenhood together. He longed to have us meet. I would be charmed with her; most of all with her voice and her power of interpretation of the subtlest music. Could I come down for dinner? He had told her of our friendship, and she waited wistfully my coming, as she was a stranger in the Santa Barbara world. From her he sent the flowers which greeted me with the note.

I studied the flowers, as if they gave some revelation of herself. No roses! Sprays of honeysuckle and jasmine twining in wild grace about a cluster of orange blossoms. Where could she find orange blossoms so late in the year? But then in Santa Barbara, with its heart of summer, orange blossoms and love dreams should unfold in every month. I sent a little note to promise my presence at dinner, and my hope in the evening to be charmed with his charmer. I have just returned from a talk in the firelight with Lorelei. She sat at dinner at another table, and the Crusader excused himself from us to sit beside her, as we had no place to give her. From my seat I could see the graceful lines of the light, swaying figure, the exquisitely formed head, the soft coil of golden hair worn low, the delicately moulded throat, soft contour of the cheek, and the small ear, in tint and line like a fair sea shell. She did not wear the

Lorelei dress to-night, but was in pure white, keeping suggestion of the sea in a quaint aqua-marine ornament at her neck; and earrings of the same stone; not the small single gem now so generally worn, but long pendants like a shower of rain drops, which quivered and gleamed with every movement of the head. After dinner, I waited their coming in my favourite chair before the drawing-room fire, for the evening was chilly and the flame on the hearth and the red light from the drawn shades gave expression to the large, lonely room.

Dorothy darted about in a kind of elfish excitement, apparently expecting Lorelei to loosen her golden hair and sing the siren song. Soon they entered: she looking most lovely in her sinuous grace beside the Crusader's martial breadth and strength. After the greeting she dropped into the "sleepy hollow" chair, and I could study her face. It was a delicate oval in form, with fine features and sensitive lips with subtle smile such as Luini loved to draw. Her hair fell low upon her brow in a kind of golden mist, from which the eyes looked up with a half veiled drooping charm. She is truly beautiful; but I felt at the first glance some fascination beyond lines of grace and fairness of colouring. We talked at first of Santa Barbara. The Crusader said, "Ultimata, my friend does not feel the charm of Santa Barbara. She misses the glamour which it has for you. You must waken her enthusiasm with your resistless love for its beauty."

"I think," said Lorelei, in a low musical voice, but with a listless languor of expression, "that it will never win me, it is not my ideal."

"What element fails in this perfect summer world?" asked Ultimata, with what seemed rude energy of tone after those soft, liquid accents. "It has cloudless sunshine, eternal roses, strength of mountains and light of the sea."

"It has too much," answered Lorelei, "its sunlight is merciless, its roses grow in crowds, the mountains in their nearness and their blankness stare with a persistent frankness, and the Pacific is too intensely blue. It lacks the varying, moody charm of the Atlantic as I know it, changing from unrest to calm. There is no mystery here. Santa Barbara greets you with a smile like one conscious of her charm. She does not wait to be won."

Ultimata flushed consciously as she answered, "It is true that Santa Barbara in her gracious sweetness meets even strangers and critics with full, frank smile; but only to a lover does she reveal her inner tenderness, her spirit beauty. These mountains can withdraw in shadow, and can be rapturous again in light. These roses may bloom in crowds, but every bud unfolds with its own thrill of joy, and sky and sea are not always unshadowed blue. Ask the Crusader if the sky and sea did not flame in glory then pale into ineffable light on our last ride. He even calls this ocean, 'The Pacific Mystery.'"

"Yes," said the Crusader, "under Santa Barbara's frank loveliness there are marvellous variations of light, and mystical gradations of shadow. I thought that I should know its beauty in a week, and hold it then a tranquil memory while I studied new scenes; but it holds me with a strange charm. In the evening I often plan to leave; but when it smiles in that sunlit way, I feel self-reproachful, like one who has won full-hearted love, and given only light, transitory friendship."

"That must be a familiar feeling to you," said Lorelei, with her suggestive smile and veiled glance, "for in the old days your life was strewn with wrecks. You held your friendships as lightly as the sea her white winged ships, gladly in sunlight or cruelly in storm; then passed on undisturbed by drift wood floating on the tide. Have Santa Barbara's sunshine and the southern sea taught you the virtue of constancy?"

"You shall see," replied the Crusader, "if you will but stay to learn loyalty also from its frank self-surrender."

"I do not need to learn loyalty of memory," answered Lorelei reproachfully. "Did I not leap to you with the old girlish gladness of greeting, when I entered the reading-room with that depressed sense of strangeness, only to be confronted with your fickle forgetfulness though disguised with chivalrous grace: yet it is only ten years since I was your guest, wearing your hot-house roses (and a great deal lovelier they were, than those flaunting garden sisters)."

"I plead guilty," said the Crusader, "not to forgetfulness, but to real constancy to my memory of your girlish self with face framed in fair, falling hair. Nothing in that memory could suggest these new phases of yourself with low brow and Greek coil."

"How can you fall from grace so hopelessly," asked Lorelei, "as to remind a lady that the years have changed her? You are demoralised indeed if you have lost the language of compliment, to speak in this ruthless, unrelenting way. This smiling, staring place has spoiled you. Do you generally speak the truth in this unbearable fashion?"

"Will you spare me two of your roses?" asked the Crusader, turning to Ultimata, who unclasped the long pin which held the big, glowing bunch. He chose one close-folded bud, one rose with unfolded petals but not fully open to disclose its centre, and handed the two to Lorelei, saying, " Santa Barbara sunshine tells the truth, when it makes the open rose fairer than the sheathed bud."

Lorelei took the rose and bud, as she quietly answered, " You were always a charming special pleader. You have won the case. I confess now, that it is flattering to be forgotten."

Ultimata interrupted the old reminiscences to remark, " You must study Santa Barbara before you close your heart against it: you must learn its real charm on horseback."

"I do not care for riding, unfortunately," replied Lorelei, " though I must of course take to the saddle again if I am to see this place; since I am told that it has few carriage roads, but many trails to the finest points of outlook. I like the long, smooth roads about Newport," she said, turning to the Crusader, "past those faultless gardens and restful lawns, with glimpses of the sea."

"I should think," said Dorothy, who had listened intently, "that you would like Venice better. Don't you think that gliding about in a gondola is like a dream?"

"Yes," answered Lorelei, lifting her eyes with their wistful charm to the child's face, "I do love Venice the best of all the Italian cities. Why did you think of Venice when we are so far away?"

Ultimata trembled lest Dorothy should make some startling revelation of her discovery of Lorelei's true individuality; for she knew Venice was suggested by her constant thought of the siren with golden hair, and her song across the sea. But Dorothy said very simply, "I think your white dress and those green stones made me think of Venice. I remember in the sunlight how white the city looked rising from the sea. Mamma calls Venice *Undine*," she added, with a questioning look into the siren's face.

"Why, I shall expect to live in a fairy story, when I am near you," said Lorelei, winning the child with that faint, rare smile.

"Oh! life is all fairyland to Dorothy," remarked Ultimata.

"Well, I love fairy stories," confessed Lorelei, "and those weird German fancies in songs and

LORELEI

poems. Dorothy and I will wander together in the wonder world."

"Will you ride to-morrow?" asked Ultimata, to divert the talk from the perils of that subject.

"No, I shall have a hammock swung on the upper piazza, which is quiet and restful," replied Lorelei, "with an awning to give shelter from what you call Santa Barbara's smile. It is a little intense and fervid for me. From there I shall have a charming, far-off glimpse of the sea over the trees, and just a sideward glance at those positive, persistent mountains. I shall swing, and sleep, and dream the first days—not literally sleep, do not think that I wish selfish, solitary dreams. Come and sit with me and bring Dorothy and her fairies."

Ultimata thought it time to withdraw the fascinated child from the spell of the siren, so said good night, while the Crusader tempted Lorelei to a moonlight walk on the porch. "You know that I hate walking," she said, "but having wounded you all by assailing the sunshine of Santa Barbara, I shall make peace by accepting its moonlight." She wrapped a vapourous white shawl about her, and looked herself like a moonlit cloud as she floated past us.

"Well, Dorothy," I said, when we were safe in the home corner, "who was bewitched to-night?"

"Oh Mamma! she is lovely, so fair, and so cool, and so dreamy! I shall swing in the hammock with her, and it will be like a boat on the sea, and she can tell stories of mermaids and naiads. You know that I mentioned *Undine* on purpose, because I thought that she might know her. But she is not like *Undine* before she won the human soul; for Lorelei is calm and still. But do you know that I think her soul is not quite awake, she has such a dreamy look and never lifts her eyes fully. I think that I should like to see her grow quite warm and human in this sunshine: but then I suppose she could not charm us with the siren's song. The charm must be that it is strange, and faint and far away. Were you afraid that I would tell her that we called her Lorelei when we talked of fairy stories?"

"Yes," I answered laughing, "I expected you to ask her if you might go to her dressing-case and bring down the golden comb; for you wanted to see her hair all down and hear her sing the song with which she lures her victims to her home in the sea."

"Mamma, you may trust me," said Dorothy gaily, "I know so much about fairies and mermaids, that I shall never startle them by my human ways. If Lorelei should draw from the sea a necklace of pearls, or an amber string, I should take it quite calmly. I have been always waiting for a fairy god-mother, and a siren is quite as charming."

CHAPTER XXIV

THE SIREN'S STORY

FOR several days Lorelei has swung in her hammock, under an artistic grey awning with pale pink lining. Of course Dorothy calls it a coral cave, and delights in its faint roseate light, as Lorelei amuses herself with the child's queer fancies, weaves for her strange sea stories, or sings to her low, rippling German songs. Perdita and Artista are charmed with her, as maidens are with the loveliness of one more fully unfolded but with the light of girlish fairness still touching the woman life. More fully unfolded, I have written of Lorelei, which is true in the grace and culture of her life: but in her dreamy misty nature she is like soft haze beside clear sunshine, when she lies with half closed eyes and soft swaying movement, while they sit beside her in their radiant, girlish gladness.

I am studying Lorelei, uncertain whether the tender brooding mystery comes from sunless depths in her nature, or is only poetic mist, giving tenderness of light and dimness of shadow to shallow waters. But I too feel her charm, and am not quite clear of vision and steady of nerve for psychological experiment. Saint Cecilia, with her simple directness and transparency of nature, is bewildered by the siren and meets her covert grace with wide open eyes, and a child's frankness of utterance. Her musical power holds the Spectator entranced when she plays "Songs without words", "Moonlight Sonata", or gives exquisite interpretation to some mystical Nocturne of Chopin. Her voice is low, with liquid softness of notes, and she sings with yearning tenderness old English ballads and German songs. Quite unconscious of the romance which Dorothy has woven about her, she one night sang the *Lorelei*. We were walking on the porch, and felt its wild, weird beauty as it floated out upon the darkness and met the sea breath of the night.

The Crusader's bearing towards Lorelei is a blending of his usual chivalrous gallantry with a tender watchfulness, as of one having right from old friendship to guard her, and a touch of pride in her beauty and bewitchment. This morning I had a foreboding of headache, and left the porch to seek a cool, shadowy spot in the drawing-room. I found the Crusader in the darkest corner, I think in a brown study; from which he roused himself with an alertness of movement like one caught napping and wishing to disprove the fact and dispel all illusions as to dreams. He moved a chair for me into the same corner. We soon spoke of Lorelei, or Lucille as he calls her. She seems the magnet towards which the social elements are being drawn; round which they are taking new forms. He told me a little of her history, which throws light upon her nature in its charming unfolding and its more charming infolding: for the sense of a power withheld, a beyond never reached, a dreamy distance of mysticism, is the spell by which she holds us.

Her father was a wealthy sea captain, owning his vessel and sailing chiefly to India. He was very unlike the conventional, bluff, florid sailor with strong voice, loud laugh and traditional sea yarns. He was of refined New England family, had been educated at Harvard, then spent three years at Heidelberg, and came home to inherit an independent fortune. But his passion for the sea prevailed over scholarly tastes and his love of leisure. He made several trips, studied navigation with enthusiasm, and eventually he bought a vessel of which he was for many years owner and captain. He was a tall, dark man of strange reserve; seeming almost imprisoned in his own individuality as if his nature lacked doors of approach and windows of outlook towards humanity. He was a lover of books, a collector of curios, and a fine musician. He lived in lonely state in the old family home in Salem; a quaint gabled house with windows in deep embrasures, and a broad hall opening upon grounds where an old-fashioned garden and orchard of gnarled apple trees seemed to touch and blend. From the porch was a glimpse of the sea, and from the upper windows a full look upon the picturesque harbour, in his early days alive with shipping and gay with foreign flags, but of late tranced and still, like phantom-haunted, deserted home. Here he lived in his brief intervals on shore, with his books, his eastern curiosities, and his organ, cared for by an antique housekeeper in harmony with the old time style of the home; and with a silent, respectful, dark-faced East Indian as personal servant. This man was his master's shadow, always near him in voiceless, noiseless service. He was an object of interest in Salem, the subject of romance and the victim of suspicion: for the traditions of witchcraft still lingered, to gather about this silent, dusky spectre, with his strange foreign dress.

When over fifty, the Captain startled Salem by bringing home a fair-haired, exquisitely beautiful, girlish wife. She was a strange, spiritual vision in the old house, sombre with its heavy, dark wainscoting, cumbersome mahogany furniture, and dim shadowy hangings—for rare tapestries was one of its owner's fancies, and the walls were heavily draped with the richness of oriental stuffs, soft and dark but with faint, lustrous light when the sun penetrated the gloom of the place. None knew the story of the wooing; but the bride was of Irish birth, and had been one season on the London stage, where her fair beauty and girlish grace won her recognition.

She lacked force and strength for many Shakespearian characters, but as Cordelia is still remembered, from her plaintive tenderness, her power of pathos, and the strange, steadfast spirit underlying the frail womanhood.

One year she brightened the old home, holding the silent lover-husband entranced in the glamour of her presence, then faded away leaving him with a baby girl. All this the Crusader knew from tradition only, as it was years later when the families met. The little child was cared for by the old housekeeper; who transferred her keys rather than the priceless baby, to that frivolous young creature, as she described the bright-faced woman of thirty who became her assistant. So Lorelei's strange childhood was passed in the gloomy old house, with the companionship of the stately dame, with solitary play in the wild, luxuriant garden, or sitting at the upper windows with face pressed against the pane, looking far out to sea and sailing in loving fancy with the dark, silent father whom she worshipped, though in a timid, appealing way. For he loved the child with a deeply hidden heart, which seldom beat outwardly in tenderness of kiss or caress. At seven her father took her on a trip to India, the old housekeeper bravely foregoing the comfort and spaciousness of the house to share the dainty little cabin, Lorelei's new home. Of the voyage her memory holds only broken visions, which give often strange foreign scenery and oriental colouring to her dreams. On her return she was sent to the convent at Georgetown; since a sister there had been in a convent of the Sacred Heart in Paris, her mother's teacher and friend. When home from the convent, spending her summer holidays in Salem, the Crusader's daughter had met her, while on a visit to that sleepiest, quaintest of sea-ports. Later she had made a long visit at the Crusader's summer home near Boston; a grand old place with grounds almost rivalling an English park, and low green banks sloping to the river.

He confessed, that in those days he was absorbed in politics and with a gay, changeful social life about him, and that he remembered Lorelei only as a fair, charming girl, whom he took rowing in the twilight, and whose songs had a strange, indefinable charm. Soon after her father died, and she came home to the stately, solitary old house which she soon left as a bride. She married a Washington lawyer of brilliant promise and with political ambition, and in her æsthetic home she became a social power. Zenobia (so I call the Crusader's daughter, from her dark imperial beauty), once visited Lucille in her home at the capital. On her return she said that the home was perfect, their life ideal, the relations of the newly-wedded most harmonious with charm of culture and social grace distinguishing both; but she felt a want—the lack of vital, human love. The husband's life was dominated by lofty ambition; and his pride in her loveliness seemed part of his own ruling passion for the finest, highest, rarest gifts which life can offer. She was symbol of his power, expression of his taste, incarnation of his ambition: but worn more as victor's wreath than as love's blossom above a throbbing, human heart.

Lucille wore her new life as becoming, exquisite drapery, finding artistic pleasure in the soft line of its folds, its changeful, glowing tints; but seemed unwarmed, untouched by any thrill of joy though always charming in her cool, shadowy grace. The married life came to a sharp, sudden end with the husband's death from brain fever, leaving only scintillating memories of his brilliant, broken career. Lucille went abroad for years, Zenobia ruled a new realm, and the girlish friends drifted apart. The Crusader confessed to finding Lucille a new study; and, as a study, fascinating.

Since coming to my room, I have woven in my fancy the strange, changeful web of Lorelei's past life. I have seen her with that mist of golden hair, those wistful, but unrevealing eyes under the apple trees in bloom, or among the sweet peas, larkspurs and carnations of the old garden: or brooding upon one of the broad window seats overlooking the harbour, with that far-off look, as she swept, in the day's waning light the awful space of that uncompanioned sea. Then I pictured her in her fair spiritual loveliness in the secluded, restful greenness of the convent garden, or moving among the dark-robed sisters like a vision of light. Next I saw her on the fair lawns, or low, green river banks, as Zenobia's guest; with her golden light of colouring and willowy grace of movement in charming contrast with the regal height of figure, the proud, dark beauty, the flashing defiant eyes of her imperial and imperious friend. Later I looked at her in the wifely home with its quiet hushed tone of exquisite refinement, its softened light and restful shadows, its rare culture, its intellectual companionship and lofty, cold pride. I saw her trailing through the spacious rooms with her undulating grace, or in dim, curtained corner holding a circle entranced with her charm.

Then still with cold, passionless face, in drapery of widow's weeds, I saw her under the shadows of Rome, in the light of Florence, gliding across the lagoons of Venice, in solitary, unstudied grace at Rolandseck of pathetic story, or bending to hear across the Rhine, the legendary song of that other *Lorelei*.

Now in the sweetness and light of Santa Barbara ungladdened by its smile, unwon by its southern sea, untouched by its mountain shadows, unloving to its full-hearted roses, she charms Dorothy with her fitful, fantastic stories; captivates Artista and Perdita with her rare beauty and mystical charm; lures the Spectator with wistful song, and I think is weaving more potent spell about the Crusader's strong, free life; and wears still that subtle smile, and looks from that golden mist with her visionary eyes. What will the end be? Will she change us all into soulless phantoms, or will she quicken into warm human life?

I thought our social world charming before, with its strong contrast of character, its freedom of companionship, its strength of friendship; but it was only real life without idealising touch of love, without glamour beyond the glad, warm sunlight: but

THE SIREN'S STORY

now it is romance—fair lady imprisoned in her own cold, passionless nature, daring knight who will free her, or perhaps wear captive chains himself. Which shall win: the Crusader's red cross, symbol of lighted faith, or the siren's song across the shining sea?

I shall be thought quite bewitched unless I give the colour and warmth of our familiar world. Themis keeps her life quite free from Lorelei's spell. She thinks her beautiful but unreal and fantastic; and declares that she dislikes veiled natures, however ethereal the sunlit haze or shadowy mist. She likes eyes which lift with full frankness, and lips which smile with unreserved gladness. I drew her the other day to Lorelei's hammock. I wished her to be won by the charm of that mystical nature, and that Lorelei should feel the steadying strength of her own unfaltering will. I led Themis captive by wheeling out a big easy chair and locating her near the charmer. Lorelei asked her to come under the awning, but Themis declined, as she likes strong, warm sunshine. I had with me a book, which I opened as apology for my withdrawal from the talk, that I might have in the conversation the contrast of that human warmth and moral steadfastness, with the sheathed power, the sunless depths of that unrevealed nature. The day was less bright than usual, the sun shone but with faint light, and dim, vaporous fog played about the mountains. Is Santa Barbara feeling the siren's spell and veiling her brightness in this entrancing way?

Lorelei remarked, "Santa Barbara is really charming to-day in this softened light and with the fog wrapping the mountains; for the first time since my coming it has the charm of ideality."

"I like better," answered Themis, "the sun's full shining, giving that fine, strong outline of the range against the sky—the individuality of every peak. I like strong light, defined lines and positive character in nature as I do in human lives."

"But," said Lorelei, "that sacrifices the charm of changefulness, the half lights, the dim shadows. To know positively, is always to accept hard, sharp limitations. Your Santa Barbara mountains are bold in line, but after all not very grand peaks in height, but with this veiling of mist just draping their summits, one can lift them to loftiest crests and can crown them with eternal snow. Yesterday they were positive facts, to-day they are infinite possibilities. I never like to see the boundaries or feel the edges."

"I can understand longing for the glory of mountains beyond the Santa Ynez range; for Alpine altitude and the snow line," answered Themis, "but I do not comprehend the charm of deluding oneself with false outlines and imaginary heights. That imagination is perilous, for it drapes fact with ideality which sacrifices truth."

"But I feel no sacredness in mere physical fact," protested Lorelei. "Why should not the Santa Ynez range lift to the most dizzy height and hold on its cold, far peaks eternal snow? It is only that

Nature was not in the mood, or failed in material, or was hurried in building these little mountains or rending these narrow cañons. To complete her work in imagination, is only to do reverence to her creative power and to express her higher thought."

"I feel on the contrary," replied Themis, "the utmost reverence for simple physical facts, for such facts are the foundation on which all scientific theories rest, the data from which all laws are discovered. The mist may give a charming poetic effect, if we call it mist; but it must not bewilder us so far that we mistake the transitoriness of fog for the mountain stability."

"Do you choose to know your friends in the same way?" asked Lorelei. "Do you not like in them the hazy effect of distance, and the charm of a far horizon?"

"I glory in the mind of a friend with a broad sweep," replied Themis, "but I wish it real and permanent, not the effect of light and shadow, or the illusion of a fog. For such atmospheric effects change; and there comes the sense of wrong and injustice in having given boundaries broader than nature. In that mistiness of impression there comes the idealising of love, and with the clearing away of the mist the disillusioning of real life. I think truth of nature, and transparent simplicity of life may sacrifice poetry, but they save from much spiritual peril."

"Still," answered the siren, "we might not find our friends lovable in that strong, realistic light of full day; but most tender in twilight shadows, by pale moonlight or in foldings of the mist. Should we not ourselves create the atmosphere of sympathy or ideality which softens their outlines and gives restful, helpful shadows?"

"That would make a masquerade of life," protested Themis, "each throwing sympathetically over one's friends, or wearing consciously oneself, this disguise of feeling and imagination."

"No, I should not like nature hidden in masks or draped with dominoes," answered Lorelei, "but only in ourselves the peculiar atmosphere, like Indian summer haze, which would give softened foreground and veiled distance."

Ultimata, who can never resist an argument, said, "Since none of us can see Nature except with our own power of vision, whether microscopic in detail or artistic in general sweep, and since we can only judge others through some mood of our own; how can we decide that the tender, idealising light may not give as true an impression as the stronger, more positive glare of critical noonday? There can be no absolute truth for any of us, but only approximate impression of truth."

"Oh, Ultimata," cried Themis, "with your accustomed sophistry you are going to prove that fog and sunlight are equally truthful in effect, that the clear view of the sea, and the distant gleam on the horizon, give in unchanged aspect, its power and unrest."

"No," said Ultimata, "my logic is not so delusive,

but I say that the gleam is as truthful as the unbroken view upon the sands, with salt waves dashing at one's feet; only it is right to know whether one's point of observation gives the full glory, or the far-off glimpse. Some minds like the bold, startling near effects, others the far-off line of blue in veiled dreamy distance. Both are true, one to the positive, one to the poetic mind."

"I wish," exclaimed Themis, "that I could draw one bold, straight line through your mind, that you might have a positive starting point, a mental equator—and you would be improved by having all the meridians drawn as well."

"But," said Ultimata, "those lines are all imaginary, to give power of measurement for finite distances to earthly voyages. Nature draws no straight lines. She gives sinuosities to her river courses, broken outlines to her hills, and gives to every wave grace of outline."

"Still," persisted Themis, "however apparently irregular the processes of Nature, we do find general laws, and we can reason from cause to effect, but only by close, scientific observation of facts."

"Yes," said Ultimata, "but scientists only reach the external facts of Nature; while artist hand and poet soul reveal its inmost secret."

"The difference between realistic fact and poetic interpretation," added Lorelei, "is the difference between the blackened craters and lifeless plains of the moon, without the tender veiling atmosphere, and our green valleys and dim blue hills: But look!

Santa Barbara decides against mystery, the fog has lifted and we have again undraped facts in the shape of those strong, barren mountains." So saying, Lorelei rose from the hammock, and in soft trailing garments and fleecy wrap, looked the incarnation of her own idealising haze.

CHAPTER XXV

FOLDED THOUGHTS

I THINK that observation is vastly more charming than experience: I like withdrawal from life's activities, to sit passive of mood, but sympathetic of spirit, while the streams of interest, of unrest, of passion flow by. So the days of seclusion when friends' thoughts reach me in bloom of roses, or in breath of violets, or in still fairer form of friendly notes, while no one demands written word or outward thanks, are, notwithstanding the depression of weakness, days of peace and pleasantness. I have an intense way of taking life, which makes needful these interludes of rest and isolation. But the social story was growing very fascinating in its development, and I should not like to miss its unfolding. From my window I watch the play of life, and our own circle do not allow me to feel excluded from the experiences, as they are so generous in expression towards me.

Lorelei has wakened from her listless dreams, or roused from her poetic reverie, and makes now one of the riding parties. I was quite impatient to see her mounted. I could not fancy her languid undulating grace transformed into the direct uprightness of the equestrienne. The first riding party which she joined was one to Cold Spring Cañon (justifying its name in cool rippling streams which give it a green leafiness even in the dry season). With sympathetic thought of my loneliness they all stopped to wave me greeting as they rode past; so I could see the grouping of the riders and study Lorelei in her new guise. She was still her charming self, with the stiff lines of the riding-habit modified by her unconscious grace. She was in green, with toque worn far back, giving her brow the usual shading of golden mist. She wore a pale, yellow gauze veil, so light as scarcely to cloud her face, brought round and tied in front with long, careless loops and floating ends. The vaporous softness of this gauze, and the yellow gloves much wrinkled over the slender wrists, relieved the severity of the habit and gave expression of herself to its conventional plainness. The Crusader was at her side, looking grand and knightly beside her spiritual fairness. The Fairy Prince on his white horse escorted Artista who rides with military erectness, and the Spectator, in his becoming rough suit and knickerbockers, rode with Perdita.

As they started, an English Colonel, known from his rôle in one of our theatrical evenings, as "the late Captain Kidd", now in faultless modern costume, was by the side of Mater Violetta, who looks, with her slim height, supremely well on horseback. But our riding parties are delightfully unconventional. As a rule, we break ranks, change companions and maintain a most harmonious *esprit de corps* instead of splitting into fragments for flirtation, or adhering to exclusive escorts.

Since that day there have been other trips on horseback, and one day a large party with four-in-hand went to Glen Annie for luncheon—later to visit the great sister ranch Elwood. Artista wished to join Mater Violetta, Perdita and other friends in the large, three-seated rock-away, so offered her village cart to Lorelei and the Crusader. The Siren had doubtless some fanciful costume, but she was draped in a long, floating India silk wrap, with soft golden ribbons knotted at the throat and confining the fulness of the loose sleeves. She wore a hat of yellow Tuscan straw, with faint, uncertain, blue facing, against the soft waves of her hair. Her colours are never positive; they have that oriental charm of always suggesting another colour. Her blues are of that faint sea tint, which in the folds look pale green (like that mystic colour caught in the soft surface of a large turquoise). Her parasol of India silk with soft lace trimmings had for lining the same ineffable blue.

I am self-consciously bewitched with the dim shining, the lustrous shadows of this strangely blended nature. It may be thought that I am chiefly in love with her costumes; but dress with her is what few have fineness of feeling and artist touch to make it, a perfect language. It is always significant of herself, with low utterance and delicate intonations. It gives no full, frank revelation, but dim, faint suggestions. I believe that under the draping and veilings of this mysticism there sleeps a strong, warm nature, which has never fully wakened. It needs a stronger touch to stir it to its depths than any which her experience has yet given. Her life has had under all its culture, a certain suppression, a shadowy unreality. Under the fervid warmth of intense feeling she would unfold with stronger line, in deeper colouring.

I think something of the idealising charm in which she wraps herself, is a dim consciousness on her part of depths unsounded in her own nature. She feels the stirrings of possible power of love and passion, which no master emotion has quickened into being; and this unknown element in herself finds expression in the veiled grace, the shadowy dimness of her dress. Only Hawthorne could analyse her, only George Fuller could paint her. Whoever remembers in the Academy, a few years ago, that picture of Winifred Dysart, with its shining of spiritual beauty through a warm, tender cloud of mystery, as of a nature which could not reveal itself in full sunlight, but suggests itself in shadow, will understand Lorelei's charm: only that face was dark through warm mist, and this face is fair, and the mist which veils it has sometimes a chill as of sea fog.

I have occasional notes during my banishment, which keep for me the thread unbroken of our social life; but during this imprisonment I have had real letters from three old friends, for life seems unfolding with a breadth of development which transcends the limits of ordinary notes. Then came a note from Lorelei, so like her in its unconscious charm, its repressed suggestiveness. I shall transcribe these, as you may perhaps touch the natures more nearly in this informal utterance of themselves, than by any description or analysis of mine. And as they all tell by hints the human story which charms me so deeply, you will, I think, like to have Lorelei studied from the standpoint of others, as you know, with me, feeling always dominates judgment; and the siren can never be only a psychological study, since I am so held by her personal spell.

I had a note from Themis which came with a basket of grapes, purple and white, as rich and ripe and full of colour as I find herself; and like herself very clear in contrast between the purple shadow and the white light:

"Dear Ultimata,

"I wish that you could come down or send for me when you are able to bear a visit. I feel as if the social foundations were falling from beneath us, everything is so changed in form and condition. You know how I like stability in the relations of life; and I felt so happy, so at rest in the companionship of our circle. Not that I had sounded each one's depths, or learned the clear outlines of each nature, but I understood the motive power and the controlling purpose in each. The Spectator sometimes in the course of conversation chills me with his sudden reserve; but when he emerges from behind his English walls (as you rightly term his power of withdrawal), he is always the same. One can build upon his firm, quiet strength, his unexpressed but absolute loyalty. Then, from his transparent purity of nature, there is a clear shining of spiritual power in his presence. I feel, when with him, through all social complications, all personal divergence of thought, the straight lines of honour and integrity. His sketches, in their firmness of outline, their accuracy of detail, are like himself in power of truth. He sometimes escapes me by beating a retreat into himself, but he never bewilders me. He is clear-cut, definite, harmonious.

"Then the Crusader with his versatility is given a strong, controlling unity by his enthusiasm for right and his devotion to social progress and political purification. He has a surface play of gallantry and compliment, which once led me to misapprehension of him; but having reached the strong, adamantine foundation of his character I rest there and leave the superficial brightness of flattery and repartee for the young, whom he always charms. But I do like his wit: it is so delicate, so trenchant, so effective; a Damascus blade in fineness and flexibility. I should not like to be his foe and feel its merciless thrust; but in social sword-play it is very charming.

"Then, I thought that I understood yourself; having found under your mercurial changes of mind, strong humanitarian sympathy, and tender personal charity. But I now think that I know none of you: I am not certain that I know myself, since this misty atmosphere wraps us all. I hate fog and its chill, grey illusions. I like clear, honest sunlight. I know Dorothy's name for the charmer, Lorelei. It tells the whole story. Now I understand the sense of chill; and the cold sea breath which I feel in her presence. She is confusing all the outlines of our life. I am all at sea: most hopelessly in the fog. Can you take your bearings? Shall we make the shore or strike on reefs? You know what I mean. The Spectator is fascinated with her music, but keeps himself quite cool of head and quite clear of vision. But the Crusader! You know his past, his long loneliness: first I believe from deep loyalty to his beautiful wife, but of late years I think with conscious enjoyment of his freedom, with its right of friendship with intellectual women, and its power of social triumph. He is popularly called fickle: outwardly it seems true, though I know with your faith in him you defend him, perhaps justly, by your recognition of his personal magnetism which strongly influences others, and his many-sidedness which gives him many points of contact with other minds. Does your faith in him falter now? Is he intent upon a new conquest, or is he himself a victim to this siren's spell? I do not like her. I do not believe in her. I think her the Jesuitical type, indirect and dangerous in her methods. She is conservative, not from conviction but from aristocratic habit, and Catholic.

"Her mind is the result of convent education, uncertain, wandering, delusive. If the Crusader is lured by her it means losing himself in the fog. With her charm upon him what will be his political future? I hoped to see him strong in the civil service reform, active in his favourite scheme for the re-organisation of political parties, and an open advocate of woman suffrage. The political world is so full of weak men, that I protest against seeing a strong man spell-bound. Do help break the chain, and save him to the rank of the world's brave workers. Your friendship with him is closer than mine; your influence more potent. Come down and give your companionship to him, as refuge from this peril.

"Yours affectionately,
"THEMIS."

I smiled at the earnestness of tone in this letter, but comprehended it; as I think two minds could hardly be more alien than her own with its sturdy strength, its clear light, and that of Lorelei, with its vagueness of outline, its twilight charm. But I feel, under this dim shining, this idealising shadow, possibilities of hidden strength, of sunlit space, if

Love once flashes its power of light across her undiscovered soul. Then, I have in my nature that fondness for a story, that passion for watching the development of lives, that I cannot repress a thrill of pleasure in the thought of a love idyll in Santa Barbara. I have been studying all the maiden faces, all the young cavaliers in hope of an unfolding of romance; but the Crusader, who is past fifty, I counted as a constant and charming element in our afternoon world. True, his is the type of nature dowered with immortal youth. One feels in his presence always the strong pulsing of the hot young blood, with which he girded his sword, and leaped, years ago, into that fierce, deathly strife. But the world accepts so fully the externals of unmarked brow, unsilvered hair, as signs of the heart of youth; and furrowed forehead and frost-touched beard as symbols of age, that we are all misled by their delusive seeming. But we whose sun dips to the west know, that the heart's strongest pulsing is not at twenty, its deepest thrill not in the morning sunlight. To the wearers of white dresses and yachting suits in the summer holidays, to whom belongs the day for fair groups on lawn and garden, and the twilight for lover loitering, or dreamy delight of sail upon near safe river, it seems a wrong done to youth and summer, that those in (what seems to them) the reaped autumn of life, should dare to love. But the power of sunlight stirs more deeply in the golden grain, than in the spring's first daisy.

I think that I feel my assurance of immortality strengthened from my own consciousness that with my riper years I feel the spring's quickening thrill and the summer's rapture; and if, in the passing of the years, the wearing of this semblance of age, there is not loss of emotional power, but its deepening—not shrouding of the spirit, but its clear shining—why fear with future failing or with deathly change, loss of the individual consciousness? If the spirit holds, by its independent being, the inner strength untouched, the inner light undimmed through passing years and the darkening life, why doubt its power to lift in winged flight from its dissolving chrysalis? Because of my apprehension of youth, not as incidental to the years of living, but as inherent in natures of strength and hope, I watch with more sympathetic interest, with more tenderness and faith, the quickening of love in older hearts, in later life, than in those to whom love is like the roses and the bird songs, part of the early summer. If the Crusader loves Lorelei, he will love her with the passion of his youth and with the power of his deepened, strengthened manhood. But, with his responsive sympathy, his chivalrous nature; this tender courtesy towards one known to him in her fair, lonely girlhood may mean but a romantic phase of friendship. But I do hear tones in his voice not known before, and see a light in his face which shone for none of us.

In the evening of the day which brought Themis' letter I received from the Spectator one of his sketch books, with views from Egypt and through Mexico, record of his wide wanderings. I had begged the loan of it for more familiar study, so it was thoughtfully sent now, to beguile the tedium of imprisonment: with it was this note:—

"DEAR FRIEND,

"You are missed, needed by us all. I am truly sorry that you are ill, but I think that I have detected in you a willingness sometimes to prolong the convalescence for sake of the silence and solitude. Are you not so contented with the long, undisturbed hours for reading, and the mountains for society, that you smile at our messages of condolence? But I think with your quick perception and warm sympathy, you would enjoy the new developments of life among us. So be human and come down. Do you want the news? It is not of the kind which will bear positive repeating, but I think that you could read new lines of an old story every day. So far from my English friends and my own people, I have come to take stronger interest in the life history of my friends here than I should have thought possible in one so withdrawn and reserved. Is it Santa Barbara air or American companionship that is working this miracle? I am growing curious about other people's affairs. You will say that it is my membership of the Club. I think that it is amiable sympathy on my part with your expressed desire for a romance. Can you throw light on the heroine? The hero needs no light. He scintillates always with his own brilliancy. I smiled when Dorothy confessed her classification of the fair charmer as a siren, christening her Lorelei. I think that I understand her better from this nomenclature. You profess not to be scientific, but in human studies you discover well genera and species. Do you remember our excited talk on Finch's Hill, when I chose the view with charming glimpses, but you and the Crusader liked sense of space and far horizon. The talk finally drifted into playful comparison of sibyls and sirens. The Crusader wished the spiritual vision and the power of inspiration of the sibyl, and you both accused me of having for ideal a siren with covert charm and mystical, veiled loveliness. Is there not some confusion of ideals, some dislocation of destinies? Is not the Crusader being charmed by the siren? I think her exquisitely lovely! She delights my artist soul, and her music might win a man from the safe shore to the fatal sea. I do not disown my ideal, the siren justifies it. But the Crusader is liberal in theology (seeming to me a pantheistic spiritualist), and a radical in politics. In temperament he is ardent and in expression vehement. How can he mate with one socially a patrician, unstirred by human sympathies beyond her world of grace and culture: one in faith a Catholic, resting upon the traditions and rites of a Church antagonistic to progress and popular rights, and with a nature so calm and dreamy? She wears life as she does those clouds of shawls, lightly and gracefully; but can one simply æsthetic respond to the Crusader's intensity of nature? Is she not as nearly Andersen's 'Ice Maiden', as the 'Lorelei'?

"My admiration for the Crusader is so strong, almost reaching reverence, that I long to see his nature met by one as broad and as deep as his own. I do not say that the Lorelei has not such possibilities. She is too hazy for positive outlines. But I should like to study her in a clear light. Now, you are sympathetic in your study of women and subtle in your discernment of nature. As Lorelei, the fair widow is perfect; but how will she be as a human woman, and wife to the Crusader? I did not mean to give positive form to my surmises, but I cannot be indirect and inferential. Do come down and warm us with a glowing argument with the Crusader, or with a flame of indignation against all men sinners, of whom I am the chief in sending this long letter. If written by a woman, it might be called gossip, but from me it is scientific, simply recording observations.

"Faithfully yours,
"SPECTATOR."

It looks serious when the Spectator breaks through his habitual reserve to write so freely. What a study the siren is, with that seductive charm, that baffling bewitchment! Who can analyse or know her? She will only be revealed in some great flame of feeling; and who lights that flame must have given his own heart to its consuming breath, before it illumines the shadows of her nature. But I believe in that revealing, the spirit will be white, and the heart warm, human red. And I think only a nature like the Crusader's, with volcanic soul of flame can give the intensity of emotion which will reveal her power to others, disclose her depths of feeling to herself.

I had a night of strange, visionary dreams, as fantastic as German *Märchen*, of volcanoes emitting chill green light, and a sea with waves of flame.

In the morning, Foo with his broad, beaming smile brought me a glorious bunch of yellow roses, with this letter from the Crusader.

"My dear Friend,

"I send the morning sunlight to greet you in these 'Cloth of Gold' roses. I know that you love yellow as the soul of light (perhaps also as the symbol of heresy), and I hold it in reverent memory as the old cavalry colour. You are missing perfect Santa Barbara days—no, not missing them, for sitting in your northern window you are revelling in their play of light and shadow. But we are missing you; for Santa Barbara sunshine needs the praise of your ardent word, the smile of your responsive rapture to be sure of its own light. Your faith in its perfect beauty has made converts of us all. Come downstairs, or I may prove a backslider from grace by a mood of longing for the restful shadows of the redwoods, the sombre grandeur of the wooded hills of Santa Cruz. Do not frown. Santa Barbara is a love song: Santa Cruz a sacred chant. That forest of mighty trees has the solemnity of twilight service in a Gothic Cathedral. Now you are sure to come down armed and equipped for a tilt with me in behalf of the peerless charm of your 'Santa'.

"I believe that my friend Lucille is yielding to the spell of the place: at least she fixes no date for her flight to the northern coast, and, by the way, her eyes wander to the hills with their caprices of light and their fantasies of shadow, I think that she is in love with the valley which she thought so narrow, the mountains so undraped, the sea so persistently blue, and the sunlight so unpoetic in its clearness. I think that her nature needs such warmth and rest. She has wandered so widely, has flitted through transitory experiences, has touched life so lightly and held her own individuality in a kind of unsunned solitude, until she seems to herself a dream. But I think that she holds in her tranced life the possibilities of warm, responsive womanhood. I see that she impresses you strongly. I think that she will charm you by her fine spiritual power, and I believe that your more humanised, more vitalised nature will win her to a broader, deeper sympathy with life as we know it—its passion and its pain. She only needs a quickened throb of feeling to be irresistible. I write freely to you. I know your idealising love of women and your freedom from small, personal jealousy. I see by your smile and the light in your eye, that you exult in her loveliness. She must, on this remote coast and in this world of strangers, seem very near to me. I see her fairness beside the dark stateliness of my own daughter; and both in the home garden of those full, strong years of my more active life.

"I wish much to see you downstairs again. Lucille is so girlish in her beauty, that I feel safer to see her under your strong, shadowing wing. For I read your spirit in your face and know that you will throw your positive power and your intense individuality about her fragile loveliness. She charms many, but unfolds to none. I think with your gift of subtle sympathy, you may win your way to her inmost self. I have joy in your strong friendship for my own sake; but more joy to-day that I feel this child, with her strange, uncompanioned past, will find in that friendship the warmth and tenderness of a spirit home.

"You have often confided to me the power of the Catholic Church over your own life in many ways. You know my intellectual antagonism to its spirit and its creed. Shall I make this letter my confessional, and avow my belief that its dim traditions, its symbolical sacraments and its solemn ritual, may hold for sensitive, shrouded spirits, the power of expression and the joy of unfolding denied in the social or personal life. I think that Lucille, in her unmothered life, sees in the Virgin Mary the smile and touch which her own childhood missed; and finds in that intercession of saints an escape from the spiritual loneliness which enthralls her. She accepts the rites and sacraments of the Church with more tender reverence, that they shine through the shadows of the centuries, and are dimmed with the mysticism of the Dark Ages. I am not suffering a reaction from the passionate protest and the unresting individualism of my own life, but I do feel the strength of accepted truth and the rest of traditional forms to drifting natures. You must not smile at this, dear Friend, dowered as you are with what Dorothy calls 'other-sidedness'.

"Sincerely yours,
"CRUSADER."

This letter touched me with its calm rest upon our friendship, its appeal to my sympathy and tenderness on behalf of the fair stranger. I am glad of the years which give me the broader experience, the deeper strength, which may seem anchorage to her drifting life, her unmoored nature. And I am glad of my intellectual companionship with the Crusader, warmed now by this confidence towards me, in this budding of his love for Lorelei.

Late in the afternoon came from herself a little bouquet of heliotrope and mignonette, tied with a ribbon of faint sea-green, and this graceful little note.

"Shall I know you only as the Crusader's friend and Dorothy's mother? Can I not hope for some personal link with your life? In your broad, warm nature is there not some shadowy corner where I can feel at home without wrong to those who claim its space and sunniness? I am tired of myself, and out of love with life. Perhaps I should say that I have never been in love with life and have never felt quite at home with myself.

"I think Santa Barbara has some gracious charm in its full smile, for I am smiling back with a gladness strange to myself. Perhaps your quaint little maiden has touched me with the wand of her childish faith, and her fairy-loving nature. Some day may I come to your room, which I hear has soft, golden glory of colouring and outlook to your idealised hills? I have made peace with Santa Barbara, so send me by Dorothy a reconciled smile.

"LUCILLE."

I should not re-write these letters, so warm hearted towards myself, but they reveal how strangely the siren holds us all by some charm. Even Themis feels, while she denies her spell. As far as the kindliness of thought towards myself, these notes have the relenting tenderness of strength towards weakness, of those in glad companionship towards friend in solitude. In truth, I have been throned and crowned by the friendships of my life. But when we sit in unbroken circle, we do not habitually talk love, but speak often the language of dissent, with wide divergence of thought. But when I fail of presence among them, and miss the familiar sunlight in which they sit; then they create for me in my shadow, by this remembering thought, by their regardful words, the summer sky and the sunlit day. In my longing across the disappointing years, when I hoped and still failed to reach this Valley, seen and loved in prevision, did I picture in its sunlight this group of waiting friends, called from afar and by touch of spiritual kinship made part of the radiant present, and warm memory through life's latest, palest years?

No, the longing failed in its winged power to reach and sweep this joy. I thought only of southern sea and cloudless sunlight, of valley fairness and mountain strength; but life, generous beyond my longing, has brought these gifts of friendships to make California truly, my Golden State.

CHAPTER XXVI

MIRAGE

YESTERDAY, in response to a note from me, Lorelei came to my room, and we had one of those womanly talks of life which always interest me, with hints and half-revealings of personal history. No one comes to an invalid's room in conventional calling costume, or in the formality of the usual, recognised social interchange. The very occupancy of a couch is a confession of outward defeat, which touches always the sweet, sympathetic fibre in a woman's nature. I think weakness is often irritating to the strength of a man, but always appealing to the tenderness of a woman. So the siren's smile was warmer in my shadowed room than in the outer sunlight. My lounge was moved into the bay window, with one shade lifted to give me a glimpse of the mountain glory. I begged Lorelei, who took the large rocking-chair near me, to draw up the other blinds, that she might have the full mountain panorama. This commenced the talk of which I shall give a broken record, between Lorelei and Ultimata. The morning was cool; not with the breath of October, which is the month of our present experience, but with the fresh hopefulness of early June. The siren wore a morning robe of soft golden cashmere, with velvet collar and cuffs of deeper shade, giving a touch of sunlit warmth to her fair pallor. Did she remember the colouring of my room that she came in this golden glamour; a perfect picture against the lustrous hangings and warm paper with glints of light?

"No," Lorelei answered to the suggestion that she should lift the shades and gain the full mountain view, "I like the shadowy dimness of the room, with just a glimpse of the hills. From the piazza there is the full sweep, and this glimpse is charming, just a suggestion of what lies beyond."

"I often wonder," replied Ultimata, "at the power of the incomplete to give more than the whole. I have felt at times, at the sight of the first violets offered by a wandering flower girl on Broadway, more fully the spring's rapture, than in fields of wild flowers, or the greenness of wood shadows. So I have found in a swallow's flight across the bit of blue framed by the window, a power of longing not quickened by the open sky with whole flocks in darkening line against its light. It is either a confession of our inadequacy to take a broad sweep, or the recognition of a power of flight beyond the utmost finite limits, that from a gleam of colour, the joy of a wild flower or a bird's note, we can create a fairer, broader world in ecstatic imagining than even earth in its summer joy."

"I love," said Lorelei, "these faint suggestions, because they seem to justify a perfect ideal; but full revelation is always disappointing. I learned long ago that the East in which my child spirit revelled, created from the soft fabrics, the sandal wood, the carved ivory and the faint, spicy odours of my father's cabinet was the true East of light and mystery. Even in my voyage when only seven, and too young to analyse, I felt the Indian Ocean was less blue, and Calcutta Harbour less foreign and mystic than my dreams had made it. I think the real disillusioning of life is its monotony. I wish not to see things clearly and fully, but far off, in a dreamy, unreal way."

"But," protested Ultimata, "in that vague, far-off gaze, you miss life's familiar warmth and sweetness. I feel, however restful the dreamy vision for poetic mood, for twilight reverie, there is joy on the near and familiar aspects of life. Do you not love to see the brown, upturned earth, with the sower in his hopeful walk, with hand of broad-cast bounty; or the lonely ploughman upon a ridge, in bold silhouette against the wistful sky of spring?

"Both seem so in harmony with Nature's processes of growth, and equally one with earth's creative power and generous gladness. Nothing thrills me more deeply in nature than waving wheat fields, a sea of changeful light, and through its fairness a thought of waiting homes and the blessedness of that daily bread; with quick suggestive pictures of mowers moving in rhythm, and mills with running water and restless wheels pouring out smooth, bountiful streams. I love the familiar and real, I think, after all, more than the faint, far-away ideal."

"I seem to miss the familiar, homely aspects of life," answered Lorelei, "I think brown fields and waving grain give me only a tired feeling of how dusty and wearisome life is to the masses. It must be so, but the only joy of being uplifted above the need of such toil is to keep the spirit calm by removal from that fervid midday glare. I miss the noon in my cool twilight world—gladly miss it. I hate strong light, loud voices, all sense of pressure; and I believe from your shadowy room, your choice of colours, that you like yourself dimness and seclusion. Now confess it."

"I do confess," said Ultimata, smiling at this discernment of her hidden self, "that as a girl I was pure idealist, my instinctive longing was to escape life's inevitable boundaries, in any dreamy distance, but I have been forced to acceptance of those limitations, and I now rejoice in what seemed adverse fate; for, only by knowing life as it is, can we know others truly, and to miss sympathetic beating with the hot human hearts about us, is to lose our own birthright."

"You will think me cold-blooded," replied Lorelei, "when I confess that I shrink from that near touch of other lives. It seems all pressure and pain. In a dumb, inarticulate way I know the suffering of life to those who struggle, who strive, who fail; but I could never express it in warm, helpful sympathy. None come to me with their grief, or with their loss. I have a sense of a strange remoteness from these stormy experiences. I cannot see clearly, I cannot feel keenly this human suffering. I could not hold my own dying canary in my hand. What fails me—a human heart, or the power of service?"

"Neither," answered Ultimata, "but the personal experience which would interpret to you human life. Your own nature has never been swept by strong emotion, to give you vibratory response to the pain of others. Then you have missed the familiar touch upon your own life, which gives warm, cordial nearness to others. Your strange, solitary childhood (for the Crusader has told me your outward life story) has been like a spell laid upon you. You missed the strong, warm sunshine of the usual child world; so have partly missed yourself—for I think a child learns itself first by its reflection in the mother's heart and eyes."

"Yes," spoke Lorelei, as if musing aloud, "it was a dim, pallid childhood, alone in all the bloom of the quaint, lonely garden, or among the weird, wrested old apple trees; too bent and grey to have much sympathy with young life, though they flushed with joy in blossom time. The housekeeper was a solemn, stately woman of whom I stood in awe; though she was truly devoted to me in her dignified way. But she never played with me—never told me a story. My father's coming home, and that one long voyage are the tender memories of my childhood: glad I cannot call them, for my father was strangely silent. His utmost tenderness was to rest his hand a moment on my curls, or to give sometimes a long, wistful look into my eyes, as if he saw through them into my dead mother's soul: for they said that I had my mother's eyes, and my father had given to her the full love of his strong, repressed nature.

"I sat much by the highest window in the house, in a queer gabled room filled with the curious accumulation of past voyages, and looked over the sea, following my father on his outward course, or watching—for ever watching, for the coming of his ship into the home harbour. When at last, during a vacation in my convent life he died at sea, I felt no poignant pain. He had drifted farther from me, gone on a longer voyage, and I grew lonelier and more wistful in following him. That was all. Yes, my life missed the mother touch. I remember sometimes stroking my own curls, to think how it would seem to feel a mother's hand brush them back to kiss the uncaressed brow.

"Those were quiet dreamy years at the convent. I loved the sisters, and the still, orderly life; the matins and the vespers, and the shadowy chapel with flowers and lights always on the altar. I should have been myself a nun: only a convent could give the withdrawal which suits my nature. But I could not bear those positive vows, that solemn, awful renunciation from which there is no appeal. I could have spent my life there in the cloistered stillness, with quiet days hushing themselves in prayer at the angelus. But I could not take the vows that meant imprisonment.

"Soon after leaving the convent, I married a man of promise and culture, whose brilliancy flashed like an electric light across my life, but never warmed it. My home was beautiful. I was proud of the power and promise of my gifted husband. For his sake I made my home a social centre, but always missed myself its glow and gaiety. My heart dwelt still in the sombre old home and the solitary garden. No child nestled against my heart, no child called me by the name which my own lips had missed. I think if the firelight had shone on a baby's face, I should have wakened from this trance into warm mother love.

"When my husband's illness came, it was brain fever, and in his delirium he was only more fiercely, fervidly brilliant, with flashing plans for his future; and when he spoke my name it was with high pride, but with no relenting of tenderness. I was part of his outward triumph, but was never treasured in his heart. I honoured him, exulted in the future which opened before him, and mourned him in death, but seemed long to follow him upon some flaming meteor track, until he faded from me. He dazzled my vision, then left it darkened. What would you call my life which has hardly felt a grief, and never clasped a joy?"

"I think that it has been like some faint, elusive mirage," said Ultimata tenderly, "but it will not always lure you. You will reach life's real shore and build your happiness on strong, deep foundations."

"I am not sure that I wish to touch the real," answered Lorelei, "at least my life is calm and restful, and these usual human lives, ardent and emotional, are so fraught with pain and loss. I have scarcely suffered heartache, but those who live and love deeply have often heart-break. Then, I am outwardly free to drift whither I will, and dream in my own world. I should not like to be limited to another's horizon."

"But," asked Ultimata, "might you not love a nature with such breadth of horizon as to give the dreamy distance you like, and yet warm, human nearness?"

"But even then," suggested Lorelei, "I might be so happy in the near, close companionship, as to miss the far, faint beauty of the ideal. No, I choose my dreams and my dehumanised life (such I know you feel it to be)."

"No," protested Ultimata, "it is not dehumanised, only not fully humanised. You have missed that central flame of love, which gives warmth of sympathy, and glow of feeling in all life's relationships."

"I do not like flame," persisted Lorelei. "I like fog better, with all its chill, its dim, fantastic shapes, than flame, heating and scorching all the life. Then, if the poets are to be trusted, this flame has a way of consuming the heart and leaving only white ash to mark its light."

"Whatever poets sing, or dreamers see in vision," said Ultimata, "power of feeling is the measure of life: and to miss its fullest throb, its utmost thrill, is to lessen that spirit force through which is developed strongest selfhood, and finest sympathy with others. I am not so sure that power of feeling is always or oftenest power of joy; since this earthly experience is not life's full and ultimate expression. But the compass of the nature must be the same for pleasure or pain. Better the full gamut of feeling, whether swept by joy or grief."

"But," asked Lorelei, "since the unfolding here is so often to loss and bitterness, why is it not safe and wise to sheath ourselves in restful calm, and find faint, visionary happiness in our dreams, and await the eternal opening into perfect power? Might not this peace be the spirit's blessedness of patience on earth, to be followed by the glad, gracious wakening into immortal life? Is not part of earth's pain this struggle to win in the finite what belongs to the infinite—to grasp more than the just measure of earthly development?"

"No," resolutely responded Ultimata, "to miss the utmost power of living here, must be to miss something eternally; since it leaves to later development that which had right to earthly growth, to earlier joy of leaf and flower. Whatever the Hereafter holds for us, it cannot give the experience of love under finite conditions: that thrill of soul which by its intensity touches the immortal, that power of faith to discern through the pain of incompleteness, the consummate glory of love. You pleaded just now for the joy gained through suggestions, the beauty caught in gleams and glimpses. Then you should believe in human love, which here, is a series of revealings, never a revelation."

"After all," said Lorelei, "we must accept life according to our natures. You will thrill and throb with intensity of emotion, not for yourself alone, but for all the hearts that touch you: and I shall dream and drift, feeling even my own life visionary and unreal. Development can only come in accordance with temperament. I am a kind of human fern, with only hidden seed on my frond, for flower and fruit. You are like the scarlet passion-flower vine you love, which embraces with close, warm clasp, climbs high and carries the symbols of the Divine Passion, in warm human red. But when I decorated my room with the sprays you sent, the blossoms folded at night in a spent, hopeless way, and all the tendrils drooped. But ferns hold their shadowy green, in cool, restful calm."

"You are escaping the argument by evasive grace of compliment," answered Ultimata, "you are no fern, though fond of shadow. You remind me rather of the water-lily leaves I watched one summer floating on a quiet lake, so near the sea that it might have been a salt inlet, and seemed to pulse with the ebb and flow of the ocean's restless heart. The calm leaves drifted idly, contented with their own green; but shy hidden buds were there, and one day they unfolded in deep-hearted chalices, their white petals flushed with tender colour, rare pink water-lilies. You will have colour in your petals too, when the sunlight touches your shrouded heart."

"But there seems some fate by which the sun never touches the hidden heart," said Lorelei, "are you sure the heart is there to thrill in answer to its light; and if thus long germinal, by what development should it unfold? My calm irresponsive life will soon complete its thirtieth unstirred year!"

"It is singular," remarked Ultimata, "that the Darwinian phraseology has taken such possession of the language, that two women cannot talk of individual life and its emotional centre, without unconsciously accepting the development hypothesis of slow, gradual change. I have never been able to feel that the theory was adequate to the interpretation of life, physical, intellectual, or spiritual.

"I feel its power and the light it throws on many dark problems, for partial development from lower forms would explain imperfect, inharmonious natures, and make Christian charity of judgment in truth a scientific classification of humanity; since there would be the inevitable acceptance of low grades on their upward line of development. If Darwinism is humiliation in retrospect, it has a hope hidden in every incomplete, transitional manifestation. But sudden inspiration, the kindling of enthusiasm, the leaping to height of heroic resolve, it does not explain. It may give, by slow, gradual evolution, the unfolding of ordinary human reason and feeling; but it fails before the wayward flame-like uplifting of those natures, whose shining is strange, clear, unique—whose lighting and whose dimming seem in far higher air than our analysed, earthly atmosphere.

"I read, some years ago, only a Tribune report of lectures, I think by Clarence King, on 'Catastrophism'. I have a mind impervious to scientific truth, but I remember that he claimed the geology of the globe could not be explained by the slow æons of development alone, but needed the acceptance of crises of sudden, swift change; the recognition of 'Catastrophism' in Nature. I read it with delighted interest, but with no thought of its application to any but the physical world—but it has held for me deep, spiritual comfort. I recognise its truth in the individual life, as in the larger national and social unfolding. Human lives have shown clearer lines through their mystery, and the events of history had more intelligent interpretation to my own mind, since studying them, not only in the course of slow development, but by the result of sudden, violent change, wrought by this force of Catastrophism.

"There are crises in Nature and humanity: and the interest of individual history centres in these surcharged, emotional experiences, which come, not by ordinary development, but by spiritual Catastrophism. The distinction between victory and defeat in life, between success and failure, may be the instant recognition by natures of these crises in fate, with swift adjustment to the changed conditions of these moral eruptions or upheavals, or their fatal irrecognition. You need the action of the second force in your life. I should like your nature to vibrate with earthquake shock, or be swept with volcanic flame."

"I really think," said Lorelei laughing, "that after such a benediction my only safety is in flight. I think I shall take a long sea voyage to escape shocks and eruptions. I thought of you in this shadowed room in quiet, mild invalidism, with only spiritual communion with your calm mountains; but I find you with incendiary instincts and explosive ambitions. I shall feel startled with the swinging of my own hammock now, knowing the possibilities of this force called in to interrupt my placid, peaceful development. I do not wonder at dear little Dorothy's vagaries of faith and feeling, after this elucidation."

"Oh, yes, Dorothy is quite the incarnation of my creed," answered Ultimata. "She accepts the flash of occasional erratic comet across her sky, as naturally as the lighting of her nightly candle. This talk of slow ascent and startling change recalls a dream of mine not long ago, which delighted Dorothy's heart. She slept with me that night, and I wakened her with my exclamation. So I pictured to her the vision, which swept across my night sky.

"I saw a high, bleak mountain, unshadowed by any tree. A road wound up its side, rough and rocky, and in fierce sunlight. An army of pilgrims toiled up that steep ascent, all in grey garb with

MIRAGE

ropes for girdles, and leaning on rough staves, which seemed rude, cumbersome crosses. Some walked in brave patience; some in resolute firmness; others in reckless defiance. Many rushed, then fainted by the way; others failed from faithlessness of finding any rest beyond; and the few still left climbed wearily. Then sudden shadow fell, and I saw trackless snow, and the few, heroic, pallid in the dim light, still winding on and on across those chill, pathless heights. My heart failed me as I watched this pilgrimage of humanity, with faltering feet and faithless hearts, all worn and wearied, all travel-stained with dust of the way and faint with heat of the merciless midday sun. Then I thought of the longer climb, the more patient pain of those who still toiled up, through twilight chill, across that far crest. Then there flashed sudden, glorious light, and with the pilgrims still struggling upward, I saw another vision. Across the cloudless sky there swept in swift winged flight, hosts of angels, luminous in light, like white cloud procession across the blue. 'Why,' I asked, 'this toiling climb for pilgrim feet, this untiring power of flight for angels' wings?'

"My own heart answered what my heart had asked, for I wakened Dorothy by exclaiming, 'His Messengers to do His will, by wearied foot or by unwearied wing!' So I think in our lives there are years that climb slowly towards spiritual light, and moments of impulse and inspiration which mount with wings. The patient climbing is brave, but also the faith to lift with power of flight in the winged hour."

Lorelei did not face the speaker as she told her dream, but with that far-away expression in her eyes she looked towards the hills. Then she turned all that mystical, veiled sweetness of gaze upon Ultimata, and said softly, "I did not like your earthquakes to startle me, but I do like your calm, white angels: I hope that I shall not miss the winged possibility in my own life."

She stood a moment in her calm, perfect grace, then came and laid her cool, white hand in Ultimata's for good-bye. But she looked so child-like with that wistful look in her face, that she was drawn down for a quick embrace and warm, human kiss. Ultimata thought that her lip trembled as they parted; but I am not responsible for Ultimata's imagination when her heart is touched, and of this I am sure, that, whether the Crusader is or is not in love with Lorelei, Ultimata's heart is lost. But falling in love with women has been her life-long weakness.

CHAPTER XXVII

RETROSPECT

THERE has been a pause in the sweet, earthly story for the telling of which you wait. After the talk in my room with Lorelei came a full, pleasant week, but rather kaleidoscopic in memory. One day Lorelei and the Crusader, the Spectator, Dorothy, Harold and myself, went a long, climbing ride over the hills, taking a road behind the Mission, following trails, and at last, under the Spectator's guidance climbing without visible path. Lorelei was as childish as Dorothy in her delight over the gophers and ground squirrels, which make with their holes the fields around the Mission, as many elsewhere, unsafe to cross at a lope; and which may be seen in swift transit or retreat, as the riding parties sweep by their haunts. Near the Mission abound also little lizards basking on the rocks, or darting with quick grace over the sun-warm weathered old walls. Lorelei's interest in the grotesque, ungainly cactus plants called our attention anew to their straggling growth and fierce, thorn-edged leaves, looking in aggressive ugliness like malicious tortured creatures, imprisoned in leafy form during their wild contortions.

This ride gives the finest view I have yet had of the mountains: sweeping the grandeur of the unbroken range and the billowy undulations of the hills, looking inland. But the sea withdraws itself into dreamy distance, too remote for sense of salt air, or sympathy with its tidal heart-beat. I like to be so near the ocean as to feel that pulse of its unrest. We did not break ranks in our usual way, as the Crusader and Lorelei were in quiet, low-voiced talk; so the Spectator accepted the situation and devoted himself to me, as Harold evinced no wish to leave that fairy world where he and Dorothy ride, for the earthly hills given to our older climbing.

The Spectator's thoughts were in England; for that day he had received from home a box with engravings, etchings, many pleasant remembrances, and, best of all (I thought), Ruskin's second course of Slade Lectures. So as we rode our talk was much of England, and our tone, even in California sunlight, was wistful, as we spoke of "the Old Home", his by birth, mine by love and adoption, for the full, blessed years of my early married life were passed there, and the friendships of English growth have been deep of root and fair of flower. How much personal experience modifies our preconceived impressions of national type!

I thought, in going to England to make it home (just when the flame of Civil War had paled upon our shores, but left, under the white ash of loss, glowing embers still of fervid resentment and fierce hatred) that my life there would be gain, in reaching the richer culture and deeper thought of an old land. But, with heart quivering still with the agony of that conflict—young heart unused to pain and unlearned in the charity which interprets aright intellectual divergence and national alienation—I thought that England, cold and critical towards our heroism and our sacrifice, could hold for me no gift of love. With my impassioned nature I should be untouched by that reserved, self-poised English character, and fail of any true revelation or justification of myself to those of colder blood, of calmer tone. I should be repressed, chilled, withdrawn. But my own English circle throbbed with vital warmth, thrilled with intellectual intensity.

I have touched on earth no soil so humanly broad, breathed no atmosphere so humanly warm as that familiar to me in London. Through art, through literature, through philanthropy, through chivalry of devotion to weak and imperilled nationalities (which glorified itself in defence of Greece and sympathy with Italy, but shadowed its clearness of vision in acceptance of "the Lost Cause") these English natures touch life at so many points. So far from being an insular world, it seemed to me universal in its connection and sympathies. And individual English friendships for years have kept their colour, like the undimmed freshness of English fields, and outreached broad branches like the stately strength of English oaks. That was to me no revelation. Stability and constancy I should have expected from the English character. But I have found in those friendships such power of tenderness, such ideality of fancy, such transfiguring charm of touch, that England is to me the land of gracious welcome, of cordial converse, of hearth-side brightness. From popular conceptions of English coldness, I appeal to my own glowing warmth of English memories, my own glad consciousness of English love. I have found far finer expression of feeling among friends there than here. Not that we are less ardent, less intense, but that we are so young, so aggressive, that we have not attained to the calm and leisure for social culture or artistic expression.

Coming from London to Chicago was like leaving the generous flame of a soft coal fire, with radiant lights and tender shadows falling upon the curtained seclusion of a home drawing-room, to experience the furnace heat, the glaring light, the unrestful atmosphere of a crowded hotel. Not but that Chicago has its warmth and beauty, its artistic homes and cultured lives, but that in its new, abundant external life, one could not escape the sense of turmoil, excitement and speculation: while London, in a cultured circle, has an insulated life, free from the disturbing currents of this material and money-making age.

However, Chicago soon escaped the atmosphere of the money-making madness of real estate speculation, to feel the fierce inferno flame of lurid ruin, when swept by that fateful fire. From material exultation, material wealth, it was lifted into tragedy of swift, utter loss. And be it said by one who never loved it in its glory, that in the light of that flame which engulfed homes and fortunes, lives stood heroic in strength, faces shone in daring hope. That fire, which left no outline of stately structure, no uplifting of church spire in its swift, awful course, revealed in startling clearness the stalwart manhood, the steadfast womanhood, which were that city's unfailing foundation. Where had been outward expression in brick and stone of civic power and pride, was field swept clear for manifestations of human nature in its naked outlines. And the human nature of Chicago in the day of awful revealing was grand in self-control, generous in self-sacrifice. In smoking ruins and grey ashes, I learned its true greatness, and thrilled with the spiritual touch of its unconquerable strength.

Still, for full, yet restful life, I should choose London; where one has links with the dim past and with the broad to-day, and yet can shield the individual life from the shock and jar of the material enterprises and excitements which vibrate too strongly in America to leave a home unshaken.

So Ultimata uttered no word of protest when the Spectator said, " It is exile: I feel it so to-day to be riding over these hills, where my future life must be, and know that my heart is at home only in Warwickshire; that the real self I can never transplant. My brother writes that I am fortunate to have a life which has necessitated so much travel, and at last found location in the freedom and pleasantness of the Pacific coast, in place of a fate like his which binds him closely to a routine life in England. How can there be any question between the rest and gladness of true home life, and this enforced wandering? You feel with me that the gain is all in the settled life?"

"No," answered Ultimata, "I am not sure that the real gain is altogether in that life. To home-loving natures like yours and mine, the pleasantness is doubtless there. I always feel that the perfect earthly experience, so far as having my intuitive longings met, would have been a daughter's place in one of those English country homes (not among the titled and undoubtedly aristocratic), but an inherited home of outward space and inner culture, with possibility of generous, gracious hospitality, and environment of park-like greenness and beauty. I can see the home, set in lawns and gardens, with drawing-room, low windowed, opening on calm, green vistas; with library shadowy and somewhat shabby, as of room where many lives had found rest and refuge; and with stables holding fine horses, responsive to touch and mood.

"There I should have matured, with a short season every year in London for the galleries and theatres, but with life rooted in the country home; with dear familiar neighbours, my own poor visited in the village, and children known and loved in those cottage homes; and the grey, ivy-grown Gothic church giving to the spirit its ritual of comfort and hope. Then I should have married the son of the squire, whose place adjoined our own, and found in marriage not so much change as a deepening and broadening of the maiden life. I should have known every tree by heart, the light with which the sun touched the hills, and the way the cool, grey fog wrapped in mystery their low, wooded crests.

"I should have found calm in the home-like culture, the steadfast green of fields, and the cool, vaporous distance: I should have had that unperturbed joy of loving a near, close circle, of resting in positive duties and in familiar pleasures; and should have known pain only by sympathy with the more refined forms of suffering. I should have escaped the uprootings of frequent change, the pain of loving with a constant heart but an inconstant fate, of feeling in every greeting the foreshadowing of farewell; have been spared the intensity of pain which comes from knowing life in its utmost pressure, its utter failure. But I should have missed the broadened knowledge of humanity, the quickened joy in its triumphs, the deepened sympathy with its defeats. There is a temptation to selfishness in those unshaken, ancestral homes, which I should not have resisted with my ease-loving nature; so I am glad that I was not allowed to drift in cool shadows on inland river, but have tossed in mid ocean, have felt the strength and awfulness of life's stormiest surge."

"I am not sure," answered the Spectator, "that I see the gain of a quickened emotional nature, without a broadened field of action. If one's power of sympathy is adjusted to the claims of duty in one's own life, does it not give more assured strength than this intensity of feeling, which only results in a sense of personal inadequacy to lessen by any real helpfulness, this awful aggregate of suffering?"

"I do not think," said Ultimata, "that one can comprehend aright a single nature, without some sympathetic insight into humanity itself, through varied experience and broadened sympathy. We are the result of so many forces, harmonious and antagonistic, that I almost feel that we miss the meaning of our own lives, unless we have touched nearly and strongly the lives of others. Therefore I rejoice in one way in the changes and dislocations of my own experience, though I crave rest and calm."

"But after all," asked the Spectator, "since life can only give a certain power of development within absolute limitations, must not that development be finer from experiences in harmony with one's natural longings, than in antagonism towards them?"

"I believe not," replied Ultimata, "if enjoyment were the end of life, it would be better met by an experience fulfilling our desires and in accordance with our instinctive tastes: but if the value of life is the possibility of development, then I comprehend the need of adverse experiences. In truth, I am struck by the fact that life usually forces upon us duties which demand the exercise of powers in which we are not strongest. I have known so many dreamy natures, thrust by relentless destiny into the current of life's activities, where the practical power, the strength of resistance must be developed, and the visionary imagination be disciplined: and I have watched ardent, impulsive natures, thrilling with eager ambition and richly dowered with positive power, restrained and repressed, by inexorable fate, until in that weariness of waiting the passive virtues of patience and fortitude had full development.

"Look at our two friends to-day. The Crusader, a born fighter, to whom life was trumpet-call to action and conflict, is now withdrawn from all fields of warfare, all glory of leadership; and Lorelei, the dreamer and visionary, needs the quickening of strong emotion, the pressure of positive duty. The one, active by temperament, must accept for a time the flag of truce and learn the lessons of peace; and the passive nature must find her own spirit a battle field."

"I cannot fancy Lorelei swept by strong feeling," said the Spectator, "she is so charming in her calm. I should not like her picturesque repose disturbed by any dramatic intensity."

"As an artist you are right," answered Ultimata. "For an artistic study she is perfect in her dreamy, slumberous charm; but as a woman she would be richer, fuller, deeper, with stronger heartbeat and more human warmth. Was she not a vision of loveliness last night?"

The night before there had been an unusually gay dance, and my eyes delighted in the individual charm, and the harmonious blending of colour in the costumes, of the dancers. Artista was in white satin, looking as stately as Juno with her erect height, her fine features and coronal of black hair. Perdita was in pink, with over-dress of white lace and blush roses; like the purity of maidenhood, just flushed with the warmth of womanly feeling. Lorelei was in a sweeping costume of old gold satin, and brocade of sea green and gold; cool in shadow but lustrous with colour in strong light. She wore exquisite lace and a long pendant necklace of amber: not clear amber like my beads of tranced sunlight, but the opaque, with translucent light and dim cloudings. She danced twice, once with the Spectator, and they looked well together, he dark and fine-featured and she a vision of golden light and green shadow. Once she danced with the Fairy Prince who evidently admires her, but with a cool, critical calmness which surprised me until Dorothy illumined my darkness, "Why, Mamma, they are from the same world and know all about each other: the Fairy Prince will not be charmed as humans are, for he knows all about sea maidens and sirens: I suppose they smile a little at each other, and wonder at meeting in the real world. But the Fairy Prince must waken a Sleeping Beauty into life with his kiss, and Lorelei must charm a human spirit to rest."

After the two dances and a chat with me, the

Crusader tempted Lorelei to a walk on the porch in the moonlight (I believe that it is always moonlight when they walk). As they stood in the door, while he with light chivalrous touch wrapped the clinging, white crape shawl about her, I thought, could you see them, you would feel that my Californian Idyll does not fail in strength of hero, or grace of heroine.

The ride was Saturday—On Sunday Lorelei went alone to Mass, and seemed to me to be strangely silent and shrouded. In the evening, after many voices had joined in the grand old hymns of Cowper and Toplady, Lorelei was begged to sing. With simple grace she yielded and sang with pathetic wistfulness of tone "Stabat Mater Dolorosa", then lifted her voice with the high spiritual triumph of the "Magnificat".

Lorelei is by manifest destiny a Catholic. In singing the hymns of the Church she interprets the spirit of its traditions; and Incarnation, Immaculate Conception, Transubstantiation, seem all the uplifting of dim, prayerful vision towards the veiled mystery of eternal truth. I watched covertly the Crusader's face as she sang. He rejects all the dogmas which she holds with unquestioning faith, but he lifts with her power of spiritual yearning, and I know that he truly worshipped as the low, vibrant tones of her voice lingered on the stately cadences of the Latin lines.

The next day, Lorelei, with Mater Violetta and Perdita, went with Artista to the ranch for a week's visit. I am glad that they parted, for I think love has often freer, finer spiritual development in absence. In the presence of the beloved, there is an element of physical charm, the warmth of touch, the light of the eye, the appeal of the voice; but in separation nature is revealed to nature, and it is easier to know how far the feeling is mere glamour cast upon the senses, and how far true, spiritual unity.

The Crusader, in Lorelei's absence, has relapsed into his genial companionship with the old circle; but with a change of mood to which I am very sensitive, through all the story telling and fun with the children, the easy chat or long arguments with Themis, the Spectator and myself. Before, he gave himself lavishly, unconsciously, blossomed out into war reminiscences, political creed or social theory. Now, he gives himself consciously, determinedly, with a resolve to live still a free, full life.

Before, he owned his own life, and controlled its manifestations with pleasant sense of his own strength of nature, his own power of expression. But his life now has, I think, its root in his love for Lorelei; and until he owns her there is loss of unity, a lack of perfect command over his own deep, intense nature. I feel the effort, the will power, now, in his companionship, where there was spontaneity and impulse. I notice, strange to say, in all his conversation, a coldness of intellectual conviction, instead of the old sympathetic warmth, as if his heart were withdrawn, held apart from his power of thought. I felt before, in all his opinions an almost emotional intensity, as if, woman-like, he thought through his heart, as well as with his head: but now there is a controlled reserve in his expression as if he watched with sense of conscious weakness his own heart, and laid a cooling hand on his own fevered thought.

For the last week before leaving I saw much of Lorelei. Sometimes I fancied a quickened feeling and perceptible warmth, as if her nature were truly touched, then again was baffled by the subtle spiritual haze in which she veils herself. Towards the Crusader, I noticed a change of manner, in the loss of her girlish ease, her ready appeal as to an old-time friend. I thought it was perhaps her womanly defiance against the deepened tenderness of his bearing towards her; for, though cold and proud in her absence, in her presence there was a thrill in his voice, a light in his eye, which no watching on his part could repress. But, with his lofty pride, I fear the chilling effect of her changed manner, her almost studied reserve. Will he think that it means indifference? Interpreted by my own woman nature, it means Lorelei's consciousness of her own change of attitude towards him. He is to her no longer the school friend's father, but the intense ardent lover—not a placid memory, but a strong personality—perhaps resistless Fate.

CHAPTER XXVIII

FOREBODING

I WISH that I had written a love story of my own, instead of waiting for real life to perplex me with one to be studied in enigmatical smiles, in unrevealing eyes, and the baffling personality of a Lorelei. I generally comprehend by intuitive glance the nature of a woman, and thrill with responsive sympathy to her variations of mood; and I generally (so asserts the Scientific Authority of our family) fail to reach the motive power in a man's life. But now I feel in touch with the Crusader's thought and feeling; and strangely alien to the chill fog in which the siren shrouds herself. I was on the porch, sitting with the Crusader, when the ranch party returned. I saw the flame leap in his eye, the colour mount to his cheek: then in an instant he stepped forward with his usual knightly grace to help the ladies from the carriage. Not a tremor stirred his proud, soldierly strength as with gay smile and courteous greeting he offered his hand to each. Lorelei was the last to leave the carriage;

and I admired the masterly self-control as with the same smiling ease he held her gloved hand for an instant, and said laughingly, "A week of ranch life, and not a touch of sunburn to tell the story! California sunlight should be discouraged at your defiance."

Truly, she looked as if no glow of sunshine, no flame of passion could quicken her to responsive warmth. It was late in the afternoon and cool in driving. Lorelei, whose costumes are always revelations of herself, was in a long, simple robe of grey cashmere (she never wears a short dress, but always gives the sweeping grace of a clinging train). It fell in straight, severe folds, giving her slender figure a look of added height. She wore a chinchilla shoulder cape, with its cloudlike shadings, and a sea gull toque. She looked herself indeed like a grey sea bird against the cold unlighted evening sky—for the sunset missed its southern glow.

I felt my own cheek burn with quick resentment, that in the home-coming (for it should be home to come back to him) there was no sympathetic flush of colour in ribbons at her throat, if not of feeling in her cheek. So pale, so phantom-like, so passionless she seemed, that I rose to meet her as one in sleep, half conscious of the unreality of the dream world. But her face lighted as she turned it towards mine, with almost infantile sweetness. I felt as I sometimes do towards Dorothy in her caprices, uncertain whether to scold or kiss her.

Could it be that she would pass like twilight

wraith or incarnate sea fog, and leave this intense, vital nature touched with deathly chill? Not the chill of death—the Crusader would never die of heart-break at a woman's feet. He will live in proud, defiant daring, but without that smile and glance which seem to have the gladness of immortal youth. If she pass, without flame of feeling to leap and meet his own, he will find life's autumn, and bear no more in his heart the eternal summer. He too will learn that the day has twilight and the year its fall of leaf, and that at last, wearied and chill, one seeks the comfort of kindled fire and lighted lamp. With his own intense vitality he has not needed yet to turn with conscious lack towards the hearth-light glow, in which tired, discouraged lives lose their sense of cold loss and twilight gloom. His life has been warm always with the flame of his own being. The world is full of grey, unlighted lives: I could not bear to see his life burn dim, or flicker into uncertainty of shadow. But if the Lorelei's heart is unwarmed, his spirit will turn pale with chill and loss.

That evening we sat in full circle in the dim drawing-room, with the firelight on the group of faces, familiar and fair in its shining. Artista and Perdita were in animated talk with the Spectator and Fairy Prince. Lorelei, in shadowy grey and white crape, with the fire-light touching her hair to a halo, looked like a twilight phantom, too unreal for home hearth.

I was not in mood for talking, so leaned back

FOREBODING

in my easy chair, hearing broken words of talk about me, studying the expression of the faces in the fitful gleams of the flame on the hearth, and feeling through the warmth and pleasantness a chill at heart, a faint foreboding. I looked at Lorelei with a wistful yearning to hold her myself so close and warm that the hidden heart would stir, and reveal itself in gracious glow towards that other life which waited its full unfolding.

I remember in my talk with the Crusader in the early days of our friendship, that he had told me that Guercino's Sibyl at Rome was his ideal woman: grand in nature, heroic in strength, with daring to utter the full word of truth given to her spirit. He spoke of having admired always the imperial type of woman, with power of command and lips of resolute will, as well as of tender sensitiveness. I smiled at his ideal, as in the soft dreamy light I studied Lorelei in her faint, indeterminate style of beauty, so suggestive, so unsatisfying. In expression, though not in colouring, I thought her in the grey shadowy robe and clinging white drapery, like one of Leonardo da Vinci's studies, with tremulous, visionary grace, subtle spirituality of smile, and mystic shadowed brow, cloudlike and unreal, as if uncertain of its own message, bearing not clear prophecy but pale premonition of truth.

At last Ultimata spoke, in answer to her own thought, not to any outward word, and said, " I am reading Hegel's 'Philosophy of History', and I find it luminous with thought. He treats the story of humanity as the development of Spirit, the justification of God in history. In his interpretation of the true Theodicæa I read the message of each nation given in its literature, its art, its form of government, to humanity. I watch the development of each race into full strength to utter in absolute harmony with its elements and environments its one sure word of truth, its sentence in the unfolding gospel of life—and then by destiny of death, the decadence when that word is spoken. That philosophy gives glorious harmony to divergent national development, and incomplete systems of faith. It is I believe also true, or should be, of individual life. The victory or defeat must be the power to give one's message, or the failure to find voice for its utterance. Lives divide themselves into the articulate and the inarticulate."

"I cannot conceive of any intelligence failing to express itself," said Themis. "Every act, every opinion, every emotion must prove the formulating power of the nature. There are varied gifts in the one accepted expression of language, but life I think must give firm, true outline of character and feeling."

"It would," remarked the Crusader, "if each nature were a unity; but each is complex and sometimes fails in controlling power to hold its own elements in harmonious form. Then this expression is broken, interrupted, incoherent. We are keen in our criticism of incertitude of nature and contradiction in utterance; but might be more charitable if we were philosophical in our recognition of the truth that each individual is an aggregate of the tastes and tempers, the moods and meanings of ancestral lives. With some, individuality is so strong, that it moulds into clear significant form these inherited elements: with others, from lack of will power or failure in that subtle something which we call personality, natures are a chaos of possibilities, never an ordered and unified cosmos. Such lives are embryonic on earth, holding promise but missing fulfilment."

"Should one," asked Lorelei, turning to Ultimata, "accept the inarticulate fate, or seek always some power of utterance?"

"I think," said Ultimata, with a tone of conscious bitterness in her voice, "that some lives are inarticulate from a kind of spiritual selfishness. They never choose to hear clearly their own message, so never utter it with full meaning. They miss themselves who have not faith and feeling to give themselves to others. I have tender sympathy with lives inarticulate by destiny, but fierce resentment towards those who, with power of articulation, fail in clear, decisive utterance."

"You must have gloried," broke in the Spectator, who had just joined our circle, "in Ruskin's recognition of the power of women in art in the last Slade Lecture. With your love for Ruskin you must be touched by this recantation of his."

"Yes," answered Ultimata, "and he retracts with such nobility of nature, such chivalry of bearing. Not that Ruskin ever valued woman lightly: he only outlined her vaguely, and the power he gave her was so subtle and spiritual as to be difficult of recognition and almost to justify an indirect and aimless life."

"Are you speaking," asked Themis, "of his general tone towards woman, or of some individual delineation of her?"

"I can only speak from dim memory," admitted Ultimata, "but his strongest statements are I think in 'Sesame and Lilies': in his lecture on 'Queens' Gardens'. I remember his beautiful tribute to woman's moral power, making her the world's spiritual magnet with unvarying truth of direction; but his idea of woman's education as outlined there, seemed not positive achievement or accomplishment, but broadest power of sympathy."

"Surely that must please you," said Lorelei, "you insisted only the other day, when I was defending cold-heartedness as a kind of spiritual armour to be wisely worn in self-defence, that power of sympathy was the measure of life. Then an education which develops power of sympathy must give the truest life."

"I believe," replied Ultimata, "that the end of all true education must be broadened sympathy: but to make such sympathy the practical aim of education would be to sacrifice singleness of purpose, and definiteness of power. How educate a woman at all, if the education is to be only quickened power of sympathy with the life of an uncertain husband of unknown profession? I do think too definite a line of education for both man and woman might limit the broad, common field of human experience and sympathy. I do also believe that a deepened, broadened nature is greater gain than mere scholarship. But scholarship we can reach by known paths and with results of intelligence and independence. Sympathy is not so much the aim of education, as the spirit of living. And I am sure the creative intellect, the artistic culture, the truth of touch, which Ruskin praises in women artists, will not lessen that womanly power of sympathy, but give to it finer expression and more helpful utterance.

"Elizabeth Thompson's heroic power he must feel, but I was doubly glad of his recognition of Miss Alexander, because it is justice to her delicate truthfulness and deep sympathy as artist and woman, and it is peace-offering to America also. He has been untender towards our youth, unloving towards our isolation. It is doubtless loss to the intellectual richness and art culture of a nation to have birth in the New World, on broad continent, unhaunted by tradition, unconsecrated by history. But it is a grand open field for political experiment. And it is true that we are 'making history', and I believe in humanitarian spirit and to heroic ends."

"You have the characteristic American sensitiveness to criticism," remarked the Crusader, "you watched our Nation through its awfulness of conflict, you felt the strength of its arm, you were part of its dauntless heart and its daring blood; yet you shiver at a stranger's adverse judgment."

"No, not at a stranger's," answered Ultimata. "But I have suffered at Ruskin's condemnation of us, for he is no student of mere external forms, but a discerner of the spirit both of men and nations. He has too long interpreted to me the symbolism of art, and the soul of nature to seem a stranger to me. I have lifted so often with the power of his inspiration, that I must feel the chill of his disowning and alienating touch upon our American life. He has helped me even in my comprehension of woman herself; for after all intellectual development, her real greatness will still be spiritual—her power more sympathetic than creative. She will be oftener the inspiration to achievement than achievement itself. I should like Ruskin to look towards our young, full, but still material life with a smile of hope."

"I would be contented with America without Ruskin's smile," said the Crusader, "as the world's field for the best and boldest political experiments of all time; as the emancipator of humanity. If we were worthy of our heritage of perfect spiritual freedom and political equality; if we could hold our continent as the home of the labouring poor; if with a bold foreign policy, a reconstructed navy, full control of the Panama Canal, and the enforcement of the Monroe Doctrine, we might hope for untrammelled development on this unshadowed continent."

"If the Crusader has reached the Monroe Doctrine and the Panama Canal," observed the Spectator, "as a solitary and undefended Englishman I decide that it is bed-time. When you grow aggressively American I always say 'Good-night'; I am sure, from the generosity of your natures towards the absent and unrepresented that there is an immediate reaction in favour of Foreign Powers."

Themis soon left, and I lingered a time with Lorelei and the Crusader. I felt that my presence was a comfort to both: that in the atmosphere of our friendship there was an escape from the constraint and chill which seem to hold them apart. The Crusader's pride has given him a responsive dignity in place of the old familiar tenderness, since Lorelei has met him with closer veilings of reserve. In their first companionship there was the glad assured tone of the old friendship, when he was host and she fair, girlish guest.

After a little time of silence the Crusader spoke as if thinking aloud, "After all, there is little use in summing up the earthly total of gain in life's activity or outward expression; when we are all so conscious that the deepest feeling finds no utterance, and the highest thought no incarnation. The finite limitation is first relentless fate, then forces the escape of winged hope. Because the development is finite, we accept the partial and incomplete; but feel our protest against it as prevision and foreshadowing of the full and final expression in the Infinite."

"I am always puzzled in acceptance of the development theory," said Ultimata, " to understand the 'divine discontent'. It would seem that each stage of our progress, without ideal of a higher, would be complete and satisfactory in itself. Without the tradition of a fall from a higher estate, or the spiritual revelation of forms of life beyond the present, why should the spirit uplift with such passion of unrest and discontent?"

"There may be, and are, mysteries of faith," answered Lorelei, "but life and the problems of human nature are more difficult to understand without a revelation and the creed of the Church, than through their acceptance. A closer relation with higher powers, once held and lost, the yearning towards us of Divine Love, and our upreaching in penitence and prayer, explain the limitations of the physical and the longings of the spiritual nature, better than the doubt of scepticism or the darkness of materialism."

"Materialism," said the Crusader, "explains nothing. It is only a blind, dumb negation. I think that previous incarnations would explain many of the mysteries of life, and be a reconcilement between the theory of development and the spiritual hope; since in each finite birth and life, one might complete one form of development, and pass into a higher form, thus evolving always a finer, nobler nature. It would be development, not by death of the lower form, but by transmigration of the freed spirit into higher existence."

"But," protested Ultimata, "an eternity of isolated finite experiences, each developing some faculty or feeling, but with no conscious, continuous identity, would be little more comforting than annihilation. It would be like a perpetual series of to-days with no memory of yesterdays. Such belief might explain faint, visionary gleams which haunt us of past experiences, and dim longings towards other developments, but it holds no promise of fully rounded completeness of life."

"If such incarnations are the mode of life, and method of individual development," responded the Crusader, "then without doubt when a certain series of finite experiences had broadened and purified the nature, in a higher life would be memory and recognition of these lower and imperfect forms of existence, and they would stand revealed as connected parts of the soul's complete cycle of experience."

"Perhaps in a series of incarnations," remarked Lorelei, "the lingering memory of the last life, or the foreshadowing of the coming fate, might sometimes give an unreality to the present experience. I often feel as if I were hardly awake, between two weird, bewildering dreams. What have I been, and what shall I be? Tell me that and I shall perhaps know what I am."

"You were a mermaid in the last, you will be a warm-blooded woman in the next; now you are a siren charmed by her own song, an unloving, but much-loved Lorelei," answered Ultimata laughing.

The Crusader turned on Ultimata his blue eyes, grown cold, steel grey, then said to Lorelei, "I see no transmigrations of spirit from form to form, but only migrations from place to place; Psyche, the winged maiden, untouched by human passion, the last estate: the next Psyche awakened and uplifted to the immortal gods; now Psyche in the dim, shadowy realm where in exile she sought Persephone, and won the box of mystical ointment, to faint with the spicy odours, and the strange awfulness of the nether world."

"Thanks," replied Lorelei, "but with my fondness for shadow, I fear that I should linger long in the dimness of Hades, without memory of the butterfly freedom, or any longing towards the immortal uplifting."

"But you must review your mythology," added Ultimata, "you will not win your own release. Psyche suffered lonely exile in Plutonian shadows, when she would look with mortal eyes on her immortal lover. But in her faint, phantom wanderings she was touched and thrilled by Eros into full-hearted life, and by him uplifted from depths and dimness of Hades to the snow heights and immortal light of Olympus."

"I have always had a horror," retorted Lorelei, "of the Chatauqua course with the text books and diplomas, and a misty reverence for the Summer School of Philosophy at Concord, but really the Esperanza is a blending of both. In spite of myself I am studying mythology, theology, philosophy and political economy. To-morrow I shall swing all day in the hammock, and Dorothy and I will tell fairy stories."

CHAPTER XXIX

MESMERISM

THE next outing was a surprise to us all. Coming out from lunch Brownie and Oscita were waiting. "With whom are you going to ride, Dorothy?" I asked. "I did not order Oscita."

"That is a secret, Mamma, but you can wait and see us start."

So I located myself in my favourite wicker rocking-chair. Soon Lorelei appeared in riding habit. The two selfish equestriennes were met by a chorus of reproaches at not making up their party publicly and including us in their comradeship, for Artista, Perdita and the Crusader were on the porch.

But Lorelei said, "This is a pilgrimage of the faithful: only Dorothy and I really believe in fairy land, and we are going this afternoon across the border into the wonder world. Nominally we shall ride in Cold Spring Cañon."

"I believe this is not your first trip into the mystic realm," said Ultimata. "Your eyes are like Kilmeny's when she came back in the gloaming after seven years with the fairies. But then those who go too often are held captive at last; so ride home before the twilight falls. I cannot spare Dorothy to 'the good folks' though I give them faith and welcome always in our own hearth-light. I am not a sceptic, Dorothy knows, only an unfortunate 'grown up' with loss of spirit vision, but longing still of the child heart. Oh! Dorothy, to think that you would leave me at home!"

"Now, Mamma, you must not be jealous: you often tell me that selfishness and jealousy are apt to be the faults of an only child, I am afraid sometimes they are the faults of an only mother too. I tell you so many stories and you shall have a new one to-night; but Lorelei and I are going to have real Arabian Nights of our own." So off they rode in triumph at the success of their selfish plot.

That evening Dorothy joined us in the drawing-room, but we pleaded in vain for the promised stories. The two invaders of Elf-land only looked unutterable things, with interchange of mystical smiles and mysterious glances. With failure to elicit any clear historical facts regarding "the wee folks", from the returned pilgrims, the talk drifted towards fairies, brownies, the banshee and ghosts. The Crusader said, "I am afraid that the advent of the electric light will send the fairies into final exile. The modern world is too strongly flooded with scientific light to give dim shadowy spots for their conclaves."

"But no illumination can banish mysticism from

the mind," answered Ultimata. "George Macdonald, Mrs. Oliphant, and Elizabeth Phelps all know life through the revelations of second sight, and America 'without castle or ruins' has produced the mind of weirdest ghostliness and most unlighted depths, in Hawthorne, who saw shadows outlined with human clearness, and living men faint and impalpable as shadows."

"But," asked Themis, "do we not all feel the unreality of this writing in our own days, and rather yield to its charm like some masquerade in which we drape modern life in quaintness of mediæval costume? Is it not like our phantom party, when we lose individuality for an hour under white shroudings, but feel all the time how warm, how human the real personal life is; and are only mildly amused, but never really chilled or mystified by the artificial ghosts?"

"I suffered," confessed Ultimata, "creeping chill of apprehension and absolute agony in reading Mrs. Mulock Craik's 'Alice Learmont'. There was the pain and peril of a soul's birth in the human child winning its way from the gaiety and glamour of the fairy world back to the homely duties and the mother heart, in the earthly cottage home. I shivered and cried as I read it; then felt my life flooded with the rapture of assured motherhood, when the brave, beleaguered maiden, tired, tearful but triumphant rested in the mother's arms."

"How strongly pain seems the foundation of all our conceptions of growth and development," said the Crusader. "Even the suffering which comes through sin at last overcome and outlived, seems more helpful to spiritual strength than unstirred calm. The mystery of the existence of evil in the universe is not greater than the mystery of its unfolding in human nature new depths of tenderness and new breadth of sympathy. However we reject the early myths, one stands endorsed by the records of humanity; that experience of sin becomes in some way the broadening of the spiritual horizon, by which comes the knowledge of good and evil. For all evil seems an experiment of the spirit towards expansion, an effort towards broadened, deepened life, a protest against finite limitations. It is the soul's defiant refusal to accept certain boundaries, recognised by custom and law, as needful to the safety of the earthly condition. It is hurtful, often fatal to the wise development of life in harmony with mundane conditions, but gives without doubt that knowledge which is the discerning of good and evil."

"No theological statement of the awfulness of sin," said Ultimata, "and no philosophical unfolding of its ultimate power in intensifying and spiritualising the nature, has ever interpreted its mystery to me so fully as Hawthorne's 'Marble Faun', where, through one act of wrong-doing, the recognition of its significance and the acceptance of its penalties, Donatello, from a sportive faun, becomes a self-conscious man."

"I have heard," observed the Spectator, "Ultimata's defence of high-spirited murder and low-spirited suicide, and various other social crimes now classified by me as 'Ultimata-peccadilloes', but I am not prepared for this alliance of powers in defence of evil in the abstract."

"I do not defend it," answered Ultimata, "but only accept it, as the ordained plan of development, through evil to higher good."

"But," asked Themis, "would not this theory glorify sin as the path of spiritual development, and make evil the condition of conscious acceptance of God?"

"I believe," answered the Crusader, "that there are natures with spiritual genius, who gain intuitively their apprehension of truth, without the need of personal knowledge of evil, its sense of alienation from, and its later deepened recognition of the Eternal Good; as those of intellectual genius gain by sympathy and imagination, that which lesser, lower lives reach only through individual experience. But to deny the educational possibility of evil and its power of spiritual enlightenment, would be to doom humanity to hopeless darkness, since sin and suffering are so universal that to miss development through their existence, would be to most natures, life's final defeat and loss."

"I feel," said Lorelei, "that the need of personal experience to learn the lessons of evil, and to consciously accept the good, is fully met by the prayers and sacraments of the Church, through which we claim the spiritual heritage of the ages."

"Yes," added the Spectator, who is most reverent towards Church creed, service and communion, "since we accept intellectually in literature and art the garnered wisdom of the ages; why deny to the spirit the possibility of equal gain, in the inner experience and the outward utterance of the Church? It offers a spiritual chart, showing the shallows and marking the reefs perilous to others: why choose to be wrecked by one's own experience in spiritual seamanship? This emphasised individualism will result in the disintegration of all form—it leads to agnosticism, communism, and the other 'isms' so dear to the American heart."

"Talking of 'isms', leads me to ask," said Ultimata, "whether you have all read the article in a late Nineteenth Century on 'Mesmerism'. The Crusader had quickened my interest in the subject, by confession of his own close study and critical observation of its phenomena. Among physicists, there is no question of the results of this mysterious power of mind upon mind, or personality upon personality; only a difficulty in analysing the power, and a difference in the scientific nomenclature."

"I hate the whole subject," proclaimed Themis vehemently, "it belongs to the realm of darkness, is part of the 'principalities and powers', which war against spiritual light. I do not disbelieve the existence of such force, but I distrust the rightfulness of its exercise."

"But its existence must prove the right of investigation," answered the Crusader, "since there can

MESMERISM

be no force or influence which is not part of the universal law. The danger is in wilful irrecognition or unwise exercise of such power."

"It is a fascinating subject," admitted Ultimata, "but seems to me full of spiritual peril. It leads to personal irresponsibility on one side, and to irresponsible power on the other. If there is loss of individuality, and possibility of misguidance in subjecting our lives to controlling influence in spiritual communion; that danger must be intensified in yielding to the domination of another mind, still held like our own under finite conditions, since we add a physical element to the peril of intellectual control."

"I can fancy," remarked Lorelei, "helpful development through mesmerism if one of vague temperament and uncertain thought, were touched and controlled by a master mind. It might give spiritual rest and concentration of power."

"Yes," said Ultimata laughing, "I can fancy the milky way under sufficiently strong magnetic influence, changing from nebulous stellar mist, to galaxy of clear, self-conscious stars."

"Your celestial pleasantry might prove scientific fact," observed the Crusader, "so little is known of magnetism, mesmerism, and other occult powers. The popular idea that mesmerism is the subjection of the weaker mind to the will-power of the stronger is erroneous. It is a sympathetic condition of mind with mind; but not of necessity, or generally, the domination of superior over inferior."

"But," argued Ultimata, "it is for the time being the abrogation of personal power, the abdication of the individual will. It is self-annihilation."

"Not more so than sleep," replied the Crusader, "to which you subject yourself with no loss of self-respect."

"It is true," confessed Ultimata, "that in sleep our mental faculties are not consciously controlled by reason, but we do not voluntarily accept the dictate or mood of some other mind."

"With the loss of consciousness, there can be no intelligent recognition of the power which dominates the mind in sleep," answered the Crusader, "but the dim memory of the dream world would often lead to the question as to whether in that passive and sensitive condition, we are not swept by spiritual influence and controlled by higher intelligence: only thus can we explain the premonitions and prophecies which have been given in dreams."

"Against such control we have no defence," said Ultimata, "since nature requires for life itself that passivity of condition in sleep, which may subject us to spiritual influence. But in mesmerism, we establish ourselves, by our acceptance of certain conditions, this relation between mind and mind which may lead to the absolute sway of one will over two natures."

"We do not, by the acceptance of conditions favourable to the development of mesmeric power establish the relation," answered the Crusader, "but only recognise a relation already existing; and I believe that the elucidation of the laws which govern spiritual affinity, in personal attraction, in magnetic power or mesmeric influence, would lead to finer social crystalisation, through helpful alliance in place of hurtful antagonism."

"Oh! that reminds me of the 'Ethics of the Dust'," cried Dorothy, " where one ounce of slime in a state of rest, by the law which attracts like to like, which the Professor (who is really Mr. Ruskin, and very funny and jolly with Egypt, Sibyl and the rest of the girls) calls the political economy of the law of co-operation, becomes a sapphire, an opal, and a diamond, set in the midst of a star of snow. I should not have remembered the hard name of the law, but you see it was all set round with jewels which kept shining in my mind."

"Nothing more in the way of illustration can be desired," said the Spectator, " since Dorothy evidently considers us in our present unmagnetised and unmesmerised condition, the original ounce of slime."

"Well, mesmerise and get crystalised," retorted the irrepressible Dorothy, who alone of us could bear personal testimony regarding the mesmeric influence. For, a few days before, she came in from a ride looking pale and tired; but she is a child incapable of rest, can never sleep in the day, and will seldom sit quiet unless most wakefully absorbed in a book. "May I hold Dorothy a moment by the fire?" asked the Crusader, "she looks cold and tired."

I assented, so she was instantly ensconced in his

lap, with her head on his shoulder. He stroked her forehead lightly, and, in a few seconds, I saw the eyes droop, then close with a restful look. I should have objected to any mesmeric experiment upon a child, but the light touch upon her brow had only been like an approach to paternal petting. She slept only two or three minutes, then unclosed her eyes in a wide open, fully-awake fashion, and said, "I believe that I had a nap, I feel so fresh and rested," and in truth she looked as if wakened from a night's sleep, so bright of face, so glad of voice: I thought the influence must have been tender and consoling, to give that sense of rest to the tired little life. I felt a hushed reverence for the strange power which could so gently cradle a child to sleep.

"Dorothy appreciates the value of spiritual law," said the Crusader. "She is the only fearless seeker of truth among us; trusts nature, keeps close to the heart of the roses, and believes in fairies. We are all too worldly wise in conceit to explore a new realm with faith and courage. Yet, in the course of human development, every fact must have recognition; and through the acceptance of facts new theories must have expression. We cannot make natural law, but only accept its manifestations. Nothing can be evolved, which in the creative plan was not first involved. Why fear any unfolding of fact, however unfamiliar, or of law, however alien to our accepted creed?"

"Is it not true," asked Themis, "that a knowledge of the laws of mesmerism would give immeasurable power to unscrupulous and ambitious minds, in schemes for the subjugation of those weak and dependent? What mental safety to any of us, if a developed mesmeric glance could control will-power and influence action?"

"And yet," said the Crusader, "we all brave that same power in social contact. The power not only in conversation, in oratory, in acting, is that subtle unmeasured influence of personal magnetism, but even in literature and art the same power is incarnate. By study of the laws of magnetism and mesmerism, we could control and modify the influence, recognise its power and its peril, and comprehend the elements in individual development which give assured strength and self-defence against invasive influence of others.

"To understand the spiritual cause of affinity and antagonism would be, as Dorothy said of the crystals, to be governed by 'the helpful law of co-operation'. All movement is from chaos towards order; but we can by cowardly, inert lives increase the confusion, or by brave, enlightened lives hasten the order of the cosmos."

"I think," remarked the Spectator, "that mesmerism may be a grand power in lessening physical suffering, if it can give rest by natural sleep in place of dependence upon nerve-shattering chlorals and bromides. It would surely be more comforting and helpful to rest from the soothing influence of another nature, than to seek unconsciousness by anodynes: but I should shrink from its influence except to lessen pain."

"But the lessening of pain is a broad field," rejoined the Crusader, "since it includes intellectual unrest and spiritual suffering. The magnetic or mesmeric influence might often hold the power of release from mental torture, or rest from soul weariness."

"But," protested Themis, "it is still a confession of weakness to escape from the pain of life by unconsciousness of self, and appropriation of the strength of another."

"I never feel," said Lorelei, "that unwillingness to confess weakness or seek strength. If an uncertain or undeveloped life longs for helpful power, a strongly dowered nature must long equally to give comfort and strength. There can be no loss in the sympathetic touch of generous strength upon appealing weakness."

"That is the true and eternal law of life," remarked the Crusader with a proud light in his eye, for Lorelei is a gracious listener, but seldom gives full expression to her feelings; and this intellectual assent to his thought, and its fine, feminine utterance, gave a more tender tone to his voice as he added, "If society gave the true adjustment of life to life, no outstretched hand would fail of strong responsive touch, no eye would lift with passionate appeal but to meet in answer a re-assuring glance, and the claim upon another strength, the acceptance of control from a firmer life, would not be loss of individuality, but a personality helpfully developed by its true relation with a more resolute will."

"I feel the truth of that," said Ultimata, "that rest and strength are in acceptance of just relation as ruler or ruled. There is only weakness in defiant rebellion against the facts of temperament and endowment which constitute inexorable fate. Once I felt in fierce pride of individuality, that I could never accept the mastery of another mind, or be reconciled to social subordination. I remember, as a child, in learning the Psalms, feeling a flame of indignation at the assertion that we are made 'a little lower than the angels'. I resented the classification. Why weariness of effort and patient endeavour, when doomed by destiny to something lower than angel-hood?

"But long ago, I learned that the joy of self-hood must be in just relation to other lives; in uplifting to the higher with glad reverence as well as down-reaching to the lower in generous sympathy."

"Still you do not bear very meekly, the suggestion of the supremacy of man," scornfully remarked the Crusader.

"I do not bear at all meekly his claim to superiority established by laws of his own making, and conditions of his own creation," retorted Ultimata. "But I would recognise with glad uplifting of my weaker life in appeal to his chivalrous strength, any inherent superiority of intellect and spirit. But I wish him to step down from his pedestal of political privilege and physical power, and measure fairly nature to nature. If in spirit stature he stand higher, I will not fail in reverence."

"But would you be willing in mesmerism to

accept the domination of another nature?" asked Themis. "I doubt it."

"I would accept the challenge to the contest of will with will, or personality against personality," answered Ultimata, "but I should probably hate the man or woman who mesmerised me."

"I can conceive no intellectual sensation so startling," observed the Crusader, "as to find you consistent in statement through one conversation. You have just glorified the strength and rest of finding one's true position in the rank of intelligences; but you would hate a man who proved, in mesmeric influence, his power to dominate you."

"I am not so inconsistent as you think," replied Ultimata, "but you fail in subtility of intellect to discern the connecting links between these statements. The rest is in the recognition of the rightfulness of the relation to those above and below: but you have asserted that the exercise of the mesmeric influence is not in strength of will, or superiority of intellect. I should be controlled by an unknown force, acting through a mind with no natural right to mastery over mine. I should hate him for the exercise of a power I could not disprove; but a power which did not justify itself by full, frank superiority of nature. I might love a man whose mesmeric influence I felt to be expression of finer spiritual force, of fuller intellectual power: but if with conscious equality or with superiority of endowment to him, I should be mesmerised, I should hate him as a protest of truth and

MESMERISM

honour against the unjustifiable tyranny by which he held me subject. I should think such hatred an expression of 'sweetness and light' against some power of darkness."

"I intended to suggest mesmeric experiments," said the Crusader, "but with Themis and Ultimata as allied antagonistic forces, it would require scientific faith and moral courage to face the humiliation of failure or the odium of success."

"You surely would not abandon your search after truth, for so trivial a reason as one woman's hatred," retorted Ultimata, "I think we should have a mesmeric séance."

The first subject was the Spectator, who faced the Crusader's constant intensity of gaze without visible effect. Themis declined personally to subject herself to the influence, though she was interested as observer in the manifestations of the power. Ultimata avowed her willingness at some future time to test her susceptibility to the influence; but confessed that she had talked herself into a mood of antagonism and self-assertion, which would render the experiment, for the time, futile. Lorelei yielded to the expressed wish of all that she should be the next subject.

An easy chair was moved for her near the piano, to withdraw her somewhat from the general circle, and a lamp placed near, with light full upon the faces of those engaged in the experiment. Lorelei was in a clinging robe of white nun's-veiling, unrelieved by any touch of colour. As she leaned back in the deep crimson chair, she looked more than ever like a fair, elusive vision. The Crusader sat opposite, and for five minutes held her hands and looked at her with earnest eyes. Then he rose and bent upon her a gaze of strangely concentrated power. I think the picture will never be dimmed in my memory, of the two in their new grouping. Lorelei was pale, calm, dreamy, with the usual half veiled expression in her unfathomable eyes. The Crusader looked strong, commanding, as he stood with eyes riveted upon her face with that intensity of expression. The lamp made a circle of light about them, and the picture suggested a scene in some mediæval tower. She looked like fair, spell-bound captive, and he like astrologer holding the secret of the stars, or alchymist with power by triumphant touch to turn all earthly dross to virgin gold.

He was not the familiar friend, not the brilliant antagonist nor the ardent crusader. He looked so intensified, so uplifted, that I recalled his own statement made once in answer to the suggestion that mesmerism might be used for ignoble ends. He avowed his belief, that the mesmeric power could only be exerted by its possessor, upon the highest plane of his being intellectual and spiritual; and that the influence emanating from the nature in that exalted condition, must be in harmony with truth and purity. He stood, with that down-looking gaze, like a steady flame touching with heat and light her pure, upturned face another five minutes, then made two or three passes in the air above her head.

Her eyes drooped, and she rested in the most tranquil, childlike sleep, a smile on her sensitive lips.

A hush fell upon the room, as if we were all tranced in a dream. The Crusader watched Lorelei, but with a quiet rested look upon his own face, free from all tension of strong feeling or concentrated willpower. Soon he made two or three upward passes. She gave a quick, almost ecstatic sigh, then opened her eyes but with a faint, far-away expression, as if she had not yet broken the spell which held her. But presently she smiled and said, "I believe the mesmeric influence is a potent sleeping potion; I think that I shall say good-night," so she rose, turned upon the Crusader a questioning look as if to determine the new relation between them, swept us all with a courteous glance, crossed the room with her unconscious grace and vanished, leaving us all somewhat dazed after the strange experience.

We said "Good-night" and parted; but I lay long awake, wondering how far that mystic influence of nature upon nature would disclose to each the inner life of the other: whether by that finer touch, that subtler communion, spirit would be revealed to spirit without that mist of doubt, that cloud of misapprehension which shrouded them. Was the mesmerised, in that strange sleep, held with dulled faculties and dimmed vision, or was that trance, by the withdrawal of the spirit from earthly environment and from thraldom of the senses, an uplifting into larger life, with finer intuition and power of unveiled vision?

CHAPTER XXX

THE SHADOW OF PARTING

SANTA BARBARA sunshine has been shadowed for me these last days, for across the outward glory creeps the dimness of personal loss and pain. I have lived here like a child, content to gather fresh roses every day: not clinging as is my heart's fashion, with sense of pathos to the faded yesterdays, or outreaching to the folded future. I have only longed to draw into this sunlight and beauty those dear to me, and then to linger tranced in this southern dream. Can you fancy the blessedness of never shivering with apprehension of the winter chill and death; to be glad in summer; with no flushing of hectic red across the autumn leaf, to foretell its fading, and the sadness of the bare, bereaved earth?

Then autumn loss and winter gloom are touched with a sadness not their own. The seasons are so symbolic of the human life, from its unfolded hope to its falling snow, that while we quicken in gladness with the world in its young leaf, and bloom with the summer's blossoming, we feel, as the years touch us with loss, more sympathetic sadness with the autumn's dying and the winter's death. It is a joy to escape the symbolism of change and decadence. Nature here does not accentuate the human fate of falling leaf and shrouding snow. The finiteness of life is less sorrowfully felt, where sunlit year is added to sunlit year, like beads on an amber rosary, with sacred meaning to each bead, and a glow and gladness of conscious light to the lengthening thread, which slips through reverent hand with voiceless prayer, or vocal praise.

But, in the sterner northern world, with its fixed limits of times and seasons, life is a Via Crucis, with solemn stations to mark the distance trodden and the lessening length of penitential path.

I am stirring with unrest through the pleasant calm, as when the keen morning light with unfriendly insistence pierces some fair dream with wakening sense of unreality. I have touched with transient thrill of ecstasy my ideal love, this Valley of my heart's prevision; but I may not hold it mine by outward right, in visible home. I am glad not to linger, since I feel the shadow of parting, the inevitable pain of uprooting. I am used to goodbye and to greeting, to missing the familiar and facing the unknown, to all the vicissitudes of a wandering life. But I have lived here in an unquestioning faith, an unreasoning rapture, as beneath a new heaven and upon a new earth, where the record should not be, and the morning and the evening were the day. But I know the end of my glad day now, by the short, sudden twilight, the grey ghostly gloom, in which I miss the strength of mountains and the calm of sea. I feel bewildered and astray, pale and still, as in the coming of night when we wandered on the hills, without road or trail, beyond the shining of home fire, or gleam of lighted lamp. The fiat of change snaps the circle of our companionship.

Themis will be the first to go, and she is firm foundation and unshaken wall in our social structure. But she leaves Santa Barbara gladly, since she returns to her own, and to Boston life with its art advantages and intellectual atmosphere. Her only daughter—who has been abroad studying art and gives great promise in her chosen career—is now on her way home from Germany with her father, who crossed to take a short trip and return with her. Themis hoped they would join her for a few months here, that her return to New England might be in summer pleasantness, not in late autumn. But the daughter—ardent in her devotion to art, and impatient to begin the independent life of action after the student years—has plans for studio life, this winter. So Themis will leave in a few days, facing in the future that which alone is fairer than Santa Babara's utmost glory of sunlight, the shining of home faces. To her strong nature, positively outlined character, and eager intellect, Santa Barbara does not give the joy which makes it so perfect to an aimless dreamer like myself. She is often restive in its calm, almost resentful towards the physical fairness, which wins one to forgetfulness of the world's thought and action. She likes the quick pulsing of life, the strong, conscious heart-beat in some centre of culture.

I know that it is well for her to be part of the strong tidal movement of life on the Atlantic coast; not lightly swayed by the gentle lapping of southern sea on sunlit shore. To me, her presence and friendship have been as invigorating as high mountain air, or strong salt breeze; and to the companionship of our circle she has given always the strength of unwavering conviction, of unfaltering will. And her strength has an element of hopefulness which gives to her intellectual power an expression of almost girlish gladness. She is the only one of our circle with native gaiety of heart. Then, her life has outward spaciousness, and much shining of clear sunlight; so she is warm and ripened in nature, with a glow at heart as well as surface gladness. She is very popular socially, from her youthfulness of spirit, her charm of personality; but feared as a critic from the keen flame in her brilliant eyes, and from the relentless sense of justice which makes her, at times, ruthless in judgment.

The Spectator, happier in fate, will find home in this valley. Since his health forbids life in England, he chooses Santa Barbara after years of world-wide wandering, and will love his new home with ideality of artist spirit and stability of English nature. He will accept his American fate and fortune with sweet hopefulness and frank friendliness of heart; but never relax his hold upon the dearer memories of his English past. I honour the spirit of faith in which he faces life, as holding still true gain of culture and of sympathy. But I honour still more the loyalty of heart in which he shrines the holier gifts of love and joy in a home now his in earthly memory and in eternal hope. Our friend has bought a charming little ranch in the Montecito Valley. It was a great pleasure to ride with him to see the new place. He seemed glad, rested, already at home in spirit; for he has an Englishman's fondness for a foothold upon the earth. The house and grounds are exquisite in taste—worthy of artist ownership.

The Cottage is a long, low structure with pretty porch and bay window; in two shades of grey, with high water-tower and windmill of the same colour. It stands in a young olive grove with its faint, silvery foliage, and at the side a group of live oaks with bank sloping to a stream, or in the dry season to the stony bed of a stream. There is a charming view of the sea over sweep of cultivated fields, and the house faces the mountains with poetic glimpses of their near grandeur, through the orchards and groves of this Arcadian Valley.

I am sorry that we leave too soon to see the Spectator in his new character as host at Warwick Ranch. But a bunch of fragrant violets came to me the other day, as breath of welcome to the beauty and bloom of the new home.

"Westward our Star of Empire will" not "take its way," so we shall turn our faces eastward, where fixed stars shine in home faces for us. I mourn more for Dorothy's loss than my own. One in the working years of life (though missing the working mood) could scarcely hope for more than such dream of joy in which to rest and be blessed, between the imperfect efforts of the past and the uncertain achievements of the future. But this is true child world, with undimmed blue of sky, low hills to climb, smooth white beach for joy of fearless dash, sea soft and caressing in measured movement, and opening buds for each unfolding day.

When I see Dorothy in this natural gladness, and think of her in the unlovely exile of city streets, I seem to see dramatised anew that old sad story of the garden's joy and the outer wilderness. She looks forward with faith to our sure return to an unchanged valley. But we, who have lived longer, know, that at the gate of every life experience, stands the invisible angel with flaming sword, forbidding all return to the lost Eden of the Past. When I see Dorothy sweep by on Brownie, I feel as if it were parting body and spirit to separate them: the little creature has danced, dashed and dared in such response to the mood of its reckless young rider.

There comes sometimes a sweet, strange sympathy of nature with our own experience of loss and longing. These last days, touched with a glow not alone of constant sun or of inconstant moon, are thrilling with a feeling not the joy of perfect light, nor the sudden gloom of southern twilight. Night after night, after the glory of sunset has faded from the west, the darkening sky thrills anew with some strange power of light. Sometimes it begins in a pale, pink flush which quickens into vivid crimson flame surging on tidal waves from west to east. Sometimes it is a swift, radiant triumph of yellow light over the coming darkness, until heavens and earth are flooded with golden glory. Again it is a pale, tender sea green, illumining the night sky, like subtle sense of joy.

Of course, scientists lay cold, critical instruments of record and measure against the heart of this mystery, and explain its ecstatic throb of pulsing colour. They say that it is the refracting power of clouds of volcanic dust from the Java eruption. To them it may be, but to me this mystical light has deeper meaning. It is spiritual ecstasy through earthly loss, it is premonition of the eternal day, through deathly darkness. This afterglow is a gleam across our human night of the near dawn of the immortal life.

We all walk out to watch this late, strange glory in the evening sky, and the transfiguration of the mountains in an unearthly vision of celestial light. I fancy that I can see in each face and feel in each nature, some faint hint of the unfolding of the Hereafter. Themis has a softened, spiritual beauty in her strong face, as of one uplifted by love; who, in that higher revelation, dares to be tender as well

THE SHADOW OF PARTING

as true. From the Spectator's face in this strange shining, lifts the cloud of natural reserve; and I discern the hidden strength, the repressed power of feeling, which will make in the full expression of the Beyond, his spirit's power glad surprise to the self of earthly limits and finite horizon.

The Crusader's face grows heroic in this light; as of one ordained to grander victory than that of remembered battle-fields, as conqueror in conflicts to eternal ends. His is always the face of fighter: but, in the revelation of the afterglow, it is lighted by the tender triumph of one who wins with light, against the leaguered powers of darkness. Lorelei's fair, unrevealing face in this mystic light shines with subtle, spiritual suggestions of her veiled, immortal self. She is no longer siren, with charm of beauty, spell of song, weaving about herself fantastic web of sea fog; but pale priestess beside dimly lighted altar, shrouded by the mystery of life, but with lifted face touched by the faith of her own luminous spirit.

Beside me always in this unearthly evening light is Dorothy, with child-face strangely grave, and in the large, full eyes a depth of feeling, a power of soul, which make me hold with closer clasp, the small, warm hand, and give to my kiss on the broad, strong brow a tender reverence of love. I do not hold with mother touch the child of to-day, nor kiss the forehead beneath which fairy stories and quaint little songs sleep and stir in dreams. I hold with largeness of love, with premonition of mother faith, the woman of the future; my lips thrill upon the brow, touched with faint, unfamiliar shadowings.—

I sigh, for the years weave many wreaths: of laurel, of willow, of thorn.

CHAPTER XXXI

THE LAST SYMPHONY

THEMIS leaves by the last boat south to-night, and we feel already as if we had lost her; for with final packing, and the looking in upon her of many Santa Barbara friends, we shall have only the hurried good-bye of the last moment. But last night we had a full, sweet evening's companionship, of all those who have touched most nearly in these months of Esperanza life. We all had a suppressed heart-ache I think, at the "beginning of the end", for this is the first break in our charmed circle. But Themis takes life with a gaiety of nature which lessens the pain of parting, or precludes the utmost expression of that pain. We gathered in the big, dim drawing-room, drew up the large easy chairs and rockers near the fire, and tried to feel as if the hearth flame and lamp light would shine still on the same group. Artista, who spends most of her time at the Esperanza, and so has watched the forming and breaking of many circles, said, "I hate to have my friends go, and I hate to see strangers come, who may win my heart, then break it again."

"Your heart bears so much breaking, my dear child," answered Themis laughing, "that I feel reasonable assurance that the fragments will soon assume a look of whole-hearted joy. One is not really missed in hotel life."

"Perhaps not in hotel life," said Ultimata, "but I hope that the companionship of our circle is not to be described as if on a level with the arrival of the omnibus, and the *menu* for the day. It does not matter greatly where natures chance to meet, if the touch is that of true friendship, and the relations not superficial contact, but intellectual sympathy."

"I feel assured," answered Themis, "that my loss is real, since I leave the circle in which has been developed so much pleasant social life: but with the coming and passing of many guests, there will be always here new elements of interest and new possibilities of companionship."

"I wonder," remarked the Fairy Prince, "from my standpoint, that of the many who casually meet in a resort like this, so few form true, recognisable social relations: they make groups upon the croquet ground, whist parties, or in porch chat; but they seem held together by chance outward circumstances, not by any force of personal attraction. I wonder again at the many who pass without leaving any lasting impression—they fade away like phantoms. Only one, now and again, is remembered by strong, distinct personality."

THE LAST SYMPHONY

"I should like the mental experiment of trying to forget Themis," said Ultimata, "after the clear way in which she has interpreted the law, given decisions in all our intellectual arguments, and settled the questionable boundaries of debatable ground."

"You should be glad to escape such tyranny," replied Themis. "I had no idea that I had exercised this autocratic sway. In truth, I have not noticed submission to law, and unanimity of opinion as characterising our debates."

"Still," said the Crusader, "we have always recognised you as the judicial element in our circle, and with your loss I feel sure that we shall lapse into the condition of a country without an authorised legal court. There may be a return to lynch law, vigilance committee or ordeal by fire. I think Ultimata is capable of extreme opinion and acts of violence when not restrained by the representative of justice."

"With your reckless ambition," retorted Ultimata, "you are already planning for a military dictatorship. Only woman suffrage can save us."

"In case of serious difficulty, I offer myself as Foreign Court of Arbitration," remarked the Spectator.

"Oh, no!" exclaimed Dorothy, "let us have a real war. The Crusader shall be Consul, then get himself made Emperor, and Mamma will be hostile legions or communists, or better still, the French Revolution. Then I shall have a chance to wear armour and ride a real war horse."

"You see, Themis," said Ultimata, "that you leave us to a Reign of Terror, in which Dorothy's mind is already a chaos of Roman legions, Imperial usurpation, mediæval armour, caparisoned war steeds, National Conventions and the Coup d'État."

"Now, Mamma, you are very unjust," cried Dorothy with her aggrieved expression, "I know very well that Napoleon was not a Roman Emperor, that the Coup d'État was not by Cæsar, and that the Crusader never wore glittering armour, and rode a horse all caparisoned in yellow, with gold trimmings, in the stupid Civil War, when soldiers wore plain blue and grey. But I like knights better than cavalry officers."

"When I am Dictator I shall remember the treason of this little rebel, and have her head cut off with a cavalry sabre," said the Crusader.

"I shall never be taken prisoner if I ride Brownie," answered Dorothy defiantly, "she would carry me to victory or death."

"Meanwhile, be quiet, Dorothy," said Ultimata, "or you will have to beat an ignominious retreat now, instead of riding your high horse to victory or death. Now," turning to Themis, "confess that you are fond of Santa Barbara, and very melancholy over the unkind fate which drives you to Boston."

"I am fond of Santa Barbara in a way, and for a time," answered Themis, "but the monotony of life here, and the very equability of the climate become wearisome."

"Well," said Ultimata, "you will escape equability of climate and enjoy the fascinating vicissitudes of New England weather, with snow, thaws, and east winds. Then sometimes you will have a vision of these sunlit hills, and smiling sea, and 'the days that are no more'."

"I shall not forget this southern world," replied Themis, " nor the companionship of these days; but this social life is not Santa Barbara, but the happy fate of one fortunate year. If I stayed, the circle would not long be unbroken. Even now, you are laying plans for flight."

"I wish," sighed Perdita, "that when friends meet, as here, in a perfect world, one could work a spell, and hold life unchanged. Why did fairy god-mothers go out of fashion? We all need one."

"Fairy god-mothers went out of fashion when people lost their faith," said Dorothy severely. "No one invites them to the christening now, or else we could all stay in the Happy Valley."

"But would not such spell reduce life to the enchanted rest which held the Sleeping Beauty and her court unstirred for a century's nap?" asked the Fairy Prince.

("He ought to know," whispered Dorothy, "for of course he woke the Princess with a kiss.")

"I can think of no fate so awful and inexorable as to be denied all possibility of change," returned the Crusader, "it would transform a possible Paradise into a positive Inferno. Such condition is inconceivable of life, it can only be predicated of death.

However perfect the blossom of to-day, its root is in the law of change, for life must be growth, and growth must find expression in change of form."

"You accused me the other day," answered Ultimata, "of preaching the gospel of disloyalty, when I defended the possible outgrowing of friendship, or the feeling called love: but now you abjure all allegiance to past or present in your glorification of change."

"I said change of form, not of necessity change of feeling," replied the Crusader.

"But," said Lorelei. "without change of environment or social elements, there still could be change in ourselves, by the growth of feeling and the unfolding of character. There might surely be unchanged love and unchanging loyalty, but with ever stronger, fuller expression of ourselves. Is not the impatient demand for outward change, a confession of the monotony of our own inner life?"

"With the intimate relations which exist between the world of sense and the world of spirit," answered the Crusader, "it is almost inevitable that monotony of external life should limit intellectual development. and lessen power of sympathy. There are doubtless natures, so fine in intuition, that they sweep a broad horizon without external experience. Such natures are clairvoyant in the true sense of the word. They apprehend spiritual truth without its external symbolism. But to most of us life is known only by its outward revelations."

"I used to wonder, at the convent," said Lorelei,

"how the passing of the quiet years, marked only by Church festivals and Saints' days, could have changed the sisters from fair, young novices to thoughtful-browed, earnest-hearted women. Some of them had reached a true, spiritual motherhood, by which they discovered the needs of young lives, and brooded over them with tireless tenderness."

"They had not gone out to study life, but life had come to them," replied the Crusader. "Their unfolding had not been so largely through ave-marias and pater-nosters, as through human contact with the glad young lives that give a semblance of home duties to the convent's isolation. The feeling of motherhood had been developed by the claims of child-life."

"That reminds me," said Ultimata, "of the vesper service, beautiful almost to heart-breaking, in the church which stands on the Pincio, in which the singing is by a choir of nuns from the adjoining convent concealed by the high gallery screen, and the responses by the little maidens of the school, all white-robed, who fill the chancel. The child voices were only young and glad; but the power of feeling, the suppressed passion in the voices of the invisible sisters, gave revelation of their lives. There were the tones of love songs denied their youth, and the plaintive tenderness of cradle songs unsung. I have not forgotten across nearly twenty years the pathetic beauty of that service, and the coming out from the church shadows and altar lamps to Rome lying below the broad, high terrace, with domes and campanilas tranced in the sunset light."

"You should have been Catholic," said Lorelei wistfully. "Your heart is only at home in the sacred mystery of the Church. Only there you find warm shadows from a living past, and mystical light which pierces the future's gloom."

"I should like to be a Catholic," exclaimed Dorothy, "for I like the rosaries and the stately sound of the Latin prayers; and I love the pictures of the Virgin Mary and the Holy Child. I do not enjoy sitting in stiff pews to hear long sermons, but I think that I might like to kneel at altars with flowers and lights, and to watch the swinging censors before the pictures of saints and angels."

"Dorothy is a strong illustration of the association between the spirit world and the world of sense," remarked the Crusader. "Her heart is won to worship by the appeal of symbolical beauty to the eye."

"I would suggest, in behalf of your Presbyterian ancestry," said Themis smiling, "that you and Dorothy should withdraw from the glamour of the Mission, or you will be lost to Protestantism and free thought."

"The American churches fail so utterly in beauty of ritual," remarked the Spectator. "A full choral service in an English cathedral leaves no part of the nature untouched. It satisfies the eye with shadowy space and glorious colour, appeals to the ear with the passionate, upward longing of fine music, and uplifts the spirit through these suggestions to the eternal beauty and the divine harmony."

"I feel more than ever the need of a change to the Boston atmosphere," observed Themis, "you are all drifting out on a sea of mysticism. I need to feel again the firmness of Plymouth Rock, regain positive political convictions, and settle the foundations of my theological creed. We have broadened our thoughts with social theories and spiritual charity for all revelations, until I feel as if we had lost all definiteness of outline."

"I do not think Boston is the place to give definiteness of outline, from the history of its transcendentalism, and the reports of the Concord School of Philosophy," said the Crusader.

"We are all trying to forget that it is the last evening," sighed Ultimata, "but the fire is dying on the hearth, and everyone's face has a faint, far-off look, as if we were already half-obliterated memories."

The Crusader piled fresh logs on the hearth, and we looked real and human again. "One of the delights that you will miss is the open wood fire," said Ultimata. "It is a cheerful, quickening presence; a warm-hearted, bright-faced friend."

"I choose not to think of what I will miss," answered Themis, "but of what I shall gain."

"That reveals the secret of your cheerfulness," remarked the Crusader. "You turn towards the future, naturally, hopefully, with out-stretched hand as one finding and giving welcome. It is the true spirit; for life must be for us in the future, not the past."

"When we part," said Ultimata to the Crusader, "I shall insist upon you writing a eulogistic epitaph for me, as I shall be part of the dead and buried past."

"This isn't a funeral, Mamma," cried Dorothy. "No one is being buried. You must not talk so. It gives me the shivers."

"Are you sure that it isn't a funeral, Dorothy, this last evening's talk?" asked Ultimata. "Something will be missing in all the to-morrows."

"In spite of my resolutions, I am growing melancholy," said Themis, "so I shall say good-night, and crowd out emotion with a little practical work. Packing is an excellent antidote to pathos."

So we parted in the firelight with a conscious shadow on each face. Themis held Lorelei's hand longer than need be with good-night words. I think that they have gained some revelation of each other. Lorelei feels the restful strength of Themis' positive character and vigorous intellect, and Themis has caught glimpses beneath the veil of Lorelei's pure spirituality. Dorothy, happier than we, in the right to give full expression to her feelings, kissed everyone good-night, and when Themis bent for the caress, put both arms round her neck with a quick, convulsive tenderness of embrace.

As we went upstairs, Dorothy said, "I am glad that you let me sit up to-night, Mamma. I seem to know them all better for this evening's talk. You are all so different, yet blend so well."

This was the last symphony.

CHAPTER XXXII

HEARTSEASE

A WEEK has passed since Themis left us, and the old familiar life seems already receding from us. Artista is for the time at the Home Ranch, Glen Annie. Mater Violetta and Perdita have left for a visit to San Diego and Los Angeles. The Spectator is still with us, though scarcely of us, as his new interests absorb him and he rides every day to the ranch; or by way of alienating himself from his own individuality, drives in a new, red-wheeled spider waggon. Then I feel that we have lost him — that he belongs no more to the group of riding tourists, exploring cañons and climbing foot-hills, but to the settled class of resident rancheros.

The house is filled with gay-voiced strangers, making up horseback parties, organising excursions in four-in-hands, and talking of Santa Barbara in a flippant way as if it were a pleasant passing acquaintance to be greeted and then forgotten. Can any other love it as I have loved, with ideal longing across the years, with thrill of recognition at meeting, as when strangers touch to find that they have been friends from the Eternities; and now, with pain of parting, which dims my exiled life with the sudden pallor of death.

Dorothy and I have taken together all our favourite rides, to the cañons, along the Los Angeles road to Montecito, to Cathedral Oaks, and to Finch's Hill where our dreams built for themselves a home. After all, the spiritual part of true companionship is more than outward dwelling-place, and the light upon faces of our own fairer than its shining on Santa Barbara hills and sea. So we are inly comforted. Dorothy has hunted up her little hammer, and plans in Denver where we meet our unrelenting Fate (who would not be won across the continent by Santa Barbara's smile), triumphant geological trips and prospecting tours. In the absence of a home on the foot-hills, she is willing to be comforted by a Colorado silver mine. And I think, with a returning smile, of long evening talks, when our memories of Santa Barbara will show him the far-off fairness of our Valley by the sea, and lure him some day to that home which I truly own upon its hills.

There is no flaw in my title. Others may buy and build, win orchards to bloom and bear, plant roses and wear their fragrant loveliness: but I shall still have spiritual ownership of my ideal home, look from its windows upon mountain shadows and feel in its uplifting, its out-looking, all its light of vision, its breadth of horizon. There is no loss. We hold our own by right of the love which claims it, the

HEARTSEASE

loyalty which keeps faith with it. I feel the same of friends as of places. Once I was inconsolable at separation, dismayed at thought of distance, and eager for assurance of unchanged and unchanging love. Now I know that in affections, as in experience and creeds, we "dwell in tents", that most of life's possessions are transient. So many friendships of real root and true growth are the roses of a summer, not the pines which lift steadfast spires against our winter sky.

I have grown less impatient towards the passing joy, less uncomforted for the inevitable loss. Of every experience, of every friendship, we hold eternally ours as much as belongs to us by true affinity, by spirit appropriation. More we dare not claim, less we cannot hold than our own. So, if I seem to lose a friendship, I know that the winning was but seeming; that I gained companionship, transient touch of life upon life, but no inner relation of spirit to spirit. If this philosophy reconciles me to the semblance of loss, it reveals also the eternal foundations of the love which endures.

There is a friendship, there is a love with elements of immortality in its own loyalty and faith. Such love smiles at the vow "until death us do part", knowing that death has no power to part those whom life has truly made one. So in leaving Santa Barbara and the dear friends made ours by daily companionship, I know that the loss of the valley's outward beauty, the loss of friend's warm hand of greeting and eye of steadfast glance is less in pain, than the spirit's gain of joy in memories of the southern world, in consciousness of the love and loyalty in which natures may meet, when lives no longer touch. The life which outwardly has much to lose, should spiritually have much to keep; since every external joy subject to change, should be the symbol of an inner joy, with living root in the immortal nature.

Still all the familiar pleasures have a strange, sweet sacredness in these last days, as in the hour of parting life's broken bread and out-poured wine become sacramental. Most of all I feel the pain of change, when I sit in my favourite north window and look towards the mountains. On the porch with the gay, passing groups, and in the drawing-room where faces shine, then fade into memories, there is always the underlying thought of transitoriness, but here, where my spirit in solitude has held communion with the everlasting hills, there has been a sense of calm and space which seemed like eternal rest. I cannot think that in the sunshine these slopes will grow lustrous with golden light, then dim with passing clouds into soft tints of tender brown; that in sunset glow the mountains will flush with crimson glory, then deepen into the regality of purple shadows against the darkening sky, and my eyes neither gladden in their joy nor sadden with their gloom; that my spirit shall neither rest itself upon the low, familiar hills, nor lift to highest crest, and to the blue beyond.

This week of broken companionship we have

missed the Crusader; and life seemed in sudden eclipse without the genial warmth, the generous light of his magnetic nature. I thought the children were less glad without his smile, the roses less gay missing his touch. But he is with us again, and in his presence I feel that spirit summer in which immortal roses bloom. There is little of outward story to tell, but I leave Santa Barbara in undimmed sunlight.

The day after Themis left there was talk of a riding party, but one after another failed, and at last only the Crusader and Lorelei went—their first ride alone. I was on the porch when they started. While Lorelei stood beside me, with the sweeping, graceful folds of her habit clinging to her slender figure, drawing on the long mousquetaire gloves, the Crusader brought her a bunch of yellow roses, and said with a smile, "Do wear them, I have taken off every thorn."

Lorelei never wears roses, she says that she hates their full-hearted fairness with hidden thorns. "When you win the secret of their hearts, it is pain," she insists, "for under the warm light of the petals is always the power to wound."

She accepted them with languid grace but with averted eyes, and pinned them so carelessly that they fell as she mounted. As the Crusader bent to pick them up from beneath her horse's feet, I said, stung for his sake with her indifference, "You should wear blood-red roses, and be pierced with all their thorns."

Lorelei gave a low, sweet laugh but when I met the Crusader's eyes they had hardened, as in mood of anger, from friendly blue to frigid grey. But as they lifted to her, in offering again the roses, they relented into tender blue. I watched them as they walked slowly towards the hills, then followed the trail to the Crusader's favourite crest. I wondered if any cloud of misapprehension, any mood of withdrawal, could withstand such sunlight, and the power of love, which I felt sure was growing in both natures.

From my window I saw them ride homeward in the sunset light. In the evening when we met I felt chilled and saddened, though my impression eluded all analysis. There seemed between them a widening distance, an alienating strangeness. Still I felt sure that the Crusader had not spoken his life's fateful word of confession, nor Lorelei the fatal word of denial. They were held apart by some impalpable influence.

I went early to my room resolved to read no more love stories in real life, and to choose carefully novels of happy ending. The next morning the Crusader was not at breakfast, and I lingered in chat on the porch, hoping for his "good morning", with power to dispel the evening's shadows, before climbing to the Spanish lesson and Calderon. But he failed to come. At noon, the Spectator told me that he was suffering from one of the severe attacks of pain in the head to which he is subject. As he is subject to these headaches, I could no rightfully feel that the suffering was due to the siren's charm, though I longed to burden her with it—to blame her for it.

What right had she to condemn the fairness of the roses with hidden thorns? Her own loveliness sheaths cruel power to wound. For three days we missed him. Lorelei unconsciously drew near to me with a wistful appeal, which I felt was confession of her loneliness, and unfolding of her repressed feeling.

In the late afternoon, Dorothy and I were swinging together in a hammock on the porch, when the Crusader startled us by speaking. He stood in the door. looking pale and stern, but his face lighted as he came towards us in answer to our eager greeting. The porch was deserted, so we met with full, glad expression of the friendship which holds us with " a three-fold cord, not lightly broken ".

I knew that Lorelei was in the garden, as she had left us to gather flowers, but she was not visible as we talked. Soon she crossed the lawn, looking so fair in the soft, sunset light. She wore the Lorelei dress of pale, vaporous sea-green, but I smiled to see that it was warmed with the glow of his favourite Cloth of Gold roses. She met the Crusader with calm sweetness, through which I thought there thrilled a quick look of rapture. But it faded almost before discovered, and she said quietly, " You are looking pale. I think you lack a *boutonnière*, may I choose in the children's place ? "

She stepped out on the lawn and returned with

a yellow pansy. As she offered it, she said, "I have chosen your own cavalry colour." He answered lightly, "But I must have its meaning: is it only a 'pansy for thought', or as maidens call it, 'love in idleness?'" She smilingly withheld the outstretched flower.

The little scene seemed only playful. Still I wished that I were elsewhere; but Dorothy, who likes to be part of every experience, called out in her unconscious child way, "Don't quarrel about names, both call it heartsease."

I saw his eyes sweep her face with flame of sudden feeling, then in low, hushed tones he asked, "Shall it be Heartsease?"

I fancied that a tremor passed over her, the last chill touch of the Lorelei nature. Then she lifted her eyes to his, and in them shone the warmth of the awakened woman soul. For answer she bent the fair head, and with tender, caressing touch, fastened on his breast that flower of perfect light, the yellow Heartsease.

FINIS

A CATALOGUE OF BOOKS AND ANNOUNCEMENTS OF METHUEN AND COMPANY PUBLISHERS : LONDON 36 ESSEX STREET W.C.

CONTENTS

	PAGE
FORTHCOMING BOOKS,	2
POETRY,	11
ENGLISH CLASSICS,	13
ILLUSTRATED BOOKS,	13
HISTORY,	14
BIOGRAPHY,	16
GENERAL LITERATURE,	19
SCIENCE,	22
PHILOSOPHY,	22
THEOLOGY,	23
LEADERS OF RELIGION,	25
FICTION,	26
BOOKS FOR BOYS AND GIRLS,	34
THE PEACOCK LIBRARY,	35
UNIVERSITY EXTENSION SERIES,	35
SOCIAL QUESTIONS OF TO-DAY,	37
CLASSICAL TRANSLATIONS,	37
EDUCATIONAL BOOKS,	38

MARCH 1897

MARCH 1897.

MESSRS. METHUEN'S ANNOUNCEMENTS

Poetry

GEORGE WYNDHAM

SHAKESPEARE'S POEMS. Edited, with an Introduction and Notes, by GEORGE WYNDHAM, M.P. *Crown 8vo.* 6s.

W. E. HENLEY

ENGLISH LYRICS. Selected and Edited by W. E. HENLEY. *Crown 8vo. Buckram.* 6s.

Also 15 copies on Japanese paper. *Demy 8vo.* £2, 2s.

Few announcements will be more welcome to lovers of English verse than the one that Mr. Henley is bringing together into one book the finest lyrics in our language. The volume will be produced with the same care that made 'Lyra Heroica' delightful to the hand and eye.

Travel and Adventure

SIR H. H. JOHNSTON, K.C.B.

BRITISH CENTRAL AFRICA. By Sir H. H. JOHNSTON, K.C.B. With nearly Two Hundred Illustrations, and Five Maps. *Crown 4to.* 30s.

CONTENTS.

(1) The history of Nyasaland and British Central Africa generally, with a detailed account of events during the last seven years.

(2) A detailed description of the various races considered anthropologically and ethnologically

(3) The languages of British Central Africa.

(4) The European settlers, their mode of life; coffee, cultivation, etc.

(5) The Missionaries.

(6) The fauna of Nyasaland, with much information concerning its big game.

(7) The flora and the minerals.

(8) The scenery (copiously illustrated to show the remarkable natural beauty of the country), and

(9) A concluding chapter on the future prospects of the country.

CAPTAIN HINDE

THE FALL OF THE CONGO ARABS. By SIDNEY L. HINDE. With Portraits and Plans. *Demy 8vo.* 12s. 6d.

This volume deals with the recent Belgian Expedition to the Upper Congo, which developed into a war between the State forces and the Arab slave raiders in Central Africa. Two white men only returned alive from the three years' war—Commandant Dhanis and the writer of this book, Captain Hinde. During the greater part of the time spent by Captain Hinde in the Congo he was amongst cannibal races in little-known regions, and, owing to the peculiar circumstances of his position, was enabled to see a side of native history shown to few Europeans. The war terminated in the complete defeat of the Arabs, seventy thousand of whom perished during the struggle.

BADEN-POWELL
SCOUTING SKETCHES IN RHODESIA. By LIEUT.-COLONEL BADEN-POWELL. With numerous Illustrations, Maps, etc. *Demy 8vo. Cloth.* 15s.

PRINCE HENRI OF ORLEANS
FROM TONKIN TO INDIA. By PRINCE HENRI OF ORLEANS. Translated by HAMLEY BENT, M.A. With over 100 Illustrations and 4 Maps. *Demy 8vo.* 21s.

The travels of Prince Henri in 1895 from China to the valley of the Bramaputra covered a distance of 2100 miles, of which 1600 was through absolutely unexplored country. No fewer than seventeen ranges of mountains were crossed at altitudes of from 11,000 to 13,000 feet. The journey was made memorable by the discovery of the sources of the Irrawaddy. To the physical difficulties of the journey were added dangers from the attacks of savage tribes. The book deals with many of the burning political problems of the East, and it will be found a most important contribution to the literature of adventure and discovery.

L. DECLE
THREE YEARS IN SAVAGE AFRICA. By LIONEL DECLE. With an Introduction by H. M. STANLEY, M.P. With 100 Illustrations and 5 Maps. *Demy 8vo.* 21s.

Few Europeans have had the same opportunity of studying the barbarous parts of Africa as Mr. Decle. Starting from the Cape, he visited in succession Bechuanaland, the Zambesi, Matabeleland and Mashonaland, the Portuguese settlement on the Zambesi, Nyasaland, Ujiji, the headquarters of the Arabs, German East Africa, Uganda (where he saw fighting in company with the late Major 'Roddy' Owen), and British East Africa. In his book he relates his experiences, his minute observations of native habits and customs, and his views as to the work done in Africa by the various European Governments, whose operations he was able to study. The whole journey extended over 7000 miles, and occupied exactly three years.

H. S. COWPER
THE HILL OF THE GRACES: OR, THE GREAT STONE TEMPLES OF TRIPOLI. By H. S. COWPER, F.S.A. With Maps, Plans, and 75 Illustrations. *Demy 8vo.* 10s. 6d.

The Turkish prohibition against all European travel in their African Pashalics has, during the last seventeen years, rendered impossible both geographical and archæological research. The author, however, was enabled to make two journeys through the hill range of Tripoli in 1895 and 1896, and this volume deals chiefly with a remarkable series of megalithic Temples and Trilithons, which he found to exist there in extraordinary numbers. These ruins have hitherto been quite uninvestigated, and to Englishmen should have an exceptional interest, from the light it is believed they will throw on our own national monument of Stonehenge. In all about one hundred sites were visited and photographed, and the volume will be fully illustrated by maps, plans, and photographs. Chapters will also be devoted to modern Tripoli, the little visited ruins of Leptes Magna, the ancient and modern geography of the district generally, and the author's personal experiences.

W. CROOKE
THE NORTH-WEST PROVINCES OF INDIA: THEIR ETHNOLOGY AND ADMINISTRATION. By W. CROOKE. With Maps and Illustrations. *Demy 8vo.* 10s. 6d.

History and Biography

MORRIS FULLER

THE LIFE AND WRITINGS OF JOHN DAVENANT, D.D. (1571-1641), President of Queen's College, Lady Margaret Professor of Divinity, Cambridge, Lord Bishop of Salisbury. By the Rev. MORRIS FULLER, B.D., Vicar of St. Mark's, Marylebone. *Crown 8vo. 7s. 6d.*

Dr. Davenant, Bishop of Salisbury, the maternal uncle of Dr. Fuller, lived at a very critical time in our history (1571-1641). He was one of the British representatives of the first great Synod of the reformed churches held at Dort, was one of Archbishop Laud's Suffragans, and assisted him in carrying out his reforms.

Précis is given of some of the Bishop's writings, and a very celebrated sermon, never before published and supposed to have been lost, is printed *in extenso*.

EDWARD GIBBON

THE DECLINE AND FALL OF THE ROMAN EMPIRE. By EDWARD GIBBON. A New Edition, edited with Notes, Appendices, and Maps by J. B. BURY, M.A., Fellow of Trinity College, Dublin. *In Seven Volumes. Demy 8vo, gilt top. 8s. 6d. each. Crown 8vo. 6s. each. Vol. III.*

J. WELLS

THE CITY AND UNIVERSITY OF OXFORD. By J. WELLS, M.A., Fellow and Tutor of Wadham College. Illustrated by E. H. NEW. *Fcp. 8vo. 2s. 6d.*

This is a Guide—chiefly historical—to the Colleges of Oxford. It contains numerous full-page illustrations.

C. H. GRINLING

A HISTORY OF THE GREAT NORTHERN RAILWAY, 1845-95. By C. H. GRINLING. With Maps and Illustrations. *Crown 8vo. 6s.*

A record of Railway enterprise and development in Northern England, containing much matter hitherto unpublished. It appeals both to the general reader and to those specially interested in railway construction and management.

Naval and Military

DAVID HANNAY

A SHORT HISTORY OF THE ROYAL NAVY, FROM EARLY TIMES TO THE PRESENT DAY. By DAVID HANNAY. Illustrated. *2 Vols. Demy 8vo. 15s.*

This book aims at giving an account not only of the fighting we have done at sea, but of the growth of the service, of the part the Navy has played in the development of the Empire, and of its inner life. The author has endeavoured to avoid the mistake of sacrificing the earlier periods of naval history—the very interesting wars with Holland in the seventeenth century, for instance, or the American War of 1779-1783—to the later struggle with Revolutionary and Imperial France.

COL. COOPER KING

THE STORY OF THE BRITISH ARMY. By Lieut.-Colonel COOPER KING, of the Staff College, Camberley. Illustrated. *Demy 8vo.* 7s. 6d.

<small>This volume aims at describing the nature of the different armies that have been formed in Great Britain, and how from the early and feudal levies the present standing army came to be. The changes in tactics, uniform, and armament are briefly touched upon, and the campaigns in which the army has shared have been so far followed as to explain the part played by British regiments in them.</small>

Theology

E. C. S. GIBSON

THE XXXIX ARTICLES OF THE CHURCH OF ENGLAND. Edited with an Introduction by E. C. S. GIBSON, D.D., Vicar of Leeds, late Principal of Wells Theological College. *In Two Volumes. Demy 8vo.* 7s. 6d. each. *Vol. II. Articles IX.-XXXIX.*

W. H. BENNETT

A PRIMER OF THE BIBLE. By Prof. W. H. BENNETT. *Crown 8vo.* 2s. 6d.

Devotional Series

C. BIGG

THE CONFESSIONS OF ST. AUGUSTINE. Newly Translated, with an Introduction, by C. BIGG, D.D., late Student of Christ Church. With a Frontispiece. *18mo.* 1s. 6d.

<small>This little book is the first volume of a new Devotional Series, the volumes of which will be edited by competent scholars, printed in clear type, and published at a very low price.

This volume contains the nine books of the 'Confessions,' which are suitable for devotional purposes. The name of the Editor is a sufficient guarantee of the excellence of the edition.</small>

F. E. BRIGHTMAN

THE DEVOTIONS OF BISHOP ANDREWES. Newly Translated, together with his 'Manual of the Sick,' with an Introduction by F. E. BRIGHTMAN, M.A., of the Pusey House, Oxford. *18mo.* 1s. 6d.

<small>The inclusion of Andrewes' 'Manual of the Sick' will greatly increase the value of this edition of the 'Preces Privatæ.'</small>

Sport

H. MORGAN BROWNE

SPORTING AND ATHLETIC RECORDS. By H. MORGAN BROWNE. *Crown 8vo.* 3s. 6d.

<small>This book gives, in a clear and complete form, accurate records of the best performances in all important branches of Sport. It is an attempt, never yet made, to</small>

present all-important sporting records in a systematic way. In many branches of athletics world's records will be properly tabulated for the first time. Records at many of the great public schools will be given. While complete lists of the winners of important events in the world of sport (*c.g.* principal horse races, English Amateur Championships, Oxford and Cambridge Boat-race, etc. etc.) will be found in an Appendix.

General Literature

ARTHUR SHERWELL

LIFE IN WEST LONDON: A STUDY AND A CONTRAST. By ARTHUR SHERWELL, M.A. *Crown 8vo.* 2s. 6d.

H. A. SALMONÉ

THE FALL AND RESURRECTION OF TURKEY. By H. ANTHONY SALMONÉ. With Portraits. *Crown 8vo.* 3s. 6d.

LAURIE MAGNUS

A PRIMER OF WORDSWORTH. By LAURIE MAGNUS. *Crown 8vo.* 2s. 6d.

R. USSHER

NEO-MALTHUSIANISM. By R. USSHER, M.A. *Cr. 8vo.* 5s.
An Enquiry into that System, with regard to its Economy and Morality.

This book deals with a very delicate but most important matter, namely, the voluntary limitation of the family, and how such action affects morality, the individual, and the nation.

Educational

C. STEPHENSON AND F. SUDDARDS

ORNAMENTAL DESIGN FOR WOVEN FABRICS. By C. STEPHENSON, of The Technical College, Bradford, and F. SUDDARDS, of The Yorkshire College, Leeds. With 65 full-page plates, and numerous designs and diagrams in the text. *Demy 8vo.* 7s. 6d.

The aim of this book is to supply, in a systematic and practical form, information on the subject of Decorative Design as applied to Woven Fabrics, and is primarily intended to meet the requirements of students in Textile and Art Schools, or of designers actively engaged in the weaving industry. Its wealth of illustration is a marked feature of the book.

R. E. STEEL
MAGNETISM AND ELECTRICITY. By R. Elliott Steel, M.A., F.C.S. With Illustrations. *Crown 8vo.* 4s. 6d.

E. E. WHITFIELD
PRÉCIS WRITING AND OFFICE CORRESPONDENCE. By E. E. Whitfield, M.A. *Crown 8vo.* 2s.
[*Commercial Series.*]

ESSENTIALS OF COMMERCIAL EDUCATION. By E. E. Whitfield, M.A. *Crown 8vo.* 1s. 6d.

A guide to Commercial Education and Examinations, which ought to prove most useful as showing what is now being done in this country to promote commercial education, and also as giving valuable information to those who may wish to enter for some of the commercial examinations now held by the London Chamber of Commerce and other bodies.

Methuen's Classical Texts

GENERAL EDITOR
E. C. MARCHANT, M.A.
OF TRINITY COLLEGE, OXFORD ; FELLOW OF PETERHOUSE, CAMBRIDGE ; ST. PAUL'S SCHOOL, LONDON.

Messrs. Methuen propose to issue a new series of Classical Texts, edited by eminent scholars, for the use of English-speaking students. The books will be well printed and bound, and will be published at a very low price. The first volume of every author will contain a brief Introduction in English, not exceeding eight pages, in which the necessary information about the MSS. will be given, and the salient features of the author's style indicated.

The critical notes, which will be at the foot of the page, will exhibit only the important MS. variants and conjectures of special value. They will contain very little argument; and there will be no explanatory notes. Every volume of the series will contain a short *Index Rerum et Nominum*

Special attention will be paid to the typography of the series.

The following, among many others, are arranged :—

AUTHOR.	EDITOR.
Aeschylus, . .	R. Y. Tyrrell, D.Litt., LL.D., Regius Professor of Greek in the University of Dublin.
Aristophanes, 2 vols.,	Professor Tyrrell.
Sophocles, . .	W. J. M. Starkie, M.A., Fellow of Trinity College, Dublin.
Euripides, 3 vols., .	W. S. Hadley, M.A., Fellow and Bursar of Pembroke College, Cambridge.
Thucydides, 2 vols., .	E. C. Marchant, M.A., Fellow of Peterhouse, Cambridge; St. Paul's School.
Demosthenes, 3 vols.,	J. E. Sandys, Litt.D., Public Orator in the University of Cambridge.

CICERO—
    Speeches, 3 vols., . . J. S. REID, Litt.D., Fellow and Tutor of Caius College, Cambridge.
    Philosophical Works, J. S. REID
    Letters, 2 vols., . L. C. PURSER, M.A., Fellow and Tutor of Trinity College, Dublin.
TACITUS, 2 vols., G. G. RAMSAY, LL.D., Litt.D., Professor of Humanity in the University of Glasgow.
TERENCE, . . . W. M. LINDSAY, M.A., Fellow of Jesus College, Oxford.
LUCRETIUS, . J. S. DUFF, M.A., Fellow of Trinity College, Cambridge.
VERGIL, . A. S. WILKINS, M.A., Professor of Latin, Owen's College, Manchester.
HORACE, . JAMES GOW, Litt.D., Master of Nottingham High School.
OVID, 3 vols., S. G. OWEN, M.A., Senior Student and Censor of Christ Church, Oxford.
JUVENAL, . S. G. OWEN, M.A.
PHAEDRUS, ROBINSON ELLIS, M.A., LL.D., Corpus Professor of Latin in the University of Oxford.
MARTIAL, . . W. M. LINDSAY, M.A.

Methuen's Byzantine Texts

GENERAL EDITOR
J. B. BURY, M.A.

FELLOW AND TUTOR OF TRINITY COLLEGE, DUBLIN, PROFESSOR OF MODERN HISTORY IN DUBLIN UNIVERSITY.

MESSRS. METHUEN propose to issue a series of texts of Byzantine Historians, edited by English and foreign scholars. It will consist mainly of Greek texts, but will also include English translations of some Oriental works which are important sources for Byzantine history. The Greek texts, which will be in all cases based on original study of MSS., will be accompanied by brief critical notes, and preceded by short introductions, containing the necessary explanations as to the material which has been used for the determination of the text. A special feature of these volumes will be very full *indices Graecitatis*, framed with a view to the collection of material for the *Lexicon totius Graecitatis* of the future. Each volume will of course also be provided with an *Index Rerum et Nominum*.

The collaboration of a considerable number of eminent foreign scholars has been secured; so that this series can justly claim to be regarded as international.

CHRONICLE OF MOREA, . . . JOHN SCHMITT, Ph.D.
CONSTANTINE PORPHYROGENNETOS, PROFESSOR J. B. BURY.
ECTHESIS CHRONICA, . . . PROFESSOR LAMBROS of Athens.
EVAGRIUS, ... PROFESSOR LÉON PARMENTIER of Liège and M. BIDEZ of Gand.
GENESIUS, ... PROFESSOR J. B. BURY.
GEORGE PISIDES, . . . PROFESSOR LEO STERNBACH of Cracow.
JOHN OF NIKIN (translated from the Ethiopic), ... REV. R. H. CHARLES.
PSELLUS (Historia), . . . MONSIEUR C. SATHAS.
THEODORE OF CYZICUS, . . PROFESSOR LAMBROS.

Fiction

MARIE CORELLI'S ROMANCES

New and Uniform Edition. Large Crown 8vo. 6s.

WORMWOOD. *Eighth Edition.*

THE SOUL OF LILITH. *Ninth Edition.*

BARABBAS: A DREAM OF THE WORLD'S TRAGEDY. *Twenty-ninth Edition.*

THE SORROWS OF SATAN. *Thirty-fourth Edition.*

The above will be issued in the uniform edition of Marie Corelli's books.

ANTHONY HOPE

PHROSO. By ANTHONY HOPE, Author of 'The Prisoner of Zenda,' etc. Illustrated by H. R. MILLAR. *Crown 8vo. 6s.*

ROBERT BARR

THE MUTABLE MANY. By ROBERT BARR, Author of 'In the Midst of Alarms,' 'A Woman Intervenes,' etc. *Crown 8vo. 6s.*

EMILY LAWLESS

A NEW BOOK. By The Hon. EMILY LAWLESS, Author of 'Hurrish,' 'Maelcho,' etc. *Crown 8vo. 6s.*

S. BARING GOULD

GUAVAS THE TINNER. By S. BARING GOULD, Author of 'The Broom Squire,' etc. Illustrated by Frank Dadd. *Crown 8vo. 6s.*

A Historical Romance of the time of Elizabeth.

W. E. NORRIS

CLARISSA FURIOSA. By W. E. NORRIS, Author of 'The Rogue,' etc. *Crown 8vo. 6s.*

GILBERT PARKER

THE POMP OF THE LAVILLETTES. By GILBERT PARKER, Author of 'The Seats of the Mighty,' etc. *Crown 8vo. 3s. 6d.*

J. MACLAREN COBBAN

WILT THOU HAVE THIS WOMAN? By J. M. COBBAN, Author of 'The King of Andaman.' *Crown 8vo. 6s.*

H. MORRAH
THE FAITHFUL CITY. By HERBERT MORRAH, Author of 'A Serious Comedy.' *Crown 8vo.* 6s.

J. F. BREWER
THE SPECULATORS. By J. F. BREWER. *Crown 8vo.* 6s.

A. BALFOUR
BY STROKE OF SWORD. By ANDREW BALFOUR. Illustrated by W. CUBITT COOKE. *Crown 8vo.* 6s.

JAMES GORDON
THE VILLAGE AND THE DOCTOR. By JAMES GORDON. *Crown 8vo.* 6s.

IDA HOOPER
THE SINGER OF MARLY. By IDA HOOPER. Illustrated by W. CUBITT COOKE. *Crown 8vo.* 6s.

A romance of adventure.

H. G. WELLS
THE PLATTNER STORY; AND OTHERS. By H. G. WELLS, Author of 'The Stolen Bacillus,' 'The Time Machine,' etc. *Crown 8vo.* 6s.

MARY GAUNT
KIRKHAM'S FIND. By MARY GAUNT, Author of 'The Moving Finger.' *Crown 8vo.* 6s.

L. S. McCHESNEY
UNDER SHADOW OF THE MISSION. By L. S. McCHESNEY. *Crown 8vo.* 6s.

M. C. BALFOUR
THE FALL OF THE SPARROW. By M. C. BALFOUR. *Crown 8vo.* 6s.

S. GORDON
A HANDFUL OF EXOTICS. By S. GORDON. *Crown 8vo.* 3s. 6d.

A volume of stories of Jewish life in Russia.

P. NEUMANN
THE SUPPLANTER. By P. NEUMANN. *Crown 8vo.* 3s. 6d.

H. A. KENNEDY
A MAN WITH BLACK EYELASHES. By H. A. KENNEDY. *Crown 8vo.* 3s. 6d.

HANNAH LYNCH
AN ODD EXPERIMENT. By HANNAH LYNCH. *Cr. 8vo.* 3s. 6d.

A LIST OF

Messrs. Methuen's
Publications

Poetry

RUDYARD KIPLING'S NEW POEMS

Rudyard Kipling. THE SEVEN SEAS. By RUDYARD KIPLING. Third Edition. *Crown 8vo. Buckram, gilt top.* 6s.

'The new poems of Mr. Rudyard Kipling have all the spirit and swing of their predecessors. Patriotism is the solid concrete foundation on which Mr. Kipling has built the whole of his work.'—*Times.*
'Full of passionate patriotism and the Imperial spirit.'—*Yorkshire Post.*
'The Empire has found a singer; it is no depreciation of the songs to say that statesmen may have, one way or other, to take account of them.'—*Manchester Guardian.*
'Animated through and through with indubitable genius.'—*Daily Telegraph.*
'Packed with inspiration, with humour, with pathos.'—*Daily Chronicle.*
'All the pride of empire, all the intoxication of power, all the ardour, the energy, the masterful strength and the wonderful endurance and death-scorning pluck which are the very bone and fibre and marrow of the British character are here.' —*Daily Mail.*

Rudyard Kipling. BARRACK-ROOM BALLADS; And Other Verses. By RUDYARD KIPLING. *Tenth Edition. Crown 8vo.* 6s.

'Mr. Kipling's verse is strong, vivid, full of character. . . . Unmistakable genius rings in every line.'—*Times.*
'The ballads teem with imagination, they palpitate with emotion. We read them with laughter and tears; the metres throb in our pulses, the cunningly ordered words tingle with life; and if this be not poetry, what is?'—*Pall Mall Gazette.*

"Q." POEMS AND BALLADS. By "Q.," Author of 'Green Bays,' etc. *Crown 8vo. Buckram.* 3s. 6d.

'His book will be read with interest by the most fastidious lovers of poetry, and it will please many who think they have no taste for poetry at all.'—*Scotsman.*

"Q." THE GOLDEN POMP: A Procession of English Lyrics from Surrey to Shirley, arranged by A. T. QUILLER COUCH. *Crown 8vo. Buckram.* 6s.

'A delightful volume: a really golden "Pomp."'—*Spectator.*

"Q." GREEN BAYS: Verses and Parodies. By "Q.," Author of 'Dead Man's Rock,' etc. *Second Edition. Crown 8vo.* 3s. 6d.

'The verses display a rare and versatile gift of parody, great command of metre, and a very pretty turn of humour.'—*Times.*

H. C. Beeching. LYRA SACRA : An Anthology of Sacred Verse. Edited by H. C. BEECHING, M.A. *Crown 8vo. Buckram.* 6s.

'An anthology of high excellence.'—*Athenæum.*
'A charming selection, which maintains a lofty standard of excellence.'—*Times.*

W. B. Yeats. AN ANTHOLOGY OF IRISH VERSE. Edited by W. B. YEATS. *Crown 8vo.* 3s. 6d.

'An attractive and catholic selection.'—*Times.*
'It is edited by the most original and most accomplished of modern Irish poets, and against his editing but a single objection can be brought, namely, that it excludes from the collection his own delicate lyrics.'—*Saturday Review.*

E. Mackay. A SONG OF THE SEA : MY LADY OF DREAMS, AND OTHER POEMS. By ERIC MACKAY, Author of 'The Love Letters of a Violinist.' *Second Edition. Fcap. 8vo, gilt top.* 5s.

'Everywhere Mr. Mackay displays himself the master of a style marked by all the characteristics of the best rhetoric. He has a keen sense of rhythm and of general balance; his verse is excellently sonorous.'—*Globe.*

Ibsen. BRAND. A Drama by HENRIK IBSEN. Translated by WILLIAM WILSON. *Second Edition. Crown 8vo.* 3s. 6d.

'The greatest world-poem of the nineteenth century next to "Faust." It is in the same set with "Agamemnon," with "Lear," with the literature that we now instinctively regard as high and holy.'—*Daily Chronicle.*

"A. G." VERSES TO ORDER. By "A. G." *Cr. 8vo.* 2s. 6d. *net.*

A small volume of verse by a writer whose initials are well known to Oxford men.
'A capital specimen of light academic poetry. These verses are very bright and engaging, easy and sufficiently witty.'—*St. James's Gazette.*

F. Langbridge. BALLADS OF THE BRAVE: Poems of Chivalry, Enterprise, Courage, and Constancy, from the Earliest Times to the Present Day. Edited, with Notes, by Rev. F. LANGBRIDGE. *Crown 8vo. Buckram.* 3s. 6d. *School Edition.* 2s. 6d.

'A very happy conception happily carried out. These "Ballads of the Brave" are intended to suit the real tastes of boys, and will suit the taste of the great majority.'—*Spectator.* 'The book is full of splendid things.'—*World.*

Lang and Craigie. THE POEMS OF ROBERT BURNS. Edited by ANDREW LANG and W. A. CRAIGIE. With Portrait. *Demy 8vo, gilt top.* 6s.

This edition contains a carefully collated Text, numerous Notes, critical and textual, a critical and biographical Introduction, and a Glossary.
'Among the editions in one volume, Mr. Andrew Lang's will take the place of authority.'—*Times.*
'To the general public the beauty of its type, and the fair proportions of its pages, as well as the excellent chronological arrangement of the poems, should make it acceptable enough. Mr. Lang and his publishers have certainly succeeded in producing an attractive popular edition of the poet, in which the brightly written biographical introduction is not the least notable feature.'—*Glasgow Herald.*

English Classics

Edited by W. E. Henley.

'Very dainty volumes are these; the paper, type, and light-green binding are all very agreeable to the eye. *Simplex munditiis* is the phrase that might be applied to them.'—*Globe*.

'The volumes are strongly bound in green buckram, are of a convenient size, and pleasant to look upon, so that whether on the shelf, or on the table, or in the hand the possessor is thoroughly content with them.'—*Guardian*.

THE LIFE AND OPINIONS OF TRISTRAM SHANDY. By LAWRENCE STERNE. With an Introduction by CHARLES WHIBLEY, and a Portrait. 2 *vols*. 7*s*.

THE COMEDIES OF WILLIAM CONGREVE. With an Introduction by G. S. STREET, and a Portrait. 2 *vols*. 7*s*.

THE ADVENTURES OF HAJJI BABA OF ISPAHAN. By JAMES MORIER. With an Introduction by E. G. BROWNE, M.A., and a Portrait. 2 *vols*. 7*s*.

THE LIVES OF DONNE, WOTTON, HOOKER, HERBERT, AND SANDERSON. By IZAAK WALTON. With an Introduction by VERNON BLACKBURN, and a Portrait. 3*s*. 6*d*.

THE LIVES OF THE ENGLISH POETS. By SAMUEL JOHNSON, LL.D. With an Introduction by J. H. MILLAR, and a Portrait. 3 *vols*. 10*s*. 6*d*.

Illustrated Books

Jane Barlow. THE BATTLE OF THE FROGS AND MICE, translated by JANE BARLOW, Author of 'Irish Idylls,' and pictured by F. D. BEDFORD. *Small 4to*. 6*s. net*.

S. Baring Gould. A BOOK OF FAIRY TALES retold by S. BARING GOULD. With numerous illustrations and initial letters by ARTHUR J. GASKIN. *Second Edition. Crown 8vo. Buckram.* 6*s*.

'Mr. Baring Gould is deserving of gratitude, in re-writing in honest, simple style the old stories that delighted the childhood of "our fathers and grandfathers." As to the form of the book, and the printing, which is by Messrs. Constable, it were difficult to commend overmuch.—*Saturday Review*.

S. Baring Gould. OLD ENGLISH FAIRY TALES. Collected and edited by S. BARING GOULD. With Numerous Illustrations by F. D. BEDFORD. *Second Edition. Crown 8vo. Buckram.* 6*s*.

A charming volume, which children will be sure to appreciate. The stories have been selected with great ingenuity from various old ballads and folk-tales, and, having been somewhat altered and readjusted, now stand forth, clothed in Mr. Baring Gould's delightful English, to enchant youthful readers.'—*Guardian*.

S. Baring Gould. A BOOK OF NURSERY SONGS AND RHYMES. Edited by S. BARING GOULD, and Illustrated by the Birmingham Art School. *Buckram, gilt top. Crown 8vo.* 6s.

'The volume is very complete in its way, as it contains nursery songs to the number of 77, game-rhymes, and jingles. To the student we commend the sensible introduction, and the explanatory notes. The volume is superbly printed on soft, thick paper, which it is a pleasure to touch; and the borders and pictures are among the very best specimens we have seen of the Gaskin school.'—*Birmingham Gazette.*

H. C. Beeching. A BOOK OF CHRISTMAS VERSE. Edited by H. C. BEECHING, M.A., and Illustrated by WALTER CRANE. *Crown 8vo, gilt top.* 5s.

A collection of the best verse inspired by the birth of Christ from the Middle Ages to the present day. A distinction of the book is the large number of poems it contains by modern authors, a few of which are here printed for the first time.

'An anthology which, from its unity of aim and high poetic excellence, has a better right to exist than most of its fellows.'—*Guardian.*

History

Gibbon. THE DECLINE AND FALL OF THE ROMAN EMPIRE. By EDWARD GIBBON. A New Edition, Edited with Notes, Appendices, and Maps, by J. B. BURY, M.A., Fellow of Trinity College, Dublin. *In Seven Volumes. Demy 8vo. Gilt top.* 8s. 6d. *each. Also crown 8vo.* 6s. *each. Vols. I. and II.*

'The time has certainly arrived for a new edition of Gibbon's great work. . . . Professor Bury is the right man to undertake this task. His learning is amazing, both in extent and accuracy. The book is issued in a handy form, and at a moderate price, and it is admirably printed.'—*Times.*

'The edition is edited as a classic should be edited, removing nothing, yet indicating the value of the text, and bringing it up to date. It promises to be of the utmost value, and will be a welcome addition to many libraries.'—*Scotsman.*

'This edition, so far as one may judge from the first instalment, is a marvel of erudition and critical skill, and it is the very minimum of praise to predict that the seven volumes of it will supersede Dean Milman's as the standard edition of our great historical classic.'—*Glasgow Herald.*

'The beau-ideal Gibbon has arrived at last.'—*Sketch.*

'At last there is an adequate modern edition of Gibbon. . . . The best edition the nineteenth century could produce.'—*Manchester Guardian.*

Flinders Petrie. A HISTORY OF EGYPT, FROM THE EARLIEST TIMES TO THE PRESENT DAY. Edited by W. M. FLINDERS PETRIE, D.C.L., LL.D., Professor of Egyptology at University College. *Fully Illustrated. In Six Volumes. Crown 8vo.* 6s. *each.*

Vol. I. PREHISTORIC TIMES TO XVI. DYNASTY. W. M. F. Petrie. *Second Edition.*

Vol. II. THE XVIITH AND XVIIITH DYNASTIES. W. M. F. Petrie.

'A history written in the spirit of scientific precision so worthily represented by Dr. Petrie and his school cannot but promote sound and accurate study, and supply a vacant place in the English literature of Egyptology.'—*Times.*

MESSRS. METHUEN'S LIST 15

Flinders Petrie. EGYPTIAN TALES. Edited by W. M. FLINDERS PETRIE. Illustrated by TRISTRAM ELLIS. *In Two Volumes. Crown 8vo. 3s. 6d. each.*

'A valuable addition to the literature of comparative folk-lore. The drawings are really illustrations in the literal sense of the word.'—*Globe.*
'It has a scientific value to the student of history and archæology.'—*Scotsman.*
'Invaluable as a picture of life in Palestine and Egypt.'—*Daily News.*

Flinders Petrie. EGYPTIAN DECORATIVE ART. By W. M. FLINDERS PETRIE, D.C.L. With 120 Illustrations. *Crown 8vo. 3s. 6d.*

'Professor Flinders Petrie is not only a profound Egyptologist, but an accomplished student of comparative archæology. In these lectures, delivered at the Royal Institution, he displays both qualifications with rare skill in elucidating the development of decorative art in Egypt, and in tracing its influence on the art of other countries.'—*Times.*

S. Baring Gould. THE TRAGEDY OF THE CÆSARS. The Emperors of the Julian and Claudian Lines. With numerous Illustrations from Busts, Gems, Cameos, etc. By S. BARING GOULD, Author of 'Mehalah,' etc. *Fourth Edition. Royal 8vo. 15s.*

'A most splendid and fascinating book on a subject of undying interest. The great feature of the book is the use the author has made of the existing portraits of the Caesars, and the admirable critical subtlety he has exhibited in dealing with this line of research. It is brilliantly written, and the illustrations are supplied on a scale of profuse magnificence.'—*Daily Chronicle.*
'The volumes will in no sense disappoint the general reader. Indeed, in their way, there is nothing in any sense so good in English. . . . Mr. Baring Gould has presented his narrative in such a way as not to make one dull page.'—*Athenæum.*

H. de B. Gibbins. INDUSTRY IN ENGLAND : HISTORICAL OUTLINES. By H. DE B. GIBBINS, M.A., D.Litt. With 5 Maps. *Demy 8vo. 10s. 6d. Pp. 450.*

This book is written with the view of affording a clear view of the main facts of English Social and Industrial History placed in due perspective. Beginning with prehistoric times, it passes in review the growth and advance of industry up to the nineteenth century, showing its gradual development and progress. The author has endeavoured to place before his readers the history of industry as a connected whole in which all these developments have their proper place. The book is illustrated by Maps, Diagrams, and Tables, and aided by copious Footnotes.

A. Clark. THE COLLEGES OF OXFORD : Their History, their Traditions. By Members of the University. Edited by A. CLARK, M.A., Fellow and Tutor of Lincoln College. *8vo. 12s. 6d.*

'A work which will certainly be appealed to for many years as the standard book on the Colleges of Oxford.'—*Athenæum.*

Perrens. THE HISTORY OF FLORENCE FROM 1434 TO 1492. By F. T. PERRENS. Translated by HANNAH LYNCH. *8vo. 12s. 6d.*

A history of Florence under the domination of Cosimo, Piero, and Lorenzo de Medicis.
'This is a standard book by an honest and intelligent historian, who has deserved well of all who are interested in Italian history.'—*Manchester Guardian.*

J. Wells. A SHORT HISTORY OF ROME. By J. WELLS, M.A., Fellow and Tutor of Wadham Coll., Oxford. With 4 Maps. *Crown 8vo.* 3s. 6d. 350 pp.

This book is intended for the Middle and Upper Forms of Public Schools and for Pass Students at the Universities. It contains copious Tables, etc.

'An original work written on an original plan, and with uncommon freshness and vigour.'—*Speaker.*

E. L. S. Horsburgh. THE CAMPAIGN OF WATERLOO. By E. L. S. HORSBURGH, B.A. *With Plans. Crown 8vo.* 5s.

'A brilliant essay—simple, sound, and thorough.'—*Daily Chronicle.*
'A study, the most concise, the most lucid, the most critical that has been produced.'
—*Birmingham Mercury.*

H. B. George. BATTLES OF ENGLISH HISTORY. By H. B. GEORGE, M.A., Fellow of New College, Oxford. *With numerous Plans. Third Edition. Crown 8vo.* 6s.

'Mr. George has undertaken a very useful task—that of making military affairs intelligible and instructive to non-military readers—and has executed it with laudable intelligence and industry, and with a large measure of success.'—*Times.*
'This book is almost a revelation; and we heartily congratulate the author on his work.'—*Daily Chronicle.*

O. Browning. A SHORT HISTORY OF MEDIÆVAL ITALY, A.D. 1250-1530. By OSCAR BROWNING, Fellow and Tutor of King's College, Cambridge. *Second Edition. In Two Volumes. Crown 8vo.* 5s. each.

    VOL. I. 1250-1409.—Guelphs and Ghibellines.
    VOL. II. 1409-1530.—The Age of the Condottieri.

'A vivid picture of mediæval Italy.'—*Standard.*
'Mr. Browning is to be congratulated on the production of a work of immense labour and learning.'—*Westminster Gazette.*

O'Grady. THE STORY OF IRELAND. By STANDISH O'GRADY, Author of 'Finn and his Companions.' *Cr. 8vo.* 2s. 6d.

'Most delightful, most stimulating. Its racy humour, its original imaginings, make it one of the freshest, breeziest volumes.'—*Methodist Times.*

Biography

S. Baring Gould. THE LIFE OF NAPOLEON BONAPARTE. By S. BARING GOULD. With over 450 Illustrations in the Text and 13 Photogravure Plates. *Large quarto. Gilt top.* 36s.

'A brilliant and attractive volume. It impresses first by reason of its bulk, and next by reason of its substantial and striking binding. Within, it is remarkable, to begin with, for the considerable number and unusual excellence of its illustrations. Never before, it is safe to say, have so many pictures relating to Napoleon been brought together within the limits of an English book. The portraits alone are multitudinous; Bonaparte is presented to us at all ages, in all sorts of costume, and amid very varied circumstances. Then there are reproductions of statuettes, busts, and medals, caricatures, portraits of his connections by birth and marriage, representations of events in which he took part, and what not. The list of illustrations in the text covers nine pages, and in addition there are a dozen full-page photogravures, in which famous paintings are reproduced. Altogether, this is a table-book of the first class. But it is more. It embodies "a study of the character and opinions of Napoleon" on which Mr. Baring Gould can be freely congratulated. The writer's plan has been to "lay on one side what concerned Napoleon's military achievements and the political importance of his life, so far as did not bear on the development of his mind and the movements of his heart." By this means a novel point of view has been secured, and the result is a narrative of which the chief characteristic is an agreeable freshness.'—*Globe.*

R. L. Stevenson. VAILIMA LETTERS. By ROBERT LOUIS STEVENSON. With an Etched Portrait by WILLIAM STRANG, and other Illustrations. *Second Edition. Crown 8vo. Buckram. 7s. 6d.*

'The Vailima Letters are rich in all the varieties of that charm which have secured for Stevenson the affection of many others besides "journalists, fellow-novelists, and boys."'—*The Times.*

'Few publications have in our time been more eagerly awaited than these "Vailima Letters," giving the first fruits of the correspondence of Robert Louis Stevenson. But, high as the tide of expectation has run, no reader can possibly be disappointed in the result.'—*St. James's Gazette.*

'For the student of English literature these letters indeed are a treasure. They are more like "Scott's Journal" in kind than any other literary autobiography.' —*National Observer.*

Victor Hugo. THE LETTERS OF VICTOR HUGO. Translated from the French by F. CLARKE, M.A. *In Two Volumes. Demy 8vo. 10s. 6d. each. Vol. I. 1815-35.*

This is the first volume of one of the most interesting and important collection of letters ever published in France. The correspondence dates from Victor Hugo's boyhood to his death, and none of the letters have been published before. The arrangement is chiefly chronological, but where there is an interesting set of letters to one person these are arranged together. The first volume contains, among others, (1) Letters to his father; (2) to his young wife; (3) to his confessor, Lamennais; (4) a very important set of about fifty letters to Sainte-Beuve; (5) letters about his early books and plays.

'A charming and vivid picture of a man whose egotism never marred his natural kindness, and whose vanity did not impair his greatness.'—*Standard.*

J. M. Rigg. ST. ANSELM OF CANTERBURY: A CHAPTER IN THE HISTORY OF RELIGION. By J. M. RIGG, of Lincoln's Inn, Barrister-at-Law. *Demy 8vo. 7s. 6d.*

This work gives for the first time in moderate compass a complete portrait of St. Anselm, exhibiting him in his intimate and interior as well as in his public life. Thus, while the great ecclesiastico-political struggle in which he played so prominent a part is fully dealt with, unusual prominence is given to the profound and subtle speculations by which he permanently influenced theological and metaphysical thought; while it will be a surprise to most readers to find him also appearing as the author of some of the most exquisite religious poetry in the Latin language.

'Mr. Rigg has told the story of the great Primate's life with scholarly ability, and has thereby contributed an interesting chapter to the history of the Norman period.' —*Daily Chronicle.*

A 3

MESSRS. METHUEN'S LIST

F. W. Joyce. THE LIFE OF SIR FREDERICK GORE OUSELEY. By F. W. JOYCE, M.A. With Portraits and Illustrations. *Crown 8vo. 7s. 6d.*

'The book gives us a complete picture of the life of one who will ever be held in loving remembrance, and who in the history of music in this country will always occupy a prominent position on account of the many services he rendered to the art.'—*Musical News.*
'This book has been undertaken in quite the right spirit, and written with sympathy, insight, and considerable literary skill.'—*Times.*

W. G. Collingwood. THE LIFE OF JOHN RUSKIN. By W. G. COLLINGWOOD, M.A., Editor of Mr. Ruskin's Poems. With numerous Portraits, and 13 Drawings by Mr. Ruskin. *Second Edition. 2 vols. 8vo. 32s.*

'No more magnificent volumes have been published for a long time.'—*Times.*
'It is long since we had a biography with such delights of substance and of form. Such a book is a pleasure for the day, and a joy for ever.'—*Daily Chronicle.*

C. Waldstein. JOHN RUSKIN: a Study. By CHARLES WALDSTEIN, M.A., Fellow of King's College, Cambridge. With a Photogravure Portrait after Professor HERKOMER. *Post 8vo. 5s.*

'A thoughtful, impartial, well-written criticism of Ruskin's teaching, intended to separate what the author regards as valuable and permanent from what is transient and erroneous in the great master's writing.'—*Daily Chronicle.*

W. H. Hutton. THE LIFE OF SIR THOMAS MORE. By W. H. HUTTON, M.A., Author of 'William Laud.' *With Portraits. Crown 8vo. 5s.*

'The book lays good claim to high rank among our biographies. It is excellently, even lovingly, written.'—*Scotsman.* 'An excellent monograph.'—*Times.*

M. Kaufmann. CHARLES KINGSLEY. By M. KAUFMANN, M.A. *Crown 8vo. Buckram. 5s.*

A biography of Kingsley, especially dealing with his achievements in social reform.
'The author has certainly gone about his work with conscientiousness and industry.— *Sheffield Daily Telegraph.*

A. F. Robbins. THE EARLY PUBLIC LIFE OF WILLIAM EWART GLADSTONE. By A. F. ROBBINS. *With Portraits. Crown 8vo. 6s.*

'Considerable labour and much skill of presentation have not been unworthily expended on this interesting work.'—*Times.*

Clark Russell. THE LIFE OF ADMIRAL LORD COLLINGWOOD. By W. CLARK RUSSELL, Author of 'The Wreck of the Grosvenor.' With Illustrations by F. BRANGWYN. *Third Edition. Crown 8vo. 6s.*

'A book which we should like to see in the hands of every boy in the country.'— *St. James's Gazette.* 'A really good book.'—*Saturday Review.*

Southey. ENGLISH SEAMEN (Howard, Clifford, Hawkins, Drake, Cavendish). By ROBERT SOUTHEY. Edited, with an Introduction, by DAVID HANNAY. *Second Edition. Crown 8vo. 6s.*

'Admirable and well-told stories of our naval history.'—*Army and Navy Gazette.*
'A brave, inspiring book.'—*Black and White.*

General Literature

S. Baring Gould. OLD COUNTRY LIFE. By S. BARING GOULD, Author of 'Mehalah,' etc. With Sixty-seven Illustrations by W. PARKINSON, F. D. BEDFORD, and F. MASEY. *Large Crown 8vo.* 10s. 6d. *Fifth and Cheaper Edition.* 6s.

'"Old Country Life," as healthy wholesome reading, full of breezy life and movement, full of quaint stories vigorously told, will not be excelled by any book to be published throughout the year. Sound, hearty, and English to the core.'—*World.*

S. Baring Gould. HISTORIC ODDITIES AND STRANGE EVENTS. By S. BARING GOULD. *Third Edition. Crown 8vo.* 6s.

'A collection of exciting and entertaining chapters. The whole volume is delightful reading.'—*Times.*

S. Baring Gould. FREAKS OF FANATICISM. By S. BARING GOULD. *Third Edition. Crown 8vo.* 6s.

'Mr. Baring Gould has a keen eye for colour and effect, and the subjects he has chosen give ample scope to his descriptive and analytic faculties. A perfectly fascinating book.'—*Scottish Leader.*

S. Baring Gould. A GARLAND OF COUNTRY SONG: English Folk Songs with their Traditional Melodies. Collected and arranged by S. BARING GOULD and H. FLEETWOOD SHEPPARD. *Demy 4to.* 6s.

S. Baring Gould. SONGS OF THE WEST: Traditional Ballads and Songs of the West of England, with their Traditional Melodies. Collected by S. BARING GOULD, M.A., and H. FLEETWOOD SHEPPARD, M.A. Arranged for Voice and Piano. In 4 Parts (containing 25 Songs each), *Parts I., II., III.,* 3s. each. *Part IV.,* 5s. *In one Vol., French morocco,* 15s.

'A rich collection of humour, pathos, grace, and poetic fancy.'—*Saturday Review.*

S. Baring Gould. YORKSHIRE ODDITIES AND STRANGE EVENTS. *Fourth Edition. Crown 8vo.* 6s.

S. Baring Gould. STRANGE SURVIVALS AND SUPERSTITIONS. With Illustrations. By S. BARING GOULD. *Crown 8vo. Second Edition.* 6s.

'We have read Mr. Baring Gould's book from beginning to end. It is full of quaint and various information, and there is not a dull page in it.'—*Notes and Queries.*

S. Baring Gould. THE DESERTS OF SOUTHERN FRANCE. By S. BARING GOULD. With numerous Illustrations by F. D. BEDFORD, S. HUTTON, etc. *2 vols. Demy 8vo.* 32s.

This book describes the great barren tableland that extends to the south of Limousin, a country of dolomite cliffs, and cañons, and subterranean rivers. The region is full of prehistoric and historic interest, relics of cave-dwellers, of mediæval robbers, and of the English domination and the Hundred Years' War.

'His two richly-illustrated volumes are full of matter of interest to the geologist, the archæologist, and the student of history and manners.'—*Scotsman.*

R. S. Baden-Powell. THE DOWNFALL OF PREMPEH. A Diary of Life with the Native Levy in Ashanti, 1895. By Lieut.-Col. BADEN-POWELL. With 21 Illustrations, a Map, and a Special Chapter on the Political and Commercial Position of Ashanti by Sir GEORGE BADEN-POWELL, K.C.M.G., M.P. *Demy 8vo.* 10s. 6d.

'A compact, faithful, most readable record of the campaign.'—*Daily News.*
'A bluff and vigorous narrative.'—*Glasgow Herald.*

G. W. Steevens. NAVAL POLICY: WITH A DESCRIPTION OF ENGLISH AND FOREIGN NAVIES. By G. W. STEEVENS. *Demy 8vo.* 6s.

This book is a description of the British and other more important navies of the world, with a sketch of the lines on which our naval policy might possibly be developed. It describes our recent naval policy, and shows what our naval force really is. A detailed but non-technical account is given of the instruments of modern warfare—guns, armour, engines, and the like—with a view to determine how far we are abreast of modern invention and modern requirements. An ideal policy is then sketched for the building and manning of our fleet; and the last chapter is devoted to docks, coaling-stations, and especially colonial defence.

'An extremely able and interesting work.'—*Daily Chronicle.*

W. E. Gladstone. THE SPEECHES AND PUBLIC ADDRESSES OF THE RT. HON. W. E. GLADSTONE, M.P. Edited by A. W. HUTTON, M.A., and H. J. COHEN, M.A. With Portraits. *8vo. Vols. IX. and X.* 12s. 6d. *each.*

Henley and Whibley. A BOOK OF ENGLISH PROSE. Collected by W. E. HENLEY and CHARLES WHIBLEY. *Cr. 8vo.* 6s.

'A unique volume of extracts—an art gallery of early prose.'—*Birmingham Post.*
'An admirable companion to Mr. Henley's "Lyra Heroica."'—*Saturday Review.*
'Quite delightful. The choice made has been excellent, and the volume has been most admirably printed by Messrs. Constable. A greater treat for those not well acquainted with pre-Restoration prose could not be imagined.'—*Athenæum.*

G. W. Steevens. MONOLOGUES OF THE DEAD. By G. W. STEEVENS. *Foolscap 8vo.* 3s. 6d.

A series of Soliloquies in which famous men of antiquity—Julius Cæsar, Nero, Alcibiades, etc., attempt to express themselves in the modes of thought and language of to-day.

'The effect is sometimes splendid, sometimes bizarre, but always amazingly clever.'
—*Pall Mall Gazette.*

J. Wells. OXFORD AND OXFORD LIFE. By Members of the University. Edited by J. WELLS, M.A., Fellow and Tutor of Wadham College. *Crown 8vo.* 3s. 6d.

This work contains an account of life at Oxford—intellectual, social, and religious—a careful estimate of necessary expenses, a review of recent changes, a statement of the present position of the University, and chapters on Women's Education, aids to study, and University Extension.

'We congratulate Mr. Wells on the production of a readable and intelligent account of Oxford as it is at the present time, written by persons who are possessed of a close acquaintance with the system and life of the University.'—*Athenæum.*

W. M. Dixon. A PRIMER OF TENNYSON. By W. M. DIXON, M.A., Professor of English Literature at Mason College. *Crown 8vo. 2s. 6d.*

'Much sound and well-expressed criticism and acute literary judgments. The bibliography is a boon.'—*Speaker.*
'No better estimate of the late Laureate's work has yet been published. His sketch of Tennyson's life contains everything essential; his bibliography is full and concise: his literary criticism is most interesting.'—*Glasgow Herald.*

W. A. Craigie. A PRIMER OF BURNS. By W. A. CRAIGIE. *Crown 8vo. 2s. 6d.*

This book is planned on a method similar to the 'Primer of Tennyson.' It has also a glossary.
'A valuable addition to the literature of the poet.'—*Times.*
'An excellent short account.'—*Pall Mall Gazette.*
'An admirable introduction.'—*Globe.*

L. Whibley. GREEK OLIGARCHIES: THEIR ORGANISATION AND CHARACTER. By L. WHIBLEY, M.A., Fellow of Pembroke College, Cambridge. *Crown 8vo. 6s.*

'An exceedingly useful handbook: a careful and well-arranged study of an obscure subject.'—*Times.*
'Mr. Whibley is never tedious or pedantic.'—*Pall Mall Gazette.*

W. B. Worsfold. SOUTH AFRICA: Its History and its Future. By W. BASIL WORSFOLD, M.A. *With a Map. Second Edition. Crown 8vo. 6s.*

'An intensely interesting book.'—*Daily Chronicle.*
'A monumental work compressed into a very moderate compass.'—*World.*

C. H. Pearson. ESSAYS AND CRITICAL REVIEWS. By C. H. PEARSON, M.A., Author of 'National Life and Character.' Edited, with a Biographical Sketch, by H. A. STRONG, M.A., LL.D. With a Portrait. *Demy 8vo. 10s. 6d.*

'These fine essays illustrate the great breadth of his historical and literary sympathies and the remarkable variety of his intellectual interests.'—*Glasgow Herald.*
'Remarkable for careful handling, breadth of view, and thorough knowledge.'—*Scotsman.* 'Charming essays.'—*Spectator.*

L. F. Price. ECONOMIC SCIENCE AND PRACTICE. By L. F. PRICE, M.A., Fellow of Oriel College, Oxford. *Crown 8vo. 6s.*

This book consists of a number of Studies in Economics and Industrial and Social Problems.
'The book is well written, giving evidence of considerable literary ability, and clear mental grasp of the subject under consideration.'—*Western Morning News.*

C. F. Andrews. CHRISTIANITY AND THE LABOUR QUESTION. By C. F. ANDREWS, B.A. *Crown 8vo. 2s. 6d.*

'A bold and scholarly survey of the principle and motive which have shaped and determined the conflicts of Labour.'—*Speaker.*

Ouida. VIEWS AND OPINIONS. By OUIDA. *Crown 8vo. Second Edition. 6s.*

'Ouida is outspoken, and the reader of this book will not have a dull moment. The book is full of variety, and sparkles with entertaining matter.'—*Speaker.*

J. S. Shedlock. THE PIANOFORTE SONATA: Its Origin and Development. By J. S. SHEDLOCK. *Crown 8vo.* 5s.

'This work should be in the possession of every musician and amateur, for it not only embodies a concise and lucid history of the origin of one of the most important forms of musical composition, but, by reason of the painstaking research and accuracy of the author's statements, it is a very valuable work for reference.' —*Athenæum.*

E. M. Bowden. THE EXAMPLE OF BUDDHA: Being Quotations from Buddhist Literature for each Day in the Year. Compiled by E. M. BOWDEN. With Preface by Sir EDWIN ARNOLD. *Third Edition.* 16mo. 2s. 6d.

J. Beever. PRACTICAL FLY-FISHING, Founded on Nature, by JOHN BEEVER, late of the Thwaite House, Coniston. A New Edition, with a Memoir of the Author by W. G. COLLINGWOOD, M.A. *Crown 8vo.* 3s. 6d.

A little book on Fly-Fishing by an old friend of Mr. Ruskin.

Science

Freudenreich. DAIRY BACTERIOLOGY. A Short Manual for the Use of Students. By Dr. ED. VON FREUDENREICH. Translated from the German by J. R. AINSWORTH DAVIS, B.A., F.C.P. *Crown 8vo.* 2s. 6d.

Chalmers Mitchell. OUTLINES OF BIOLOGY. By P. CHALMERS MITCHELL, M.A., F.Z.S. *Fully Illustrated. Crown 8vo.* 6s.

A text-book designed to cover the new Schedule issued by the Royal College of Physicians and Surgeons.

G. Massee. A MONOGRAPH OF THE MYXOGASTRES. By GEORGE MASSEE. With 12 Coloured Plates. *Royal 8vo.* 18s. net.

'A work much in advance of any book in the language treating of this group of organisms. It is indispensable to every student of the Myxogastres. The coloured plates deserve high praise for their accuracy and execution.'—*Nature.*

Philosophy

L. T. Hobhouse. THE THEORY OF KNOWLEDGE. By L. T. HOBHOUSE, Fellow and Tutor of Corpus College, Oxford. *Demy 8vo.* 21s.

' The most important contribution to English philosophy since the publication of Mr. Bradley's "Appearance and Reality." Full of brilliant criticism and of positive theories which are models of lucid statement.'—*Glasgow Herald.*

' An elaborate and often brilliantly written volume. The treatment is one of great freshness, and the illustrations are particularly numerous and apt.'—*Times.*

W. H. Fairbrother. THE PHILOSOPHY OF T. H. GREEN. By W. H. FAIRBROTHER, M.A., Lecturer at Lincoln College, Oxford. *Crown 8vo.* 3s. 6d.

> This volume is expository, not critical, and is intended for senior students at the Universities and others, as a statement of Green's teaching, and an introduction to the study of Idealist Philosophy.

> 'In every way an admirable book. As an introduction to the writings of perhaps the most remarkable speculative thinker whom England has produced in the present century, nothing could be better.'—*Glasgow Herald.*

F. W. Bussell. THE SCHOOL OF PLATO : its Origin and its Revival under the Roman Empire. By F. W. BUSSELL, M.A., Fellow and Tutor of Brasenose College, Oxford. *Demy 8vo.* 10s. 6d.

> 'A highly valuable contribution to the history of ancient thought.'—*Glasgow Herald.*
> 'A clever and stimulating book, provocative of thought and deserving careful reading.'—*Manchester Guardian.*

F. S. Granger. THE WORSHIP OF THE ROMANS. By F. S. GRANGER, M.A., Litt.D., Professor of Philosophy at University College, Nottingham. *Crown 8vo.* 6s.

> The author delineates that group of beliefs which stood in close connection with the Roman religion, and among the subjects treated are Dreams, Nature Worship, Roman Magic, Divination, Holy Places, Victims, etc.

> 'A scholarly analysis of the religious ceremonies, beliefs, and superstitions of ancient Rome, conducted in the new instructive light of comparative anthropology.'—*Times.*

Theology

E. C. S. Gibson. THE XXXIX. ARTICLES OF THE CHURCH OF ENGLAND. Edited with an Introduction by E. C. S. GIBSON, D.D., Vicar of Leeds, late Principal of Wells Theological College. *In Two Volumes. Demy 8vo.* 7s. 6d. each. Vol. I. *Articles I.-VIII.*

> 'The tone maintained throughout is not that of the partial advocate, but the faithful exponent.'—*Scotsman.*
> 'There are ample proofs of clearness of expression, sobriety of judgment, and breadth of view. . . . The book will be welcome to all students of the subject, and its sound, definite, and loyal theology ought to be of great service.'—*National Observer.*
> 'So far from repelling the general reader, its orderly arrangement, lucid treatment, and felicity of diction invite and encourage his attention.'—*Yorkshire Post.*

R. L. Ottley. THE DOCTRINE OF THE INCARNATION. By R. L. OTTLEY, M.A., late Fellow of Magdalen College, Oxon., Principal of Pusey House. *In Two Volumes. Demy 8vo.* 15s.

> 'Learned and reverent : lucid and well arranged.'—*Record.*
> 'Accurate, well ordered, and judicious.'—*National Observer.*
> 'A clear and remarkably full account of the main currents of speculation. Scholarly precision . . . genuine tolerance . . . intense interest in his subject—are Mr. Ottley's merits.'—*Guardian.*

F. B. Jevons. AN INTRODUCTION TO THE HISTORY OF RELIGION. By F. B. JEVONS, M.A., Litt.D., Tutor at the University of Durham. *Demy 8vo.* 10s. 6d.

Mr. F. B. Jevons' 'Introduction to the History of Religion' treats of early religion, from the point of view of Anthropology and Folk-lore; and is the first attempt that has been made in any language to weave together the results of recent investigations into such topics as Sympathetic Magic, Taboo, Totemism, Fetishism, etc., so as to present a systematic account of the growth of primitive religion and the development of early religious institutions.

'Displays mental power of no ordinary kind, and is the result of much and well-directed study.'—*Scotsman.*

S. R. Driver. SERMONS ON SUBJECTS CONNECTED WITH THE OLD TESTAMENT. By S. R. DRIVER, D.D., Canon of Christ Church, Regius Professor of Hebrew in the University of Oxford. *Crown 8vo.* 6s.

'A welcome companion to the author's famous 'Introduction.' No man can read these discourses without feeling that Dr. Driver is fully alive to the deeper teaching of the Old Testament.'—*Guardian.*

T. K. Cheyne. FOUNDERS OF OLD TESTAMENT CRITICISM: Biographical, Descriptive, and Critical Studies. By T. K. CHEYNE, D.D., Oriel Professor of the Interpretation of Holy Scripture at Oxford. *Large crown 8vo.* 7s. 6d.

This important book is a historical sketch of O. T. Criticism in the form of biographical studies from the days of Eichhorn to those of Driver and Robertson Smith. It is the only book of its kind in English.

'A very learned and instructive work.'—*Times.*

C. H. Prior. CAMBRIDGE SERMONS. Edited by C. H. PRIOR, M.A., Fellow and Tutor of Pembroke College. *Crown 8vo.* 6s.

A volume of sermons preached before the University of Cambridge by various preachers, including the Archbishop of Canterbury and Bishop Westcott.

'A representative collection. Bishop Westcott's is a noble sermon.'—*Guardian.*

H. C. Beeching. SERMONS TO SCHOOLBOYS. By H. C. BEECHING, M.A., Rector of Yattendon, Berks. With a Preface by Canon SCOTT HOLLAND. *Crown 8vo.* 2s. 6d.

Seven sermons preached before the boys of Bradfield College.

E. B. Layard. RELIGION IN BOYHOOD. Notes on the Religious Training of Boys. With a Preface by J. R. ILLINGWORTH. By E. B. LAYARD, M.A. 18mo. 1s.

W. Yorke Faussett. THE *DE CATECHIZANDIS RUDIBUS* OF ST. AUGUSTINE. Edited, with Introduction, Notes, etc., by W. YORKE FAUSSETT, M.A., late Scholar of Balliol Coll. *Crown 8vo.* 3s. 6d.

An edition of a Treatise on the Essentials of Christian Doctrine, and the best methods of impressing them on candidates for baptism. The editor bestows upon this patristic work the same care which a treatise of Cicero might claim. There is a general Introduction, a careful Analysis, a full Commentary, and other useful matter. No better introduction to the study of the Latin Fathers, their style and diction, could be found than this treatise, which also has no lack of modern interest.

'Ably and judiciously edited on the same principle as the ordinary Greek and Latin texts.'—*Glasgow Herald.*

Devotional Books

*With Full-page Illustrations. Fcap. 8vo. Buckram. 3s. 6d.
Padded morocco, 5s.*

THE IMITATION OF CHRIST. By THOMAS À KEMPIS. With an Introduction by DEAN FARRAR. Illustrated by C. M. GERE, and printed in black and red. *Second Edition.*

'Amongst all the innumerable English editions of the "Imitation," there can have been few which were prettier than this one, printed in strong and handsome type by Messrs. Constable, with all the glory of red initials, and the comfort of buckram binding.'—*Glasgow Herald.*

THE CHRISTIAN YEAR. By JOHN KEBLE. With an Introduction and Notes by W. LOCK, M.A., Sub-Warden of Keble College, Ireland Professor at Oxford, Author of the 'Life of John Keble.' Illustrated by R. ANNING BELL.

'The present edition is annotated with all the care and insight to be expected from Mr. Lock. The progress and circumstances of its composition are detailed in the Introduction. There is an interesting Appendix on the MSS. of the "Christian Year," and another giving the order in which the poems were written. A "Short Analysis of the Thought" is prefixed to each, and any difficulty in the text is explained in a note.—*Guardian.*

'The most acceptable edition of this ever-popular work.'—*Globe.*

Leaders of Religion

Edited by H. C. BEECHING, M.A. *With Portraits, crown 8vo.*

A series of short biographies of the most prominent leaders of religious life and thought of all ages and countries.

3/6

The following are ready—

CARDINAL NEWMAN. By R. H. HUTTON
JOHN WESLEY. By J. H. OVERTON, M.A.
BISHOP WILBERFORCE. By G. W. DANIEL, M.A.
CARDINAL MANNING. By A. W. HUTTON, M.A.
CHARLES SIMEON. By H. C. G. MOULE, M.A.
JOHN KEBLE. By WALTER LOCK, M.A.
THOMAS CHALMERS. By Mrs. OLIPHANT.
LANCELOT ANDREWES. By R. L. OTTLEY, M.A.
AUGUSTINE OF CANTERBURY. By E. L. CUTTS, D.D.
WILLIAM LAUD. By W. H. HUTTON, M.A.
JOHN KNOX. By F. M'CUNN.
JOHN HOWE. By R. F. HORTON, D.D.
BISHOP KEN. By F. A. CLARKE, M.A.
GEORGE FOX, THE QUAKER. By T. HODGKIN, D.C.L.

Other volumes will be announced in due course.

Fiction

SIX SHILLING NOVELS

Marie Corelli's Novels
Crown 8vo. 6s. each.

A ROMANCE OF TWO WORLDS. *Fourteenth Edition.*

VENDETTA. *Twelfth Edition.*

THELMA. *Sixteenth Edition.*

ARDATH. *Tenth Edition.*

THE SOUL OF LILITH. *Ninth Edition.*

WORMWOOD. *Eighth Edition.*

BARABBAS: A DREAM OF THE WORLD'S TRAGEDY. *Twenty-ninth Edition.*

'The tender reverence of the treatment and the imaginative beauty of the writing have reconciled us to the daring of the conception, and the conviction is forced on us that even so exalted a subject cannot be made too familiar to us, provided it be presented in the true spirit of Christian faith. The amplifications of the Scripture narrative are often conceived with high poetic insight, and this "Dream of the World's Tragedy" is, despite some trifling incongruities, a lofty and not inadequate paraphrase of the supreme climax of the inspired narrative.'—*Dublin Review.*

THE SORROWS OF SATAN. *Thirty-fourth Edition.*

'A very powerful piece of work. . . . The conception is magnificent, and is likely to win an abiding place within the memory of man. . . . The author has immense command of language, and a limitless audacity. . . . This interesting and remarkable romance will live long after much of the ephemeral literature of the day is forgotten. . . . A literary phenomenon . . . novel, and even sublime.'—W. T. STEAD in the *Review of Reviews.*

Anthony Hope's Novels
Crown 8vo. 6s. each.

THE GOD IN THE CAR. *Seventh Edition.*

'A very remarkable book, deserving of critical analysis impossible within our limit; brilliant, but not superficial; well considered, but not elaborated; constructed with the proverbial art that conceals, but yet allows itself to be enjoyed by readers to whom fine literary method is a keen pleasure.'—*The World.*

A CHANGE OF AIR. *Fourth Edition.*

'A graceful, vivacious comedy, true to human nature. The characters are traced with a masterly hand.'—*Times.*

A MAN OF MARK. *Fourth Edition.*

'Of all Mr. Hope's books, "A Man of Mark" is the one which best compares with "The Prisoner of Zenda."'—*National Observer.*

THE CHRONICLES OF COUNT ANTONIO. *Third Edition.*

'It is a perfectly enchanting story of love and chivalry, and pure romance. The outlawed Count is the most constant, desperate, and withal modest and tender of lovers, a peerless gentleman, an intrepid fighter, a very faithful friend, and a most magnanimous foe.'—*Guardian.*

S. Baring Gould's Novels
Crown 8vo. 6s. each.

'To say that a book is by the author of "Mehalah" is to imply that it contains a story cast on strong lines, containing dramatic possibilities, vivid and sympathetic descriptions of Nature, and a wealth of ingenious imagery.'—*Speaker.*

'That whatever Mr. Baring Gould writes is well worth reading, is a conclusion that may be very generally accepted. His views of life are fresh and vigorous, his language pointed and characteristic, the incidents of which he makes use are striking and original, his characters are life-like, and though somewhat exceptional people, are drawn and coloured with artistic force. Add to this that his descriptions of scenes and scenery are painted with the loving eyes and skilled hands of a master of his art, that he is always fresh and never dull, and under such conditions it is no wonder that readers have gained confidence both in his power of amusing and satisfying them, and that year by year his popularity widens.'—*Court Circular.*

ARMINELL : A Social Romance. *Fourth Edition.*

URITH : A Story of Dartmoor. *Fifth Edition.*
'The author is at his best.'—*Times.*

IN THE ROAR OF THE SEA *Fifth Edition.*
'One of the best imagined and most enthralling stories the author has produced.—*Saturday Review.*

MRS. CURGENVEN OF CURGENVEN. *Fourth Edition.*
'The swing of the narrative is splendid.'—*Sussex Daily News.*

CHEAP JACK ZITA. *Fourth Edition.*
'A powerful drama of human passion.'—*Westminster Gazette.*
'A story worthy the author.'—*National Observer.*

THE QUEEN OF LOVE. *Fourth Edition.*
'You cannot put it down until you have finished it.'—*Punch.*
'Can be heartily recommended to all who care for cleanly, energetic, and interesting fiction.'—*Sussex Daily News.*

KITTY ALONE. *Fourth Edition.*
'A strong and original story, teeming with graphic description, stirring incident, and, above all, with vivid and enthralling human interest.'—*Daily Telegraph.*

NOÉMI : A Romance of the Cave-Dwellers. Illustrated by R. CATON WOODVILLE. *Third Edition.*
'"Noémi" is as excellent a tale of fighting and adventure as one may wish to meet. The narrative also runs clear and sharp as the Loire itself.'—*Pall Mall Gazette.*
'Mr. Baring Gould's powerful story is full of the strong lights and shadows and vivid colouring to which he has accustomed us.'—*Standard.*

THE BROOM-SQUIRE. Illustrated by FRANK DADD. *Fourth Edition.*
'A strain of tenderness is woven through the web of his tragic tale, and its atmosphere is sweetened by the nobility and sweetness of the heroine's character.'—*Daily News.*
'A story of exceptional interest that seems to us to be better than anything he has written of late.'—*Speaker.*

THE PENNYCOMEQUICKS. *New Edition.*

DARTMOOR IDYLLS.
'A book to read, and keep and read again; for the genuine fun and pathos of it will not early lose their effect.'—*Vanity Fair.*

Gilbert Parker's Novels
Crown 8vo. 6s. each.

PIERRE AND HIS PEOPLE. *Third Edition.*
'Stories happily conceived and finely executed. There is strength and genius in Mr. Parker's style.'—*Daily Telegraph.*

MRS. FALCHION. *Fourth Edition.*
'A splendid study of character.'—*Athenæum.*
'But little behind anything that has been done by any writer of our time.'—*Pall Mall Gazette.* 'A very striking and admirable novel.'—*St. James's Gazette.*

THE TRANSLATION OF A SAVAGE.
'The plot is original and one difficult to work out; but Mr. Parker has done it with great skill and delicacy. The reader who is not interested in this original, fresh, and well-told tale must be a dull person indeed.'—*Daily Chronicle.*

THE TRAIL OF THE SWORD. *Fourth Edition.*
'Everybody with a soul for romance will thoroughly enjoy "The Trail of the Sword."'—*St. James's Gazette.*
'A rousing and dramatic tale. A book like this, in which swords flash, great surprises are undertaken, and daring deeds done, in which men and women live and love in the old straightforward passionate way, is a joy inexpressible to the reviewer.'—*Daily Chronicle.*

WHEN VALMOND CAME TO PONTIAC: The Story of a Lost Napoleon. *Fourth Edition.*
'Here we find romance—real, breathing, living romance, but it runs flush with our own times, level with our own feelings. The character of Valmond is drawn unerringly; his career, brief as it is, is placed before us as convincingly as history itself. The book must be read, we may say re-read, for any one thoroughly to appreciate Mr. Parker's delicate touch and innate sympathy with humanity.'—*Pall Mall Gazette.*
'The one work of genius which 1895 has as yet produced.'—*New Age.*

AN ADVENTURER OF THE NORTH: The Last Adventures of 'Pretty Pierre.' *Second Edition.*
'The present book is full of fine and moving stories of the great North, and it will add to Mr. Parker's already high reputation.'—*Glasgow Herald.*

THE SEATS OF THE MIGHTY. *Illustrated. Sixth Edition.*
The best thing he has done; one of the best things that any one has done lately.'—*St. James's Gazette.*
'Mr. Parker seems to become stronger and easier with every serious novel that he attempts. . . . In "The Seats of the Mighty" he shows the matured power which his former novels have led us to expect, and has produced a really fine historical novel. . . . Most sincerely is Mr. Parker to be congratulated on the finest novel he has yet written.'—*Athenæum.*
'Mr. Parker's latest book places him in the front rank of living novelists. "The Seats of the Mighty" is a great book.'—*Black and White.*
'One of the strongest stories of historical interest and adventure that we have read for many a day. . . . A notable and successful book.'—*Speaker.*
'An admirable romance. The glory of a romance is its plot, and this plot is crowded with fine sensations, which have no rest until the fall of the famous old city and the final restitution of love.'—*Pall Mall Gazette.*

Conan Doyle. ROUND THE RED LAMP. By A. CONAN DOYLE, Author of 'The White Company,' 'The Adventures of Sherlock Holmes,' etc. *Fourth Edition. Crown 8vo. 6s.*

'The book is, indeed, composed of leaves from life, and is far and away the best view that has been vouchsafed us behind the scenes of the consulting-room. It is very superior to "The Diary of a late Physician."'—*Illustrated London News.*

Stanley Weyman. UNDER THE RED ROBE. By STANLEY WEYMAN, Author of 'A Gentleman of France.' With Twelve Illustrations by R. Caton Woodville. *Eleventh Edition. Crown 8vo. 6s.*

'A book of which we have read every word for the sheer pleasure of reading, and which we put down with a pang that we cannot forget it all and start again.'—*Westminster Gazette.*
'Every one who reads books at all must read this thrilling romance, from the first page of which to the last the breathless reader is haled along. An inspiration of "manliness and courage."'—*Daily Chronicle.*
'A delightful tale of chivalry and adventure, vivid and dramatic.'—*Globe.*

Lucas Malet. THE CARISSIMA. By LUCAS MALET, Author of 'The Wages of Sin,' etc. *Third Edition. Crown 8vo. 6s.*

This is the first novel which Lucas Malet has written since her very powerful 'The Wages of Sin.'
'A very able story. Only a very few of our novelists can write so well.'—*Sketch.*

Lucas Malet. THE WAGES OF SIN. By LUCAS MALET. *Thirteenth Edition. Crown 8vo. 6s.*

Mrs. Clifford. A FLASH OF SUMMER. By Mrs. W. K. CLIFFORD, Author of 'Aunt Anne,' etc. *Second Edition. Crown 8vo. 6s.*

'The story is a very sad and a very beautiful one, exquisitely told, and enriched with many subtle touches of wise and tender insight. It will, undoubtedly, add to its author's reputation—already high—in the ranks of novelists.'—*Speaker.*

Emily Lawless. HURRISH. By the Honble. EMILY LAWLESS, Author of 'Maelcho,' etc. *Fifth Edition. Crown 8vo. 6s.*
A reissue of Miss Lawless' most popular novel, uniform with 'Maelcho.'

Emily Lawless. MAELCHO: a Sixteenth Century Romance. By the Honble. EMILY LAWLESS, Author of 'Grania,' 'Hurrish,' etc. *Second Edition. Crown 8vo. 6s.*

'A really great book.'—*Spectator.*
'There is no keener pleasure in life than the recognition of genius. Good work is commoner than it used to be, but the best is as rare as ever. All the more gladly, therefore, do we welcome in "Maelcho" a piece of work of the first order, which we do not hesitate to describe as one of the most remarkable literary achievements of this generation. Miss Lawless is possessed of the very essence of historical genius.'—*Manchester Guardian.*

J. H. Findlater. THE GREEN GRAVES OF BALGOWRIE. By JANE H. FINDLATER. *Third Edition. Crown 8vo. 6s.*

'A powerful and vivid story.'—*Standard.*
'A beautiful story, sad and strange as truth itself.'—*Vanity Fair.*
'A work of remarkable interest and originality.'—*National Observer.*
'A very charming and pathetic tale.'—*Pall Mall Gazette.*
'A singularly original, clever, and beautiful story.'—*Guardian.*
'"The Green Graves of Balgowrie" reveals to us a new Scotch writer of undoubted faculty and reserve force.'—*Spectator.*
'An exquisite idyll, delicate, affecting, and beautiful.'—*Black and White.*

E. F. Benson. DODO : A DETAIL OF THE DAY. By E. F. BENSON. *Sixteenth Edition. Crown 8vo. 6s.*

'A delightfully witty sketch of society.'—*Spectator.*
'A perpetual feast of epigram and paradox.'—*Speaker.*

E. F. Benson. THE RUBICON. By E. F. BENSON, Author of 'Dodo.' *Fifth Edition. Crown 8vo. 6s.*

'An exceptional achievement ; a notable advance on his previous work.'—*National Observer.*

M. M. Dowie. GALLIA. By MÉNIE MURIEL DOWIE, Author of 'A Girl in the Carpathians.' *Third Edition. Crown 8vo. 6s.*

'The style is generally admirable, the dialogue not seldom brilliant, the situations surprising in their freshness and originality, while the subsidiary as well as the principal characters live and move, and the story itself is readable from title-page to colophon.'—*Saturday Review.*

Mrs. Oliphant. SIR ROBERT'S FORTUNE. By MRS. OLIPHANT. *Crown 8vo. 6s.*

'Full of her own peculiar charm of style and simple, subtle character-painting comes her new gift, the delightful story before us. The scene mostly lies in the moors, and at the touch of the authoress a Scotch moor becomes a living thing, strong, tender, beautiful, and changeful.'—*Pall Mall Gazette.*

Mrs. Oliphant. THE TWO MARYS. By MRS. OLIPHANT. *Second Edition. Crown 8vo. 6s.*

W. E. Norris. MATTHEW AUSTIN. By W. E. NORRIS, Author of 'Mademoiselle de Mersac,' etc. *Fourth Edition. Crown 8vo. 6s.*

'"Matthew Austin" may safely be pronounced one of the most intellectually satisfactory and morally bracing novels of the current year.'—*Daily Telegraph.*

W. E. Norris. HIS GRACE. By W. E. NORRIS. *Third Edition. Crown 8vo. 6s.*

'Mr. Norris has drawn a really fine character in the Duke of Hurstbourne, at once unconventional and very true to the conventionalities of life.'—*Athenæum.*

W. E. Norris. THE DESPOTIC LADY AND OTHERS. By W. E. NORRIS. *Crown 8vo. 6s.*

'A budget of good fiction of which no one will tire.'—*Scotsman.*
'An extremely entertaining volume—the sprightliest of holiday companions.'—*Daily Telegraph*

H. G. Wells. THE STOLEN BACILLUS, and other Stories. By H. G. WELLS, Author of 'The Time Machine.' *Crown 8vo. 6s.*

'The ordinary reader of fiction may be glad to know that these stories are eminently readable from one cover to the other, but they are more than that ; they are the impressions of a very striking imagination, which, it would seem, has a great deal within its reach.'—*Saturday Review.*

Arthur Morrison. TALES OF MEAN STREETS. By ARTHUR MORRISON. *Fourth Edition. Crown 8vo. 6s.*

'Told with consummate art and extraordinary detail. He tells a plain, unvarnished tale, and the very truth of it makes for beauty. In the true humanity of the book lies its justification, the permanence of its interest, and its indubitable triumph.'—*Athenæum.*

'A great book. The author's method is amazingly effective, and produces a thrilling sense of reality. The writer lays upon us a master hand. The book is simply appalling and irresistible in its interest. It is humorous also ; without humour it would not make the mark it is certain to make.'—*World.*

Arthur Morrison. A CHILD OF THE JAGO. By ARTHUR MORRISON, Author of 'Tales of Mean Streets.' *Second Edition. Crown 8vo.* 6s.

This, the first long story which Mr. Morrison has written, is like his remarkable 'Tales of Mean Streets,' a realistic study of East End life.

'The book is a masterpiece.'—*Pall Mall Gazette.*
'Told with great vigour and powerful simplicity.'—*Athenæum.*

J. Maclaren Cobban. THE KING OF ANDAMAN: A Saviour of Society. By J. MACLAREN COBBAN. *Crown 8vo.* 6s.

'An unquestionably interesting book. It would not surprise us if it turns out to be the most interesting novel of the season, for it contains one character, at least, who has in him the root of immortality, and the book itself is ever exhaling the sweet savour of the unexpected. . . . Plot is forgotten and incident fades, and only the really human endures, and throughout this book there stands out in bold and beautiful relief its high-souled and chivalric protagonist, James the Master of Hutcheon, the King of Andaman himself.'—*Pall Mall Gazette.*

H. Morrah. A SERIOUS COMEDY. By HERBERT MORRAH. *Crown 8vo.* 6s.

'There are many delightful places in this volume, which is well worthy of its title. The theme has seldom been presented with more freshness or more force.'—*Scotsman.*

L. B. Walford. SUCCESSORS TO THE TITLE. By MRS. WALFORD, Author of 'Mr. Smith,' etc. *Second Edition. Crown 8vo.* 6s.

'The story is fresh and healthy from beginning to finish; and our liking for the two simple people who are the successors to the title mounts steadily, and ends almost in respect.'—*Scotsman.*

T. L. Paton. A HOME IN INVERESK. By T. L. PATON. *Crown 8vo.* 6s.

'A book which bears marks of considerable promise.'—*Scotsman.*
'A pleasant and well-written story.'—*Daily Chronicle.*

John Davidson. MISS ARMSTRONG'S AND OTHER CIRCUMSTANCES. By JOHN DAVIDSON. *Crown 8vo.* 6s.

'Throughout the volume there is a strong vein of originality, a strength in the handling, and a knowledge of human nature that are worthy of the highest praise.'—*Scotsman.*

J. A. Barry. IN THE GREAT DEEP: TALES OF THE SEA. By J. A. BARRY. Author of 'Steve Brown's Bunyip.' *Crown 8vo.* 6s.

'A collection of really admirable short stories of the sea, very simply told, and placed before the reader in pithy and telling English.'—*Westminster Gazette.*

J. B. Burton. IN THE DAY OF ADVERSITY. By J. BLOUNDELLE BURTON, Author of 'The Hispaniola Plate.' *Second Edition. Crown 8vo.* 6s.

'Unusually interesting and full of highly dramatic situations.'—*Guardian.*
'A well-written story, drawn from that inexhaustible mine, the time of Louis XIV.'—*Pall Mall Gazette.*

J. Bloundelle Burton. DENOUNCED. By J. BLOUNDELLE BURTON, Author of 'In the Day of Adversity,' etc. *Second Edition. Crown 8vo.* 6s.

'The plot is an extremely original one, and the local colouring is laid on with a delicacy of touch and an accuracy of detail which denote the true artist.'—*Broad Arrow.*

H. Johnston. DR. CONGALTON'S LEGACY. By HENRY JOHNSTON. *Crown 8vo.* 6s.
'The story is redolent of humour, pathos, and tenderness, while it is not without a touch of tragedy.'—*Scotsman.*
'A worthy and permanent contribution to Scottish creative literature.'—*Glasgow Herald.*

Julian Corbett. A BUSINESS IN GREAT WATERS. By JULIAN CORBETT, Author of 'Forgotten Gold,' 'Kophetua XIII,' etc. *Crown 8vo.* 6s.
'Mr. Corbett writes with immense spirit, and the book is a thoroughly enjoyable one in all respects. The salt of the ocean is in it, and the right heroic ring resounds through its gallant adventures.'—*Speaker.*

L. Cope Cornford. CAPTAIN JACOBUS: A ROMANCE OF THE ROAD. By L. COPE CORNFORD. Illustrated. *Crown 8vo.* 6s.
'An exceptionally good story of adventure and character.'—*World.*

C. Phillips Wolley. THE QUEENSBERRY CUP. A Tale of Adventure. By CLIVE PHILLIPS WOLLEY, Author of 'Snap,' Editor of 'Big Game Shooting.' *Illustrated. Crown 8vo.* 6s.
'A book which will delight boys: a book which upholds the healthy schoolboy code of morality.'—*Scotsman.*

Robert Barr. IN THE MIDST OF ALARMS. By ROBERT BARR, Author of 'From Whose Bourne,' etc. *Third Edition. Crown 8vo.* 6s.
'A book which has abundantly satisfied us by its capital humour.'—*Daily Chronicle.*
'Mr. Barr has achieved a triumph whereof he has every reason to be proud.'—*Pall Mall Gazette.*

L. Daintrey. THE KING OF ALBERIA. A Romance of the Balkans. By LAURA DAINTREY. *Crown 8vo.* 6s.
'Miss Daintrey seems to have an intimate acquaintance with the people and politics of the Balkan countries in which the scene of her lively and picturesque romance is laid. On almost every page we find clever touches of local colour which differentiate her book unmistakably from the ordinary novel.'—*Glasgow Herald.*

M. A. Owen. THE DAUGHTER OF ALOUETTE. By MARY A. OWEN. *Crown 8vo.* 6s.
A story of life among the American Indians.
'A fascinating story.'—*Literary World.*

Mrs. Pinsent. CHILDREN OF THIS WORLD. By ELLEN F. PINSENT, Author of 'Jenny's Case.' *Crown 8vo.* 6s.
'Mrs. Pinsent's new novel has plenty of vigour, variety, and good writing. There are certainty of purpose, strength of touch, and clearness of vision.'—*Athenæum.*

Clark Russell. MY DANISH SWEETHEART. By W. CLARK RUSSELL, Author of 'The Wreck of the Grosvenor,' etc. *Illustrated. Fourth Edition. Crown 8vo.* 6s.

G. Manville Fenn. AN ELECTRIC SPARK. By G. MANVILLE FENN, Author of 'The Vicar's Wife,' 'A Double Knot,' etc. *Second Edition. Crown 8vo.* 6s.

Ronald Ross. THE SPIRIT OF STORM. By RONALD ROSS, Author of 'The Child of Ocean.' *Crown 8vo.* 6s.
A romance of the Sea. 'Weird, powerful, and impressive.'—*Black and White.*

R. Pryce. TIME AND THE WOMAN. By RICHARD PRYCE, Author of 'Miss Maxwell's Affections,' 'The Quiet Mrs. Fleming,' etc. *Second Edition. Crown 8vo. 6s.*

Mrs. Watson. THIS MAN'S DOMINION. By the Author of 'A High Little World.' *Second Edition. Crown 8vo. 6s.*

Marriott Watson. DIOGENES OF LONDON, AND OTHER SKETCHES. By H. B. MARRIOTT WATSON, Author of 'The Web of the Spider.' *Crown 8vo. Buckram. 6s.*

M. Gilchrist. THE STONE DRAGON. By MURRAY GILCHRIST. *Crown 8vo. Buckram. 6s.*
'The author's faults are atoned for by certain positive and admirable merits. The romances have not their counterpart in modern literature, and to read them is a unique experience.'—*National Observer.*

E. Dickinson. A VICAR'S WIFE. By EVELYN DICKINSON. *Crown 8vo. 6s.*

E. M. Gray. ELSA. By E. M'QUEEN GRAY. *Crown 8vo. 6s.*

THREE-AND-SIXPENNY NOVELS 3/6
Crown 8vo.

DERRICK VAUGHAN, NOVELIST. By EDNA LYALL.
MARGERY OF QUETHER. By S. BARING GOULD.
JACQUETTA. By S. BARING GOULD.
SUBJECT TO VANITY. By MARGARET BENSON.
THE SIGN OF THE SPIDER. By BERTRAM MITFORD.
A story of South Africa.
'Far superior to any of the tales of the Transvaal with which we are acquainted. Not for a moment is the interest allowed to slacken.'—*World.*

THE MOVING FINGER. By MARY GAUNT.
JACO TRELOAR. By J. H. PEARCE.
THE DANCE OF THE HOURS. By 'VERA,' Author of 'Blue Roses.'
A WOMAN OF FORTY. By ESMÉ STUART.
A CUMBERER OF THE GROUND. By CONSTANCE SMITH.
THE SIN OF ANGELS. By EVELYN DICKINSON.
'The story is extremely well told; it holds the attention and is decidedly clever.'—*Leeds Mercury.*

AUT DIABOLUS AUT NIHIL. By X. L.
THE COMING OF CUCULAIN. A Romance of the Heroic Age of Ireland. By STANDISH O'GRADY. *Illustrated.*
THE GODS GIVE MY DONKEY WINGS. By ANGUS EVAN ABBOTT.
THE STAR GAZERS. By G. MANVILLE FENN.

THE POISON OF ASPS. By R. ORTON PROWSE.
THE QUIET MRS. FLEMING. By R. PRYCE.
DISENCHANTMENT. By F. MABEL ROBINSON.
THE SQUIRE OF WANDALES. By A. SHIELD.
  'Vastly interesting . . . Capitally written.'—*Black and White.*
A REVEREND GENTLEMAN. By J. M. COBBAN.
A DEPLORABLE AFFAIR. By W. E. NORRIS.
A CAVALIER'S LADYE. By Mrs. DICKER.
THE PRODIGALS. By Mrs. OLIPHANT.

HALF-CROWN NOVELS   2/6
A Series of Novels by popular Authors.

1. HOVENDEN, V.C. By F. MABEL ROBINSON.
2. ELI'S CHILDREN. By G. MANVILLE FENN.
3. A DOUBLE KNOT. By G. MANVILLE FENN.
4. DISARMED. By M. BETHAM EDWARDS.
5. A MARRIAGE AT SEA. By W. CLARK RUSSELL.
6. IN TENT AND BUNGALOW. By the Author of 'Indian Idylls.'
7. MY STEWARDSHIP. By E. M'QUEEN GRAY.
8. JACK'S FATHER. By W. E. NORRIS.
9. JIM B.
10. THE PLAN OF CAMPAIGN. By F. MABEL ROBINSON.
11. MR. BUTLER'S WARD. By F. MABEL ROBINSON.
12. A LOST ILLUSION. By LESLIE KEITH.

Lynn Linton. THE TRUE HISTORY OF JOSHUA DAVIDSON, Christian and Communist. By E. LYNN LINTON. *Eleventh Edition. Post 8vo.* 1s.

Books for Boys and Girls   3/6
A Series of Books by well-known Authors, well illustrated.

1. THE ICELANDER'S SWORD. By S. BARING GOULD.
2. TWO LITTLE CHILDREN AND CHING. By EDITH E. CUTHELL.
3. TODDLEBEN'S HERO. By M. M. BLAKE.
4. ONLY A GUARD-ROOM DOG. By EDITH E. CUTHELL.
5. THE DOCTOR OF THE JULIET. By HARRY COLLINGWOOD.
6. MASTER ROCKAFELLAR'S VOYAGE. By W. CLARK RUSSELL.
7. SYD BELTON: Or, The Boy who would not go to Sea. By G. MANVILLE FENN.

The Peacock Library

A Series of Books for Girls by well-known Authors, handsomely bound in blue and silver, and well illustrated. **3/6**

1. A PINCH OF EXPERIENCE. By L. B. WALFORD.
2. THE RED GRANGE. By Mrs. MOLESWORTH.
3. THE SECRET OF MADAME DE MONLUC. By the Author of 'Mdle Mori.'
4. DUMPS. By Mrs. PARR, Author of 'Adam and Eve.'
5. OUT OF THE FASHION. By L. T. MEADE.
6. A GIRL OF THE PEOPLE. By L. T. MEADE.
7. HEPSY GIPSY. By L. T. MEADE. 2s. 6d.
8. THE HONOURABLE MISS. By L. T. MEADE.
9. MY LAND OF BEULAH. By Mrs. LEITH ADAMS.

University Extension Series

A series of books on historical, literary, and scientific subjects, suitable for extension students and home-reading circles. Each volume is complete in itself, and the subjects are treated by competent writers in a broad and philosophic spirit.

Edited by J. E. SYMES, M.A.,
Principal of University College, Nottingham.
Crown 8vo. Price (with some exceptions) 2s. 6d.
The following volumes are ready:—

THE INDUSTRIAL HISTORY OF ENGLAND. By H. DE B. GIBBINS, D.Litt., M.A., late Scholar of Wadham College, Oxon., Cobden Prizeman. *Fourth Edition. With Maps and Plans.* 3s.

'A compact and clear story of our industrial development. A study of this concise but luminous book cannot fail to give the reader a clear insight into the principal phenomena of our industrial history. The editor and publishers are to be congratulated on this first volume of their venture, and we shall look with expectant interest for the succeeding volumes of the series.'—*University Extension Journal.*

A HISTORY OF ENGLISH POLITICAL ECONOMY. By L. L. PRICE, M.A., Fellow of Oriel College, Oxon. *Second Edition.*

PROBLEMS OF POVERTY: An Inquiry into the Industrial Conditions of the Poor. By J. A. HOBSON, M.A. *Third Edition.*

VICTORIAN POETS. By A. SHARP.

THE FRENCH REVOLUTION. By J. E. SYMES, M.A.

PSYCHOLOGY. By F. S. GRANGER, M.A., Lecturer in Philosophy at University College, Nottingham.

THE EVOLUTION OF PLANT LIFE: Lower Forms. By G. MASSEE, Kew Gardens. *With Illustrations.*
AIR AND WATER. Professor V. B. LEWES, M.A. *Illustrated.*
THE CHEMISTRY OF LIFE AND HEALTH. By C. W. KIMMINS, M.A. Camb. *Illustrated.*
THE MECHANICS OF DAILY LIFE. By V. P. SELLS, M.A. *Illustrated.*
ENGLISH SOCIAL REFORMERS. H. DE B. GIBBINS, D.Litt., M.A.
ENGLISH TRADE AND FINANCE IN THE SEVENTEENTH CENTURY. By W. A. S. HEWINS, B.A.
THE CHEMISTRY OF FIRE. The Elementary Principles of Chemistry. By M. M. PATTISON MUIR, M.A. *Illustrated.*
A TEXT-BOOK OF AGRICULTURAL BOTANY. By M. C. POTTER, M.A., F.L.S. *Illustrated.* 3s. 6d.
THE VAULT OF HEAVEN. A Popular Introduction to Astronomy. By R. A. GREGORY. *With numerous Illustrations.*
METEOROLOGY. The Elements of Weather and Climate. By H. N. DICKSON, F.R.S.E., F.R. Met. Soc. *Illustrated.*
A MANUAL OF ELECTRICAL SCIENCE. By GEORGE J. BURCH, M.A. *With numerous Illustrations.* 3s.
THE EARTH. An Introduction to Physiography. By EVAN SMALL, M.A. *Illustrated.*
INSECT LIFE. By F. W. THEOBALD, M.A. *Illustrated.*
ENGLISH POETRY FROM BLAKE TO BROWNING. By W. M. DIXON, M.A.
ENGLISH LOCAL GOVERNMENT. By E. JENKS, M.A., Professor of Law at University College, Liverpool.
THE GREEK VIEW OF LIFE. By G. L. DICKINSON, Fellow of King's College, Cambridge.

'Sensible, accurate, and interesting . . . Written with great clearness and real insight . . . We think highly of this little volume.'—*Pall Mall Gazette.*

Social Questions of To-day

Edited by H. DE B. GIBBINS, D.Litt., M.A.
Crown 8vo. 2s. 6d.

2/6

A series of volumes upon those topics of social, economic, and industrial interest that are at the present moment foremost in the public mind. Each volume of the series is written by an author who is an acknowledged authority upon the subject with which he deals.

The following Volumes of the Series are ready:—

TRADE UNIONISM—NEW AND OLD. By G. HOWELL, Author of 'The Conflicts of Capital and Labour.' *Second Edition.*

THE CO-OPERATIVE MOVEMENT TO-DAY. By G. J. HOLYOAKE, Author of 'The History of Co-Operation.' *Second Edition.*

MUTUAL THRIFT. By Rev. J. FROME WILKINSON, M.A., Author of 'The Friendly Society Movement.'

PROBLEMS OF POVERTY: An Inquiry into the Industrial Conditions of the Poor. By J. A. HOBSON, M.A. *Third Edition.*

THE COMMERCE OF NATIONS. By C. F. BASTABLE, M.A., Professor of Economics at Trinity College, Dublin.

THE ALIEN INVASION. By W. H. WILKINS, B.A., Secretary to the Society for Preventing the Immigration of Destitute Aliens.

THE RURAL EXODUS. By P. ANDERSON GRAHAM.

LAND NATIONALIZATION. By HAROLD COX, B.A.

A SHORTER WORKING DAY. By H. DE B. GIBBINS, D.Litt., M.A., and R. A. HADFIELD, of the Hecla Works, Sheffield.

BACK TO THE LAND: An Inquiry into the Cure for Rural Depopulation. By H. E. MOORE.

TRUSTS, POOLS AND CORNERS: As affecting Commerce and Industry. By J. STEPHEN JEANS, M.R.I., F.S.S.

THE FACTORY SYSTEM. By R. COOKE TAYLOR.

THE STATE AND ITS CHILDREN. By GERTRUDE TUCKWELL.

WOMEN'S WORK. By LADY DILKE, Miss BULLEY, and Miss WHITLEY.

MUNICIPALITIES AT WORK. The Municipal Policy of Six Great Towns, and its Influence on their Social Welfare. By FREDERICK DOLMAN.

SOCIALISM AND MODERN THOUGHT. By M. KAUFMANN.

THE HOUSING OF THE WORKING CLASSES. By R. F. BOWMAKER.

MODERN CIVILIZATION IN SOME OF ITS ECONOMIC ASPECTS. By W. CUNNINGHAM, D.D., Fellow of Trinity College, Cambridge.

THE PROBLEM OF THE UNEMPLOYED. By J. A. HOBSON, B.A., Author of ' The Problems of Poverty.' *Crown 8vo. 2s. 6d.*

'A very good book—the work of an evidently sincere man, and one who carefully weighs his words.'—*Spectator.*

Classical Translations

Edited by H. F. FOX, M.A., Fellow and Tutor of Brasenose College, Oxford.

Messrs. Methuen are issuing a New Series of Translations from the Greek and Latin Classics. They have enlisted the services of some of the best Oxford and Cambridge Scholars, and it is their intention that the Series shall be distinguished by literary excellence as well as by scholarly accuracy.

ÆSCHYLUS—Agamemnon, Chöephoroe, Eumenides. Translated by LEWIS CAMPBELL, LL.D., late Professor of Greek at St. Andrews, 5s.

CICERO—De Oratore I. Translated by E. N. P. MOOR, M.A., Assistant Master at Clifton. 3s. 6d.

CICERO — Select Orations (Pro Milone, Pro Murena, Philippic II., In Catilinam). Translated by H. E. D. BLAKISTON, M.A., Fellow and Tutor of Trinity College, Oxford. 5s.

CICERO—De Natura Deorum. Translated by F. BROOKS, M.A., late Scholar of Balliol College, Oxford. 3s. 6d.

LUCIAN—Six Dialogues (Nigrinus, Icaro-Menippus, The Cock, The Ship, The Parasite, The Lover of Falsehood). Translated by S. T. IRWIN, M.A., Assistant Master at Clifton; late Scholar of Exeter College, Oxford. 3s. 6d.

SOPHOCLES—Electra and Ajax. Translated by E. D. A. MORSHEAD, M.A., late Scholar of New College, Oxford; Assistant Master at Winchester. 2s. 6d.

TACITUS—Agricola and Germania. Translated by R. B. TOWNSHEND, late Scholar of Trinity College, Cambridge. 2s. 6d.

Educational Books

CLASSICAL

TACITI AGRICOLI. With Introduction, Notes, Map, etc. By R. F. DAVIS, M.A., Assistant Master at Weymouth College. *Crown 8vo.* 2s.

TACITI GERMANIA. By the same Editor. *Crown 8vo.* 2s.

HERODOTUS: EASY SELECTIONS. With Vocabulary. By A. C. LIDDELL, M.A., Assistant Master at Nottingham High School. *Fcap. 8vo.* 1s. 6d.

SELECTIONS FROM THE ODYSSEY. By E. D. STONE, M.A., late Assistant Master at Eton. *Fcap. 8vo.* 1s. 6d.

PLAUTUS: THE CAPTIVI. Adapted for Lower Forms by J. H. FRESSE, M.A., late Fellow of St. John's, Cambridge. 1s. 6d.

DEMOSTHENES AGAINST CONON AND CALLICLES. Edited with Notes and Vocabulary, by F. DARWIN SWIFT, M.A., formerly Scholar of Queen's College, Oxford; Assistant Master at Denstone College. *Fcap. 8vo.* 2s.

GERMAN

A COMPANION GERMAN GRAMMAR. By H. DE B. GIBBINS, D.Litt., M.A., Assistant Master at Nottingham High School. *Crown 8vo.* 1s. 6d.

GERMAN PASSAGES FOR UNSEEN TRANSLATION. By E. M'QUEEN GRAY. *Crown 8vo.* 2s. 6d.

SCIENCE

THE WORLD OF SCIENCE. Including Chemistry, Heat, Light, Sound, Magnetism, Electricity, Botany, Zoology, Physiology, Astronomy, and Geology. By R. ELLIOTT STEEL, M.A., F.C.S. 147 Illustrations. *Second Edition. Crown 8vo.* 2s. 6d.

'Mr. Steel's Manual is admirable in many ways. The book is well calculated to attract and retain the attention of the young.'—*Saturday Review.*

'If Mr. Steel is to be placed second to any for this quality of lucidity, it is only to Huxley himself; and to be named in the same breath with this master of the craft of teaching is to be accredited with the clearness of style and simplicity of arrangement that belong to thorough mastery of a subject.'—*Parents' Review.*

ELEMENTARY LIGHT. By R. E. STEEL. With numerous Illustrations. *Crown 8vo.* 4s. 6d.

ENGLISH

ENGLISH RECORDS. A Companion to the History of England. By H. E. MALDEN, M.A. *Crown 8vo.* 3s. 6d.

A book which aims at concentrating information upon dates, genealogy, officials, constitutional documents, etc., which is usually found scattered in different volumes.

THE ENGLISH CITIZEN: HIS RIGHTS AND DUTIES. By H. E. MALDEN, M.A. 1s. 6d.

'The book goes over the same ground as is traversed in the school books on this subject written to satisfy the requirements of the Education Code. It would serve admirably the purposes of a text-book, as it is well based in historical facts, and keeps quite clear of party matters.'—*Scotsman.*

METHUEN'S COMMERCIAL SERIES

Edited by H. DE B. GIBBINS, D.Litt., M.A.

BRITISH COMMERCE AND COLONIES FROM ELIZABETH TO VICTORIA. By H. DE B. GIBBINS, D.Litt., M.A., Author of 'The Industrial History of England,' etc., etc., 2s.

COMMERCIAL EXAMINATION PAPERS. By H. DE B. GIBBINS, D.Litt., M.A., 1s. 6d.

THE ECONOMICS OF COMMERCE. By H. DE B. GIBBINS, D.Litt., M.A. 1s. 6d.

A MANUAL OF FRENCH COMMERCIAL CORRESPONDENCE. By S. E. BALLY, Modern Language Master at the Manchester Grammar School. 2s.

GERMAN COMMERCIAL CORRESPONDENCE. By S. E. BALLY, Assistant Master at the Manchester Grammar School. *Crown 8vo.* 2s. 6d.

'A thorough-going and practical work, that covers the ground of the usual examinations in its subject.'—*Scotsman.*

A FRENCH COMMERCIAL READER. By S. E. BALLY. 2s.

COMMERCIAL GEOGRAPHY, with special reference to Trade Routes, New Markets, and Manufacturing Districts. By L. W. LYDE, M.A., of the Academy, Glasgow. 2s.

A PRIMER OF BUSINESS. By S. JACKSON, M.A. 1s. 6d.

COMMERCIAL ARITHMETIC. By F. G. TAYLOR, M.A. 1s. 6d.

WORKS BY A. M. M. STEDMAN, M.A.

INITIA LATINA: Easy Lessons on Elementary Accidence. *Second Edition. Fcap 8vo.* 1s.

FIRST LATIN LESSONS. *Fourth Edition. Crown 8vo.* 2s.

FIRST LATIN READER. With Notes adapted to the Shorter Latin Primer and Vocabulary. *Third Edition. Crown 8vo.* 1s. 6d.

EASY SELECTIONS FROM CAESAR. Part I. The Helvetian War. 18mo. 1s.

EASY SELECTIONS FROM LIVY. Part I. The Kings of Rome. 18mo. 1s. 6d.

EASY LATIN PASSAGES FOR UNSEEN TRANSLATION. *Fourth Edition. Fcap. 8vo.* 1s. 6d.

EXEMPLA LATINA. First Lessons in Latin Accidence. With Vocabulary. *Crown 8vo.* 1s.

www.ingramcontent.com/pod-product-compliance
Lightning Source LLC
Chambersburg PA
CBHW022105300426
44117CB00007B/592